Theology
The Basic Readings

Also by Alister E. McGrath from Wiley Blackwell

Theology: The Basics, 3rd edn (2012)
Luther's Theology of the Cross, 2nd edn (2011)
Darwinism and the Divine (2011)
The Christian Theology Reader, 4th edn (2011)
Christian Theology: An Introduction, 5th edn (2011)
Science and Religion: A New Introduction, 2nd edn (2009)
Christianity: An Introduction, 2nd edn (2006)
The Blackwell Companion to Protestantism (edited with
    Darren C. Marks, 2003)
The Intellectual Origins of the European Reformation, 2nd edn (2003)
A Brief History of Heaven (2003)
The Future of Christianity (2002)
Christian Literature: An Anthropology (edited, 2000)
Reformation Thought: An Introduction, 3rd edn (1999)
Christian Spirituality: An Introduction (1999)
Historical Theology: An Introduction (1998)
The Blackwell Encyclopedia of Modern Christian Thought (1995)

For a complete list of Alister E. McGrath's publications from
Wiley Blackwell, visit www.alistermcgrathwiley.com

Theology
The Basic Readings
Third Edition

Edited by

Alister E. McGrath

WILEY Blackwell

This edition first published 2018
Editorial material and organization © Alister E. McGrath

Edition History: Blackwell Publishing Ltd (1e, 2008), Wiley-Blackwell (2e, 2012)

The right of Alister E. McGrath to be identified as the author of the editorial material in this work has been asserted in accordance with law.

Registered Offices
John Wiley & Sons, Inc., 111 River Street, Hoboken, NJ 07030, USA
John Wiley & Sons Ltd, The Atrium, Southern Gate, Chichester, West Sussex, PO19 8SQ, UK

Editorial Office
9600 Garsington Road, Oxford, OX4 2DQ, UK

For details of our global editorial offices, customer services, and more information about Wiley products visit us at www.wiley.com.

Wiley also publishes its books in a variety of electronic formats and by print-on-demand. Some content that appears in standard print versions of this book may not be available in other formats.

Library of Congress Cataloging-in-Publication Data

Names: McGrath, Alister E., 1953- editor.
Title: Theology : the basic readings / edited by Alister E. McGrath.
Description: Third edition. | Hoboken, NJ : John Wiley & Sons, 2018. |
    Includes bibliographical references and index. |
Identifiers: LCCN 2017030739 (print) | LCCN 2017038130 (ebook) | ISBN
    9781119158172 (pdf) | ISBN 9781119158189 (epub) | ISBN 9781119158158 (pbk.)
Subjects: LCSH: Theology, Doctrinal. | Theology–History.
Classification: LCC BT21.3 (ebook) | LCC BT21.3 .M34 2018 (print) | DDC
    230–dc23
LC record available at https://lccn.loc.gov/2017030739

Cover image: ImageBROKER / Alamy Stock Photo
Cover design by Wiley

Set in 10.5/12pt BemboStd by Aptara Inc., New Delhi, India
Printed and bound in Malaysia by Vivar Printing Sdn Bhd

10 9 8 7 6 5 4 3 2 1

Brief Contents

Contents

Acknowledgments

The editor and publisher gratefully acknowledge the permission granted to reproduce the copyright material in this book:

1.4 Karl Barth, *The Göttingen Dogmatics: Instruction in the Christian Religion* (Grand Rapids, MI: Eerdmans, 1991), 14–16. Reproduced with permission from Wm. B. Eerdmans Publishing Company.

1.5 Emil Brunner, *Revelation and Reason* (London: SCM Press, 1947), 416–17. © SCM Press. Reproduced with permission from SCM Press.

1.6 Paul Tillich, *The Shaking of the Foundations* (London: SCM Press, 1949), 127–9. Reproduced with permission from Wipf and Stock Publishers.

1.7 C. S. Lewis, "Is Theology Poetry?," in *C. S. Lewis: Essay Collection* (London: Collins, 2000), 1–21. © C. S. Lewis Pte. Ltd. Reproduced with permission from C. S. Lewis Pte. Ltd.

1.8 Encyclical letter *Fides et Ratio* of John Paul II to the Catholic bishops of the world, issued on September 18, 1998, paras 16–17. Reproduced with permission from the Vatican.

2.4 Hans Urs von Balthasar, *The Glory of the Lord: A Theological Aesthetics*, 7 vols (Edinburgh: T&T Clark, 1989), vol. 7, 268–70. © T&T Clark International, an imprint of Bloomsbury Publishing Plc. Reproduced with permission from Bloomsbury Publishing Plc.

2.5 Elizabeth A. Johnson, *She Who Is: The Mystery of God in Feminist Theological Discourse* (New York: Crossroad, 1992), 55–7. Reproduced with permission from Crossroad Publishing.

2.6   Sarah Coakley, *Powers and Submissions: Spirituality, Philosophy and Gender* (Oxford: Blackwell, 2002), 32–6. Reproduced with permission from John Wiley & Sons.

3.6   Dorothy L. Sayers, *The Mind of the Maker* (London: Methuen, 1941), 81–3. Reproduced with permission from David Higham Associates.

3.7   John Polkinghorne, *The Faith of a Physicist* (Princeton, NJ: Princeton University Press, 1994), 73–5. Reproduced with permission from Princeton University Press.

4.5   Austin Farrer, *Love Almighty and Ills Unlimited: An Essay on Providence and Evil* (London: Collins, 1962), 124–30. Reprinted by permission of HarperCollins Publishers Ltd © Farrer 1962. Reproduced with permission from HarperCollins Publishers Ltd and from Doubleday, an imprint of the Knopf Doubleday Publishing Group, a division of Penguin Random House LLC.

4.6   Morna D. Hooker, "Chalcedon and the New Testament," in *The Making and Remaking of Christian Doctrine*, ed. Sarah Coakley and David A. Pailin (Oxford: Clarendon Press, 1993), 73–93. Reproduced with permission from Oxford University Press.

4.7   N. T. Wright, "Jesus and the Identity of God," *Ex Auditu* 14 (1998): 42–56. Reproduced with permission from N. T. Wright and from Wipf & Stock Publishers.

5.5   Bernard Lonergan, *The Collected Works of Bernard Lonergan, vol. 6: Philosophical and Theological Papers, 1958–1964* (Toronto: University of Toronto Press, 1996), 8–13. Reproduced with permission from University of Toronto Press.

5.6   Colin E. Gunton, *The Actuality of Atonement* (Edinburgh: T&T Clark, 1988), 47–51. Reproduced with permission from Bloomsbury Publishing Plc.

5.7   Rosemary Radford Ruether, *Introducing Redemption in Christian Feminism* (Sheffield: Sheffield Academic Press, 1998), 97–100. Reproduced with permission from Bloomsbury Publishing Plc.

6.6   John Webster, "The Identity of the Holy Spirit: A Problem in Trinitarian Theology," *Themelios* 9, no. 1 (1983): 4–7. Reproduced with permission from The Gospel Coalition.

6.7   John Meyendorff, *The Byzantine Legacy in the Orthodox Church* (Crestwood, NY: St Vladimir's Seminary Press, 1982), 154–6. Reproduced with permission from St Vladimir's Seminary Press.

7.4   Karl Rahner, "Remarks on the Dogmatic Treatise 'De trinitate'," in *Theological Investigations* (London: Darton, Longman &

Todd, 1966), 77–102. Reproduced with permission from Darton, Longman & Todd.

7.5 John Macquarrie, *Principles of Christian Theology*, rev. ed. (London: SCM Press, 1977), 190–2. Reproduced with permission from SCM Press.

7.6 Robert Jenson, "The Triune God," in *Christian Dogmatics*, ed. C. E. Braaten and R. W. Jenson, vol. 1 (Philadelphia, PA: Fortress Press, 1984), 87–92. Reproduced with permission from 1517 Media.

7.7 Catherine Mowry LaCugna, "The Practical Trinity," *Christian Century* 109, no. 22 (1992), 678–82. Reproduced with permission from The Christian Century.

8.2 Lesslie Newbigin, *The Household of God: Lectures on the Nature of the Church* (London: SCM Press, 1953), 140–1.

8.3 Second Vatican Council, *Lumen Gentium* ("Dogmatic Constitution on the Church"), 6, 8. Reproduced with permission from the Vatican.

8.4 George Dragas, "Orthodox Ecclesiology in Outline," *Greek Orthodox Theological Review* 26 (1981), 185–92. Hellenic College Holy Cross.

8.5 Stanley Hauerwas, *A Community of Character: Toward a Constructive Christian Social Ethic* (Notre Dame, IN: University of Notre Dame Press, 1981), 91–2. Reproduced with permission from University of Notre Dame Press.

8.6 Leonardo Boff, *Ecclesiogenesis: The Base Communities Reinvent the Church* (Maryknoll, NY: Orbis, 1986), 23–4. Reproduced with permission from Orbis Books.

9.4 World Council of Churches, *Baptism, Eucharist and Ministry*, Faith and Order Paper 111 (Geneva: World Council of Churches, 1982), 2–3. Reproduced with permission from World Council of Churches.

9.5 Rowan Williams, *On Christian Theology* (Oxford: Blackwell, 2000), 203–4. Reproduced with permission from John Wiley & Sons.

9.6 Benedict XVI, "Post-Synodal Apostolic Exhortation *Sacramentum Caritatis*," given at Saint Peter's, Rome, on February 22, 2007, http://w2.vatican.va/content/benedict-xvi/en/apost_exhortations/documents/hf_ben-xvi_exh_20070222_sacramentum-caritatis.html. Reproduced with permission from the Vatican.

10.5   *Catechism of the Catholic Church* (Collegeville, MN: Liturgical Press, and other publishers, 1994), paras 992–1001. Reproduced with permission from the Vatican.

10.6   Wolfhart Pannenberg, *Systematic Theology*, 3 vols (Grand Rapids, MI: Eerdmans, 1988–98), vol. 3, 637–40. Reproduced with permission from Wm. B. Eerdmans Publishing Company.

10.7   Kathryn Tanner, *Jesus, Humanity and the Trinity: A Brief Systematic Theology* (Minneapolis, MN: Fortress Press, 2001), 108–10. Reproduced with permission from 1517 Media.

Every effort has been made to trace copyright holders and to obtain their permission for the use of copyright material. The publisher apologizes for any errors or omissions in the above list and would be grateful if notified of any corrections that should be incorporated in future reprints or editions of this book.

How to Use This Book

Theology is "talk about God"; Christian theology is thus "talk about God" from a Christian perspective. In practice, however, the term "Christian theology" has developed a wider meaning than simply the Christian understanding of God, referring to the study of the fundamental themes of the Christian faith. The eleventh-century theologian Anselm of Canterbury (ca. 1033–1109) spoke of theology as "faith seeking understanding." Theology can be thought of as a Christian discipleship of the mind. Christian theologians have generally distinguished two senses of the word "faith." Faith can be understood both as *a set of beliefs* and as *an act of believing*. Theology is basically Christian reflection on the ideas of faith.

Christian theology is one of the most fascinating subjects that you can hope to study. Yet most people find it an intimidating subject. It often seems to use words that nobody else uses or understands. Its ideas often seem strange or inaccessible. The demand for a short, simple, and accessible introduction to this invigorating subject led to the production of my textbook *Theology: The Basics* in 2004. Now in its fourth edition, this short and highly accessible work has proved an invaluable resource to many who are starting the serious study of theology.

It is very helpful to have the basic themes, debates, and personalities of Christian theology introduced by a skilled and unbiased commentator. This, however, is only a starting point for the journey of theological reflection. It lays a foundation for something more helpful and important – namely, interacting with these theological themes, debates, and personalities at a deeper and more satisfying level *through reading and interacting with original texts*. Yet many students often find themselves reduced to despair, as they try to understand texts that they realize are important, but find impossibly difficult to understand. What are they meant to be looking for? What is the importance of these texts? This collection of readings is designed to provide a reliable, helpful, and accessible way of engaging with original texts.

This collection of readings provides students with a substantial amount of help as they encounter primary sources. Much thought has been given to how best to do this. In the first place, the texts have been selected with great care, to make sure that they are not merely representative of the debates, but are both *interesting* and *accessible*. This means that I have often chosen pieces from authors – such as G. K. Chesterton and Dorothy L. Sayers – who are lucid and engaging writers, yet who do not often find their way into more traditional theological anthologies. To allow a wide variety of theological voices, every item in this collection comes from a different theological source. The first edition of this collection, which was well received by its users, did not include a separate chapter on the theology of the Holy Spirit. In response to helpful feedback from those users, the second and third editions include a chapter dedicated to this important topic.

In the second place, each reading needs to be introduced and explained to the reader, who then needs guidance about how best to interact with it. This book aims to do exactly that, by providing an introduction to each individual reading, followed by a commentary designed to enable readers to get the most from interacting with it. Although this book can be used to great effect in taught courses, it has been developed with the needs of those studying on their own particularly in mind. To allow easy correlation with *Theology: The Basics*, this collection of readings is divided into ten chapters which reflect the basic structure of the latest edition of this textbook.

Engaging with these readings is one of the best ways of understanding how Christians have tried to express their faith, develop its ideas, and weave its themes together into a systematic whole. Each reading is accompanied by an introduction, comment, and study questions, designed to make this process of engagement as straightforward, interesting, and profitable as possible. I have made my own translations of Greek, Latin, and German texts written before 1800, aiming primarily at conceptual clarity, rather than literary elegance. My main concern is to allow readers to grasp the theological significance of these readings.

This collection of readings *aims* to introduce you to some key ideas, personalities, and schools of thought within Christian theology by direct engagement with original theological texts. It *assumes* that you know virtually nothing about the subject. It *provides* 68 readings, each from a different source, spread throughout the two thousand years of Christian history. Every attempt has been made to ensure that the work is broadly representative of the two thousand years of sustained critical reflection within western Christianity. Although this collection includes readings from every period of Christian history, it includes a very high proportion – nearly two in three – of readings dating from the last two hundred years. This ensures that students have access to classical approaches, while being introduced to more recent developments.

This book is deliberately pitched at an introductory level, and may well leave many readers longing for more after they have completed it. Such readers will find ample material in two more detailed and comprehensive textbooks from the present author and publisher: *Christian Theology: An Introduction* and *The Christian Theology Reader*. The former, now in its sixth edition, provides a thorough university-level introduction to Christian theology, including comprehensive coverage of the history of theology, the basics of theological method, and detailed engagement with ten major areas of theology. The latter, now in its fifth edition, provides more than 375 primary texts of relevance to the study of theology, along with individual introductions, commentary, and study questions. Readers who enjoy the present collection of texts may want to move on to this larger collection, once they have mastered the contents of this shorter work.

It remains for me to thank my students at Oxford and London who have given me much advice and feedback on various readings under consideration for this collection, and Rebecca Harkin, my editor at Wiley Blackwell, for her encouragement and guidance as it was developed. I hope it will enable its users to take their reading further, and to enjoy exploring the vast collection of theological resources now at their disposal. I am deeply grateful to users of the first two editions of this work for their detailed feedback on the work, which has been invaluable in revising and expanding the material for this new edition, and welcome further feedback on this new edition.

Alister E. McGrath
Oxford, July 2017

How to Engage a Reading

How should you interact with a text? Many people find the idea difficult, even intimidating. Where do you start? What do you do? What are you meant to be looking for? This book assumes that you've never done this sort of thing before, and tries to make it as easy, interesting, and rewarding as possible.

Let me begin by explaining how this collection of readings is arranged. The texts are arranged *thematically* by chapter and *chronologically* within each chapter. In other words, all the readings dealing with the doctrine of the Trinity are grouped together in a single chapter. Within this chapter the readings are presented in the order in which they were written. The earliest comes first; the most recent comes last.

The first chapter, dealing with some basic issues of faith, is introductory. It is designed to help you find your feet as you begin to engage with original sources. Not only does it provide more readings than the chapters which follow; it also offers a much greater degree of guidance and direction as you engage with the readings. This will help set you up for later chapters, where less direct guidance is provided. You are strongly recommended to work your way through this first chapter before moving on to explore other themes later in the work. It will help you work out how to interact with primary sources, and what to expect from engaging them.

The best way of using this book is simply to adopt a thematic approach and work your way through each chapter. Each reading has its own introduction, which will help you get an idea of what it's all about. Sometimes these are quite detailed; sometimes, they are short – it all depends on how much background knowledge you need to make sense of the text. So read the introduction first, then move on to the text itself. After you've read it through, try interacting with it like this.

1. Make sure that you can identify the author. When did she live? In which part of the world was he based? There is much helpful material available on the Internet that will be helpful here, particularly in providing full biographical details of writers.
2. Spend a little time thinking about the work from which the reading is taken. What kind of a work is it? For example, is it academic, polemical, pastoral, or popular? Who is the author writing for?
3. Try to summarize the passage, noting the flow of the argument and any assumptions which seem to be especially important. Make a note of any phrases used that you think are interesting – for example, by underlining or highlighting them in the text. If you come across words that puzzle you, try looking them up in the glossary at the end of this book.
4. Now close the book and see if you can summarize the reading. The more information you can retain, the better. In particular, try to recall the main points of any arguments used.
5. Write down your summary in a single paragraph.

This kind of exercise will help you test your own understanding of the passage, and also enable you to make the best possible use of the information for yourself.

You don't need to agree with a writer's perspective to benefit from exploring the approach they adopt. Sometimes the most useful texts to engage are those that take positions we disagree with. Why? Because they force us to ask ourselves why we take the position that we do, and how we would respond to the points they make. This collection of readings draws from a wide variety of sources, and will certainly force you to think about your own ideas. Nobody is asking you to change your mind about anything (though you may do so as a result of interacting with some of these texts). Hopefully, you will find these texts interesting and stimulating, opening up new ways of thinking or offering new illustrations or approaches that will prove to be helpful.

Christian Theology: A Historical Overview

This reader brings together a collection of readings drawn from the first two thousand years of Christian theology. Although two in every three of these readings are drawn from very recent sources, you will find material from each of the great periods of Christian history represented here. To get the most out of these readings, you need a basic understanding of the main features of the development of Christian theology. If you are using this reader alongside my textbook *Christian Theology: An Introduction*, now in its sixth edition, you will find that this provides you with a detailed road map which will allow you to get the most from this collection of readings. It will help you make much more sense of what you read, and allow you to appreciate the context in which it was written. The four introductory chapters of this larger work provide a survey of historical theology. The following four chapters deal with issues of sources and interpretation, dealing with material covered in the first two chapters of this reader. The remaining chapters present a detailed engagement with the major themes of Christian theology, providing an in-depth introduction to the readings.

However, not all will want to make use of this specific introduction to Christian theology. For those not using this companion volume, the brief section which follows will give you something of a panoramic view of the main landmarks of this process of development, and identify readings that will help you understand some of its features. While this can only highlight some of the many themes of Christian theology (passing over many topics, debates, and schools of thought that fully deserve discussion), it will nevertheless help readers to get their bearings in the midst of this vast landscape of ideas.

For the sake of convenience, historians of Christian thought tend to break its first two thousand years down into more manageable sections. While everyone has their own views about how best to divide Christian history, many use a framework which looks something like this.

The apostolic period

The first hundred years are often referred to as the *apostolic* period. This is the period during which the works now included in the New Testament were written. During this time, Christianity was spreading throughout the Mediterranean region and beyond. The missionary journeys of St Paul, described in the Acts of the Apostles, are an excellent example of this activity. This reader does not include readings from the New Testament, as this document is so readily accessible in traditional and digital forms.

The patristic period

This is followed by the *patristic* period, which is usually held to begin about the year 100. There is no firm agreement about when this period ended: some scholars suggest it ends in the fifth century, while others extend it by at least two centuries. The Council of Chalcedon (451) marked a landmark in Christian thinking, especially over the identity of Jesus Christ, and is seen by many writers as bringing this important period of theological development to a close. The unusual word "patristic" derives from the Greek word *pater* ("father"), and designates a group of writers who are often collectively known as the "fathers of the church." (Sadly, there were very few women among them.) The readings chosen for inclusion here are representative of all the major writers of this period – such as Irenaeus of Lyons, Athanasius of Alexandria, and Augustine of Hippo.

The patristic period witnessed important theological explorations of the relation of faith and classical culture, clarifying the place of the Bible in Christian theology (including establishing the New Testament canon), the identity of Jesus Christ, the doctrine of God (including the Trinity), the doctrine of the church, and the relation of grace and free will. Most of these are represented in this reader. In what follows, we will look at each of them in a little more detail.

Faith and classical culture. As Christianity expanded in its first centuries, it moved from a Palestinian context into the Greek-speaking world of the eastern Mediterranean, establishing a presence in the great cities of Alexandria and Antioch. It also began to grow in the western Latin-speaking Roman empire, including North Africa. This raised the question of how Christianity related to ideas already present in this region – for example, classical philosophy.

The place of the Bible. One of the most important achievements of the patristic period was establishing which books dating from the apostolic period were to be regarded as "canonical" or "biblical." Considerable attention was also paid to the question of how the Bible was to be interpreted, and especially the role of tradition in combating unorthodox interpretations of the Bible. During this period, "creeds" began to emerge as communally accepted and authorized summaries of the Christian faith.

The identity of Jesus Christ. The patristic period saw clarification of the identity and significance of Jesus as being of the utmost importance. Where was he to be placed on a theological map? The period witnessed growing acceptance of the "two natures" doctrine, along with exploration of how best to make sense of Jesus Christ being both divine and human.

The doctrine of God. Classical Greek philosophy already had its ideas about what "God" was like. One of the most important tasks of Christian theology was to differentiate the Christian idea of God from its philosophical rivals. Many early debates concentrated on what it meant to say that God was creator, the role of the Holy Spirit, or how the existence of evil was consistent with a good God. However, the most significant discussions concerned the doctrine of the Trinity – the distinctively Christian idea of one God in three persons. How was this to be understood?

The doctrine of the church. Patristic writers initially paid relatively little attention to the doctrine of the church, tending to focus attention on developing a coherent understanding of the sacraments. The Donatist controversy of the fourth century forced the western church to reconsider the nature of the church, and who was authorized to administer the sacraments. These debates would break out once more during the Reformation period.

The Middle Ages

The Middle Ages, or medieval period, are regarded as extending from the end of the patristic era to about the year 1500. This long period was immensely creative culturally, and productive theologically, producing theological classics such as Peter Lombard's *Four Books of the Sentences* and Thomas Aquinas' great thirteenth-century work, the *Summa Theologiae* ("The Totality of Theology"). Peter Lombard's medieval theological textbook was the subject of many commentaries, which used its material to develop increasingly sophisticated theological ideas.

Among the many issues to be explored in detail during this period were the relation between faith and reason, how to interpret the Bible, and the theology of the sacraments. Alongside this, there was continuing exploration of issues debated during the patristic period, such as the relation of grace and free will.

Faith and reason. The Middle Ages saw new attention being given to a whole range of issues concerning the relation of faith and reason, theology and philosophy. One reason for this was the emergence of universities in western Europe, particularly the University of Paris. The debates over whether God's existence could be proved are good examples of this concern.

Biblical interpretation. The rise of the monasteries led to a new interest in the correct interpretation of the Bible. The constant use of the Bible in corporate worship and private devotion raised important questions about how the Bible was to be understood and applied.

The institution of the church. The rise of the papacy raised increasingly important questions about the church and its sacramental system. Major issues debated during the Middle Ages included the definition of a sacrament, and the vexed question of how Christ could be present in the eucharist. The growing political power of the church raised important theological questions about the relation of church and state.

The Reformation and post-Reformation period

The sixteenth century marked a period of radical change in the western church. This period of *reformation* witnessed the birth of Protestantism, through writers such as Martin Luther and John Calvin. Certain theological debates became especially heated around this time, especially the place of the Bible in theological reflection, the doctrine of the church, and the question of what it is necessary to do in order to be saved. The doctrine of justification by faith alone became of especial importance around this time, rapidly becoming a characteristic of the Protestant Reformation. The Catholic church also went through a period of reformation around this time, with the Council of Trent setting out the definitive Catholic position on issues of importance at this time. Many scholars also include the seventeenth century in this period, arguing that this represents the Protestant and Catholic consolidation of the developments that began in the previous century. It was during this century that Christians emigrated to North America, and began to establish that region as a major player in theological debates.

A number of significant theological developments take place during this period, most of which relate to Protestantism. Two new styles of theological texts make their appearance, both generally (though not exclusively) associated with Lutheranism and Calvinism respectively – Melanchthon's *Loci Communes* ("Commonplaces") and Calvin's *Institutes of the Christian Religion*. The "catechism," with its distinctive "question and answer" format, became of major importance at this time as a means of encouraging popular theological education.

Among the debates that took place at this time, we may note the following as being of particular importance.

The authority of the Bible. A major debate between Protestants and Catholics concerned whether, in the first place, the Bible had an authority independent of that of the church; and, in the second, whether the Bible could be interpreted without the guidance of the church. Alongside these specific debates, there was continued discussion over methods for the interpretation of Scripture.

The church. Three major debates concerning the church became of particular importance around this time. In the first place, what were the marks of the true church? Was the church defined by institutional, historical continuity with the past – or by the faithful preaching of the gospel? Second, how many sacraments were there? Protestants tended to identify only two gospel sacraments; the Catholic church recognized seven. Third, in what sense, if any, was Christ present at the eucharist? The Catholic church maintained its commitment to the specific doctrine of transubstantiation, while various viewpoints emerged within Protestantism.

The modern era

The period since about 1800 is often referred to as the "modern era" – a period of considerable instability in western Europe, especially following the French Revolution of 1789, and later through the rise of Marxism in eastern Europe in the twentieth century. Despite these anxieties, it was a period of remarkable theological creativity throughout western Europe and North America. In addition, a growing Christian presence in Africa and Asia during the twentieth century led to an increasing interest in developing "local theologies" in these new regions. These local theologies would be grounded in the Christian tradition, but sensitive to their local situations. Although this reader cannot hope to document the emergence of these distinctive theologies outside the west, there is no doubt that this has been a development of major importance, which will become increasingly significant in the twenty-first century.

Most of the readings in this volume are drawn from this period, especially the last hundred years. A wide range of theological issues have come to the fore during the modern period. Many traditional issues have continued to be debated, including the relation of faith and reason, the authority and interpretation of Scripture, the doctrine of the Trinity, the identity of Christ, the grounds of salvation, and the nature of the church. In most cases, these debates have been shaped by the concerns of the Enlightenment, which stressed the importance of reason, and was generally suspicious of theological arguments involving an appeal to church tradition or divine revelation. A number of additional issues have begun to emerge as characteristic of this period. In what follows, we shall note some of these new debates.

The rise of rationalism within western culture has led to a critique of a number of aspects of traditional Christian theology. The most important of these has been the rise of the "historical Jesus movement" as a result of the belief that there was a massive gap between an essentially simple, rational "Jesus of history" and the church's rather more complex "Christ of faith." As rationalism began to lose its influence in the early twentieth century, Christian theology began to rediscover the idea of revelation, and to regain confidence in the doctrine of the Trinity as a means of expressing the distinctive identity of the Christian God.

A final factor of importance has been the growing realization of the importance of issues raised by feminist writers, who have pointed out the need to explore further issues relating to the traditional use of male language about God, the maleness of Christ as the central figure of the Christian faith, or essentially masculine approaches to biblical interpretation or theological concepts.

This very brief survey of theological history can only identify, in a very cursory and unsatisfactory manner, some of the great themes to have been explored and debated during Christian history. It is hoped that it will help you appreciate and begin to engage with the 68 readings collected in this volume. Once you have mastered them, you may feel ready to move on to deal with the much larger and more comprehensive set of more than 375 readings gathered in the latest edition of *The Christian Theology Reader*, which will open up new areas of theological debate and exploration for you.

The Apostles' Creed

The structure of this collection of readings is loosely modeled on the Apostles' Creed, one of the most familiar and widely cited summaries of the Christian faith. It is regularly included in public worship, and is often the subject of sermons, textbooks, and study guides. Its simple structure creates an ideal framework for exploring some of the central themes of Christian theology. Although many earlier versions of the Apostles' Creed are known, this creed reached its final form in the eighth century.

> I believe in God, the Father Almighty,
> creator of heaven and earth.
>
> I believe in Jesus Christ, God's only Son, our Lord,
> who was conceived by the Holy Spirit,
> born of the Virgin Mary,
> suffered under Pontius Pilate,
> was crucified, died, and was buried;
> he descended to the dead.
> On the third day he rose again;
> he ascended into heaven,
> he is seated at the right hand of the Father,
> and he will come to judge the living and the dead.
>
> I believe in the Holy Spirit,
> the holy catholic Church,
> the communion of saints,
> the forgiveness of sins,
> the resurrection of the body,
> and the life everlasting. Amen.

CHAPTER 1

Faith

What is faith? We have already seen that there are two senses of the word "faith": *a set of beliefs* and *an act of believing*. This opening chapter considers some basic issues that lie behind any attempt to reflect on the contents of faith, including some reflections on the nature of faith, and the sources and methods that might be used to establish and explore basic Christian beliefs.

One of the central questions that will be considered in this opening chapter is how theology develops its ideas. Where do they come from? Traditionally, three main sources of Christian theology are recognized: the collection of texts usually known as "the Bible," tradition, and reason. There is widespread agreement within the Christian tradition that the most fundamental source is the Bible. One of the most important questions in Christian theology therefore relates to the authority and interpretation of Scripture. (Note that many theological writings tend to use the term "Scripture" or "Holy Scripture" in preference to "the Bible," even though these terms refer to exactly the same collection of writings.) Some of the readings assembled in this chapter deal directly with this issue.

However, from the earliest of times, it was realized that Scripture was open to a series of interpretations of varying degrees of reliability, some of which were not even remotely Christian. This insight is especially associated with the Gnostic controversies of the second century, during which

Gnostic writers put forward some intensely speculative interpretations of Scripture. In response to this, writers such as Irenaeus emphasized the need to interpret Scripture within the bounds of the living tradition of the church. This led to growing interest in the way in which tradition was to be understood as a source for theology.

The role of reason has also featured prominently in Christian theological reflection. The early church witnessed an important discussion of the extent to which theology should interact with secular philosophy. This later developed into debates about whether the existence of God could be proved by an appeal to reason. The debate over the relation of faith and reason continues in contemporary theology, reflecting the church's ongoing dialogue with secular culture over the rationality of faith.

In this chapter, we shall consider a number of issues concerning the nature and sources of theology. We begin by looking at a classic discussion of the relation between Christian theology and secular philosophy, found in the writings of Augustine of Hippo.

1.1   Augustine of Hippo on the theological use of secular philosophy

One of the most divisive debates within early Christianity concerned the extent to which the church should make use of secular cultural ideas or values. It was a debate of immense significance, as it raised the question of whether Christianity would turn its back on the classical heritage, or appropriate it, even if in a modified form. As the Roman imperial authorities distrusted Christianity, often subjecting it to repressive controls, many early theologians saw little point in exploring this question. The third-century theologian Tertullian, for example, saw it as a waste of time. It is important to appreciate that Christianity had a decidedly ambiguous legal status in the Roman empire at this time. On the one hand, it was not legally recognized, and so did not enjoy any special rights; on the other, it was not forbidden. However, its growing numerical strength led to periodic attempts to suppress it by force. Sometimes these persecutions were local, restricted to regions such as North Africa; sometimes, they were sanctioned throughout the Roman empire as a whole.

Things changed with the conversion of the Roman emperor Constantine in 313, which opened the way to a much more positive evaluation of the relation of every aspect of Christian life and thought to classical culture. Rome was now the servant of the gospel; might not the same be true of its culture? If the Roman state could be viewed positively by Christians, why not also its cultural heritage? It seemed as if a door had opened upon some very interesting possibilities. Prior to 313, this situation could only have been dreamed of. After 313, its exploration became a matter of urgency for leading Christian thinkers – supreme among whom was Augustine of Hippo (354–430).

Widely regarded as the most influential Latin patristic writer, Augustine was converted to Christianity in the northern Italian city of Milan in the summer of 386. He returned to North Africa, and was made bishop of Hippo in 395. He was involved in two major controversies: the Donatist controversy, focusing on the church and sacraments; and the Pelagian controversy, focusing on grace and sin. He also made substantial contributions to the development of the doctrine of the Trinity, the Christian understanding of history, and – as in this passage – the theological appropriation of secular philosophy.

In his work *On Christian Doctrine*, Augustine argued for the "critical appropriation of classical culture." For Augustine, the situation is comparable to Israel fleeing from captivity in Egypt at the time of the

Exodus. Although they left the idols of Egypt behind them, they carried the gold and silver of Egypt with them, in order to make better and proper use of such riches, which were thus liberated in order to serve a higher purpose than before. In much the same way, the philosophy and culture of the ancient world could be appropriated by Christians, where this seemed right, and thus allowed to serve the cause of the Christian faith. Augustine clinched his argument by pointing out how several recent distinguished Christians had made use of classical wisdom in advancing the gospel.

> If those who are called philosophers, particularly the Platonists, have said anything which is true and consistent with our faith, we must not reject it, but claim it for our own use, in the knowledge that they possess it unlawfully. The Egyptians possessed idols and heavy burdens, which the children of Israel hated and from which they fled; however, they also possessed vessels of gold and silver and clothes which our fore-bears, in leaving Egypt, took for themselves in secret, intending to use them in a better manner (Exodus 3:21–2; 12:35–6), not doing this on their own authority, but by the command of God. The Egyptians themselves, in their ignorance, thus provided them with things which they themselves were not using well. In the same way, pagan learning is not entirely made up of false teachings and superstitions, or heavy burdens of unnecessary difficulty, which every one of us, when going out under the leadership of Christ from the fellowship of the heathen, ought to abhor and avoid. It contains also some excellent teachings, well suited to be used by truth, and excellent moral values. Indeed, some truths are even found among them which relate to the worship of the one God. Now these are, so to speak, their gold and their silver, which they did not invent themselves, but which they dug out of the mines of the prov-idence of God, which are scattered throughout the world, yet which are improperly and unlawfully prostituted to the worship of demons. The Christian, therefore, can separate these truths from their unfortu-nate associations, take them away, and put them to their proper use for the proclamation of the gospel. We must also take their "garments" – that is, human institutions such as are adapted to human relationships which are indispensable in this life – and put them to a Christian use.
>
> What else have many good and faithful people from amongst us done? Look at the wealth of gold and silver and clothes which Cyprian – that eloquent teacher and blessed martyr – brought with him when he left Egypt! And think of all that Lactantius brought with him, not to mention Marius Victorinus, Optatus and Hilary of Poitiers,

and others who are still living! And look at how much the Greeks have borrowed! And before all of these, we find that Moses, that most faithful servant of God, had done the same thing: after all, it is written of him that "he was learned in all the wisdom of the Egyptians" (Acts 7:22). Pagan superstition (especially in those times when, kicking against the yoke of Christ, it was persecuting the Christians) would never have allowed us access to those branches of knowledge it held useful, if it had suspected they were about to hand them over to the use of worshipping the One God, and thereby overturning the vain worship of idols. But they gave their gold and their silver and their garments to the people of God as they were going out of Egypt, not knowing how the things they gave would be turned to the service of Christ. For what was done at the time of the exodus was no doubt a type, prefiguring what happens now.

Read the text slowly. Note how Augustine adopts a critical yet positive attitude to philosophy. It asserts some things which are true, and others which are false. It cannot be totally rejected on the one hand; on the other, neither can it be uncritically accepted.

Augustine affirms that Christians are free to make use of philosophical ideas, which can be detached from their pagan associations. Augustine's argument is that philosophical ideas can be extricated from their historical associations with the pagan culture which persecuted earlier generations of Christians. Although this persecution had ended nearly a century before Augustine's time, it was still an important theme in Christian thinking. Augustine's approach allowed a more positive attitude to the ideas and values of secular culture to be adopted.

Finally, notice how Augustine appeals to a series of distinguished Christians who were converted to Christianity from paganism, yet were able to make good use of their pagan upbringing in serving the church. Cyprian is of especial importance for Augustine, in that Cyprian had been martyred by the Romans in the third century. The fact he had made use of philosophy in this way is seen by Augustine as an important confirmation of his basic approach.

1.2   Vincent of Lérins on tradition and theology

The word "tradition" comes from the Latin term *traditio* which bears such senses as "handing over," "handing down," or "handing on." At one level, it is a thoroughly biblical idea. Paul reminded his readers that he was handing on to them core teachings of the Christian faith which he had received from others (1 Corinthians 15:1–4). The term can refer both to the action of passing teachings on to others – something which Paul insists must be done within the church – and to the body of teachings which are passed on in this manner. Tradition can thus be understood as a process as well as a body of teaching. The Pastoral Epistles in particular stress the importance of "guarding the good deposit which was entrusted to you" (2 Timothy 1:14).

If any controversy served to emphasize the importance of tradition, it was the Gnostic debates of the second century. Faced with repeated assertions from his Gnostic critics that he had misrepresented the Bible, Irenaeus of Lyons (ca. 130–ca. 200) argued that they had simply chosen to interpret the Bible according to their own taste. What had been handed down, he insisted, was not merely the biblical texts, but a certain way of reading and understanding those texts.

Irenaeus' point is that a continuous stream of Christian teaching, life, and interpretation can be traced from the time of the apostles to his own period. The church is able to point to those who have maintained the teaching of the church, and to certain public standard creeds which set out the main lines of Christian belief. This, he argues, contrasts with the secret and mystical teaching of the Gnostics, which is not available for public inspection, and which cannot be traced back to the apostles themselves. Tradition is thus the guarantor of faithfulness to the original apostolic teaching, a safeguard against the innovations and misrepresentations of biblical texts on the part of the Gnostics.

This point was further developed in the early fifth century by Vincent of Lérins, who was concerned that certain doctrinal innovations were being introduced without adequate reason. Writing in the year 434, Vincent (who died at an unknown date before 450) expressed his belief that the controversies of his age had given rise to dangerous theological innovations. But how could such doctrinal innovations be identified as such? There was a need to have public standards by which such doctrines could be judged. So what standard was available, by which the church could be safeguarded from such errors? For Vincent, the answer was clear – tradition.

Developing this point, Vincent set out a triple criterion by which authentic Christian teaching may be established: *universality* (being believed everywhere), *antiquity* (being believed always), and *consensus* (being believed by all people).

> Therefore I have devoted considerable study and much attention to enquiring, from men of outstanding holiness and doctrinal correctness, in what way it might be possible for me to establish a kind of fixed and, as it were, general and guiding principle for distinguishing the truth of the catholic faith from the depraved falsehoods of the heretics. And the answer I receive from all can be put like this: if I or anyone else wishes to detect the deceits of the heretics or avoid their traps, and to remain healthy and intact in a sound faith, we ought, with the help of the Lord, to strengthen our faith in two ways; first, by the authority of the divine law, and then by the tradition of the catholic church.
>
> Now at this point someone may ask: since the canon of the scriptures is complete, and is in itself adequate, why is there any need to join to its authority the understanding of the church? Because Holy Scripture, on account of its depth, is not accepted in a universal sense. The same statements are interpreted in one way by one person, in another by someone else, with the result that there seem to be as many opinions as there are people. [...] Therefore, on account of the number and variety of errors, there is a need for someone to lay down a rule for the interpretation of the prophets and the apostles in such a way that is directed by the rule of the catholic church.
>
> Now in the catholic church itself the greatest care is taken that we hold that which has been believed everywhere, always, and by all people [*quod ubique, quod semper, quod ab omnibus creditum est*]. This is what is truly and properly catholic. This is clear from the force of the word and reason, which understands everything universally. We shall follow "universality" in this way, if we acknowledge this one faith to be true, which the entire church confesses throughout the world. We affirm "antiquity" if we in no way depart from those understandings which it is clear that the greater saints and our fathers proclaimed. And we follow "consensus" if in this antiquity we follow all (or certainly nearly all) the definitions of the bishops and masters.
>
> So what should a catholic Christian do if a small part of the church cuts itself off from the communion of the universal faith? Surely the soundness of the whole body is to be preferred to the unsoundness of a pestilent and corrupt part! What, if some new contamination were

to try and infect not merely a small part of the church, but its entirety? Then the Christian must hold fast to antiquity, which in this day cannot possibly be seduced by any fraudulent novelty.

But what if some error is found in antiquity on the part of two or three men, or even in a city or a province? In that case, the Christian should give priority to the decrees of an ancient General Council (if there are any) over the foolishness and ignorance of a few people. But what if some error should arise, and no such decree is found to be of relevance? Then the Christian must assemble and consult and interrogate the opinions of ancient writers – that is, those who, though living in various times and places, stood firmly within the communion and faith of the one catholic church, and were recognized and acknowledged to be approved authorities. The Christian can believe without any doubt or hesitation whatever can be established to have been held, written, and taught, not just by one or two of these, but by all, equally, with one consent, openly, frequently, and persistently.

Read the text carefully, making sure that you understand the problem that Vincent is trying to solve. How does Vincent arrive at the need for a publicly agreed standard of Christian orthodoxy?

Now consider this statement: "Christian orthodoxy is just repeating what the Bible says." How would Vincent respond to such a suggestion?

What does Vincent mean by "that which has been believed everywhere, always, and by all people"? Do you think that this is a workable definition of orthodoxy? What problems can you see with it?

1.3   John Calvin on the nature of faith

One of the tasks of theology is to clarify the meaning of its vocabulary. What do we mean, for example, when we use the word "God"? Or what is faith? It is very easy to use the term loosely, without bothering to reflect on what it means. An excellent example of critical reflection on how this important theological term is to be understood can be found in John Calvin's *Institutes of the Christian Religion*, which was first published in 1536 and went through many editions until the final, definitive edition of 1559. It is widely regarded as one of the most significant works of Protestant theology. Calvin (1509–64) is a very precise and logical theologian, who is generally very easy to read and understand.

Calvin's discussion of the nature of faith in the *Institutes* is set in the context of his analysis of redemption. Having shown how redemption is related to the person and work of Jesus Christ, Calvin proceeds to discuss "the manner of obtaining the grace of Christ, the benefits which it confers, and the effects which result from it." Calvin argues that the benefits of Christ remain external to us unless something happens by which they can be internalized. So long as we are separated from Christ, all that he achieved upon the cross is of no importance. It is by faith, Calvin argues, that these benefits are appropriated by the believer. This leads him to move on to a discussion of the nature of faith, as follows.

It is now proper to consider the nature of this faith, by means of which those who are adopted into the family of God gain possession of the heavenly kingdom. For the accomplishment of such a great goal, it is obvious that no mere opinion or persuasion is good enough. Particular care and diligence are necessary in discussing the true nature of faith on account of the serious delusions concerning it which are held by many in the present day. Lots of people, on hearing the term, think that it means nothing more than a certain common assent to the history of the gospel. [...]

Faith is the knowledge of the divine will in regard to us, as ascertained from his Word. And the foundation of it is a previous persuasion of the truth of God. So long as your mind entertains any misgivings as to the certainty of the Word, its authority will be weak and dubious, or rather it will have no authority at all. Nor is it sufficient to believe that God is true, and that he cannot lie or deceive, unless you feel firmly persuaded that every word which comes from him is sacred, inviolable truth.

But since the human heart is not brought to faith by every word of God, we must therefore consider what it is that faith specifically relates to in this word. The declaration of God to Adam was, "You shall surely die" (Genesis 2:17); and to Cain, "The voice of your brother's blood cries out to me from the ground" (Genesis 4:10). These, however, instead of being intended to establish faith, tend only to shake it. At the same time, we do not deny that it is the purpose of faith to assent to the truth of God whenever, whatever, and in whatever way God speaks. We are only inquiring what faith can find in the word of God to lean and rest upon. When conscience sees only wrath and indignation, how can it but tremble and be afraid? How can it do anything except avoid the God whom it dreads in this way? But faith ought to seek God, not avoid him. It is evident, therefore, that we have not yet obtained a full definition of faith, since it is impossible to use this word to refer to every kind of knowledge of the divine will. [...]

Now we shall have a right definition of faith if we say that it is a steady and certain knowledge of the divine benevolence towards us which is founded upon the truth of the gracious promise of God in Christ, and is both revealed to our minds and sealed in our hearts by the Holy Spirit.

Read this through, and take in what Calvin is saying. Try to follow the flow of his argument, as he sets out to pin down precisely what faith means by exploring various possibilities, and rejecting those that he considers to be inadequate. First of all, note how Calvin's definition of faith is *trinitarian*. Calvin ascribes different aspects of faith to each of the three persons of the Trinity – Father, Son, and Spirit. Try to identify each of these aspects. What role is played by each person of the Trinity, according to Calvin?

Now note that the first part of this definition declares that faith is a "steady and certain knowledge of the divine benevolence towards us." It is significant here that Calvin uses language that expresses confidence in God, and stresses God's reliability. Notice also how faith is defined as "knowledge'" – but a certain very specific kind of knowledge. It is not just "knowledge"; in fact, it is not even "knowledge of God." It is specifically "knowledge of *God's benevolence towards us*." Calvin's language is very specific and intentional. Faith is grounded and based in God's *goodness*. It is not simply about accepting that God exists, but about encountering God's kindness to us. Do you agree with Calvin at this point?

The definition now goes on to declare that faith is "founded upon the truth of the gracious promise of God in Christ." Notice how faith is again affirmed to be about knowledge – the use of the word "truth" is very important here. Calvin wants to make it absolutely clear that faith is not a human invention or delusion, but something that is grounded in the bedrock of truth. But notice how Calvin then proceeds to link this with a "gracious promise of God." For Calvin, we are dealing with a God who makes promises to us – promises which can be trusted and relied upon. Interestingly, Calvin identifies Christ as the confirmation or means of disclosure of these promises. You might like to look up 2 Corinthians 1:20, and see how Calvin's approach relates to that text.

Finally, Calvin clearly holds that faith involves both mind and heart. Note how, once more, Calvin affirms that faith is indeed about knowledge – something that affects the way in which we think, affecting our minds. Yet it is more than this: it is something that transforms us internally. Calvin's language about the human "heart" points to a deeper change within us than just mental acceptance of an idea. Calvin sees God as active throughout the process of coming to faith. Faith is not human insight; it is personal knowledge of God made possible by the Holy Spirit.

1.4   Karl Barth on revelation and the Word of God

The Swiss Protestant theologian Karl Barth (1886–1968) is widely regarded as one of the most significant theologians of the twentieth century. His *Church Dogmatics*, one of the most substantial and influential recent works of Christian theology, was originally delivered as lectures to his students at the University of Bonn and later at the University of Basel.

One of Barth's major themes is the priority of divine revelation. God speaks; the discipline of theology is the response of intellectual attentiveness and moral obedience that God's words demand and deserve. Unlike some earlier Protestant writers, Barth does not directly equate this "Word of God" with the text of the Bible. Rather, he develops the notion of the "three-fold form of the Word of God" in Jesus Christ, Scripture, and the preaching of the church. On this approach, the Bible is a witness to God's self-revelation in Christ, and is not itself to be identified with "revelation."

These ideas, although more fully developed in the *Church Dogmatics*, are found in an earlier form in a course of lectures given by Barth at the University of Göttingen during the academic year 1924/5. Our extract is taken from an early stage in those lectures, when Barth wrestles with the question of how one is to understand the idea of the "Word of God," and its implications for how Christian theology is to be done.

In a secondary introductory subsection I would like to say more explicitly what I mean by "reflection" on the Word of God. First, I must say something about the addition I have made to "Word of God" in the thesis of this first section: "which is spoken by God in revelation, which is recorded in the holy scripture of the prophets and apostles, and which now both is and should be proclaimed and heard in Christian preaching." You can see compressed in this addition all that I am trying to say this semester in the form of prolegomena to dogmatics. For this reason any supporting or expounding of the addition would anticipate my whole series. At this point I can only show logically and grammatically what is meant.

I am distinguishing the Word of God in a first address in which God himself and God alone is the speaker, in a second address in which it is the Word of a specific category of people (the prophets and apostles), and in a third address in which the number of its human agents or proclaimers is theoretically unlimited. But God's Word abides forever (Isaiah 40:8; 1 Peter 1:25). It neither is nor can be different whether it has its first, its second, or its third form, and always when it is one of the three it is also in some sense the other two as well. The Word of God on which dogmatics reflects — I need only refer to the common formula to show the point at issue — is one in three and three in one: revelation, scripture, and preaching — the Word of God as revelation, the Word of God as scripture, and the Word of God as preaching, neither to be confused nor separated. One Word of God, one authority, one power, and yet not one but three addresses. Three addresses of God in revelation, scripture, and preaching, yet not three Words of God, three authorities, truths, or powers, but one. Scripture is not revelation, but from revelation. Preaching is not revelation or scripture, but from both. But the Word of God is scripture no less than it is revelation, and it is preaching no less than it is scripture. Revelation is from God alone, scripture is from revelation alone, and preaching is from revelation and scripture. Yet there is no first or last, no greater or less. The first, the second, and the third are all God's Word in the same glory, unity in trinity and trinity in unity. I will not go on to say with the Athanasian Creed that those who would be saved must think thus of the Trinity, for as yet I have only said and not shown that this is so and why it is so. But I think that this statement, which must simply stand until it can be confirmed or not in the course of our discussion, will be enough to show what I have in mind when I call the object of the reflection which is the dogmatic task the Word of God.

I must add two observations. At this third point I have tried to indicate that God's Word is to be regarded as a living, actual, and present factor, the Word of God which now both is and should be proclaimed and heard. Now! Should be! Note in these expressions first of all the movement, the qualified temporal element, the turning from past to present denoted by them. The Word of God is God's speaking. It is ongoing as Christian preaching. It is not ongoing as revelation in the strict sense. It never took place as such. The statement "God revealed himself" means something different from the statement "revelation took place." Revelation is what it is in time, but as the frontier of time, remote from us as heaven is from earth. Nor is God's Word ongoing as holy scripture. It is in time as such. It took place as the witness given to revelation. But in itself it is a self-enclosed part of history which is as far from us as everything historical and past. Our experiences are not a continuation of those of the prophets and apostles. Theoretically one might declare the continuation of the biblical canon to be possible (e.g., if two lost epistles to the Corinthians were found again, or if an ecumenical council received the *Didache* into the [New Testament]). But this would not be an ongoing of scripture, only an extension of the concept of scripture, or of what the concept means. All conceivable extensions of scripture would still belong to the past, not to the present. They would not be a step out of the past into the future. But as Christian preaching, which proceeds from revelation and scripture (as the Holy Spirit proceeds from the Father and the Son), the Word of God is ongoing. It is present. Naturally, in, with, and under Christian preaching, revelation and scripture are present too, but not otherwise. In this regard we are not restricting the term "Christian preaching" to sermons from the pulpit, or to the work of pastors, but including in it whatever we all "preach" to ourselves in the quiet of our own rooms.

Barth's thought is relatively easy to follow, once his agenda has been understood. (Note that the *Didache* is an early Christian work, which was widely respected within the early church, but is not included in the canon of the New Testament.) One of the core themes is the relation of divine revelation, the Bible, and Christian preaching. How would you summarize this relationship?

Barth sets out a threefold account of the nature of God's self-disclosure in terms of the "addresses of God in revelation, scripture, and preaching." Notice how he hints at some kind of correspondence or analogy between these three "addresses of God" and the three persons of the Trinity. On the basis of this passage, how committed do you think he is to this analogy? What might its implications be?

One of Barth's concerns in this discussion is to avoid "freezing" revelation in a fixed set of statements, which determine and limit its scope and application. Where in the passage do you find this concern addressed? Do you think he is right to be concerned about this? How does the idea of the Word of God being "ongoing" address this?

1.5 Emil Brunner on revelation and reason

One of the most interesting theological debates of the twentieth century took place in 1934, between two Swiss Protestant theologians: Karl Barth and Emil Brunner (1889–1966). The debate concerned "natural theology" – the area of theology which considers what humanity can naturally know about God. Brunner and Barth had many theological similarities – for example, both stressed the priority of God's revelation, and resisted the idea that humanity could discover the nature and character of God through the use of pure reason. Yet there were some significant differences, as this reading will make clear.

Emil Brunner began his career as a pastor in the eastern Swiss village of Obstalden. An impressive series of publications led to him being appointed professor of theology at the University of Zurich from 1924 to 1955, during which time he produced many works of significance. One of their leading themes is the priority of divine revelation over natural human reason. Brunner, like Barth, places an emphasis upon the idea of revelation as the "word of God." But an important question emerges: is this "word of God" something that impacts immediately and directly on humanity? Or does it need to be interpreted?

One of the most fundamental differences between Barth and Brunner, which becomes clear in the passage to be studied, concerns whether the "word of God" overwhelms humanity, commanding assent and eliciting an appropriate response (Barth), or whether it addresses humanity, inviting them to make such a response (Brunner). The passage for study is taken from the work *Revelation and Reason*, which Brunner published in 1941, following his controversy with Barth on natural theology.

Since the Bible describes revelation as the "Word of God," this shows clearly that revelation presupposes a receptive spiritual subject. The manner in which the Word works is different from all subjective-causal, concrete-magical influences. The Word does not overwhelm, it does not coerce, it does not ignore the one "over against us," but it calls, addresses, threatens, and entreats; it "calls forth" or evokes decision. It appeals to hearing and understanding. The proclamation through the Word therefore applies only to the human creation which is endowed with reason. Certainly, "God can of these stones raise up children to Abraham" (Matthew 3:9). He can create humanity out of nothing by His almighty Word. But that is not our concern here; for God does not ordain that His Gospel shall be proclaimed to stones, plants, and animals, but to human beings alone; for they alone are *logikoi*, beings designed for the reception of words. God can redeem even idiots who are without reason; but this does not take place through the preaching of the Word. For an idiot, in the strict sense of the word, is a creature who is incapable of understanding words; he is open to the working of God's mighty power, but not to the Word of God, because he cannot understand speech at all.

God, when He became a human being, came down to the level of humanity, in order that humanity might be able to meet Him. He has adapted His revelation to humanity, in that He clothed it in the human word of the Apostles. He chose this form of revelation because communication through speech is the proper way in which human communication is carried on. Human beings use words, wherever they awaken to their human identity; as *humanus* they use language, that is, they can speak and understand the speech of others. This capacity was given to humanity as its own in the creation. Wherever the Gospel is proclaimed this capacity is presupposed. Capacity for speech is not given to us by the message of Christ, but it is claimed and used for the message of Christ.

Human capacity for speech belongs to the *lumen naturale*; indeed, it is the primary token by which we perceive the presence and the operation of the natural light, or the light of reason. But this *lumen naturale* is not without an original relation to the divine Word, which in Jesus Christ became flesh. It is not the same, but it comes from the same source, from the Logos of God. When God created humanity as a rational being, as a *logikos*, those who can understand and use words, He created them for the reception of His Word of revelation. As the personal being of humanity is a reflection of the divine personal Being, *imago Dei*, so the human word is *imago verbi divini*. The human capacity for speech is intended by the Creator as receptivity for His Word; that is its most original and direct meaning. "God is our nearest relation," says Pestalozzi. So also the Word of God is that which alone makes us "human" in the fullest sense of the word.

The Word of God comes to us as a human word – as the word of an Isaiah, a Paul, or a John. It makes use of a definite human language that is already in existence, with its vocabulary and its grammar. The Prophet speaks Hebrew, the Hebrew which every Hebrew understands; the Apostle speaks the Greek which every Greek and every educated man of his day understands. The Word of God makes use of these languages, and thus presupposes the understanding of these languages. It turns to the understanding of the hearer with his own particular language and mentality. It claims this understanding of language for itself. This adaptation, this consideration of that which man already has, comes out very clearly in the "translation" of the Hebrew–Greek Bible into other languages. Without this translation the Word of God remains closed and unknown. To such an extent does the Word of God presuppose an understanding of man – namely, of language – that it remains completely ineffective where this understanding cannot be presupposed. The Word of God submits to the process of translation into all the languages of the world; this shows how seriously God takes man. For God wills that human beings as subjects should not be overwhelmed, but that they should come into communion with Himself. That is why He speaks to us in a word that we are able to understand.

Read the passage slowly, and try to identify Brunner's central concerns. Can you identify any sentences that seem to sum up his general approach in this passage? Note how John Calvin's notion of God accommodating the form of revelation to take account of human weakness features prominently in Brunner's discussion, especially in his statement that God "has adapted His revelation to humanity."

Brunner clearly regards the human capacity for language as immensely important. Note how he reflects on the significance of biblical translation. The Bible, he argues, needs to be translated into languages that people can understand. Can you see the theological point that he draws out from this observation?

If not, the following discussion may help you. Suppose that the "word of God" was capable of breaking through human incomprehension, as Brunner believes Barth to teach. Since the "word of God" was originally given in Hebrew or Greek, the languages of the Bible, should not this suggest that translation is unnecessary? Yet we all know that translation is needed. This, Brunner, suggests, leads to the conclusion that God "speaks to us in a word that we are able to understand." Locate this sentence in the passage, and make sure you understand the argument that leads to this conclusion.

Finally, try to reflect on the broader implications of this point. If God indeed "speaks to us in a word that we are able to understand," does this imply that a human failure to understand what God speaks makes revelation impossible? Does this suggest that humanity is active in revelation, in that humans have to make sense of what God is saying?

1.6   Paul Tillich on the nature of theology

What is theology? And what is the task of the theologian? Many answers have been given throughout the long history of Christian theology, reflecting longstanding debates about the nature of Christianity, the place of critical reflection within the church, and the way in which the Christian faith engages the mind, imagination, and emotions. There is no obvious right answer – yet trying to answer the question illuminates the issues.

One answer was given by Paul Tillich (1886–1965), one of the twentieth century's most notable theologians. Tillich was a German Lutheran theologian who was sacked for his opposition to Adolf Hitler in 1933. He emigrated to the United States, initially holding a chair in theology at Union Theological Seminary, New York, before being appointed professor of religion at Harvard University.

Our reading is taken from one of three sermons delivered during the 1940s on the topic of "the theologian," aimed especially at students of theology at Union Seminary. Tillich opens his reflections on his theme by referring to the "Areopagus Address," delivered by Paul in Athens (Acts 17:16–34), and notes how theology can be considered to articulate the Christian response to the "ultimate questions" that are asked within a culture.

> The famous scene in which Paul speaks from the central place of Greek wisdom shows us a man who is the prototype of the *answering* theologian. Paul has been asked about his message, partly because the Athenians were always curious about novelties, and partly because they knew that they did *not* know the truth, and seriously desired to know it. There are three stages in Paul's answer, which reveal the three tasks of the *answering* theologian. The first stage of Paul's answer consists in the assertion that those who ask him the ultimate question are not unconscious of the answer: these men adore an unknown God and thus witness to their religious knowledge in spite of their religious ignorance. That knowledge is not astounding, because God is close to each one of us; it is in *Him* that we live and move and exist; these *also* belong to His race. The first answer, then, that we must give to those who ask us about such a question is that they themselves are already aware of the answer. We must show to them that neither they nor we are outside of God, that even the atheists stand in God – namely, that power out of which they live, the truth for which they grope, and the ultimate meaning of life in which they believe. It is bad theology and religious cowardice

ever to think that there may be a place where we could look *at* God, as though He were something outside of us to be argued for or against. Genuine atheism is not humanly possible, for God is nearer to a man than that man is to himself. *A* God can only be denied in the name of another God; and God appearing in *one* form can be denied only by God appearing in another form. That is the first answer that we must give to ourselves and to those who question us, not as an abstract statement, but rather as a continuous interpretation of our human existence, in all its hidden motions and abysses and certainties.

God is nearer to us than we ourselves. We cannot find a place outside of Him; but we can *try* to find such a place. The second part of Paul's answer is that we can be in the condition of continuous flight from God. We can imagine one way of escape after another; we can replace God by the products of our imagination; and we do. Although mankind is not strange to God, it is estranged from Him. Although mankind is never without God, it perverts the picture of God. Although mankind is never without the knowledge of God, it is ignorant of God. Mankind is separated from its origin; it lives under a law of wrath and frustration, of tragedy and self-destruction, because it produces one distorted image of God after another, and adores those images. The answering theologian must discover the false gods in the individual soul and in society. He must probe into their most secret hiding-places. He must challenge them through the power of the Divine Logos, which makes him a theologian. Theological polemic is not merely a theoretical discussion, but rather a spiritual judgement against the gods which are not God, against those structures of evil, those distortions of God in thought and action. No compromise or adaptation or theological self-surrender is permitted on this level. For the first Commandment is the rock upon which theology stands. There is no synthesis possible between God and the idols. In spite of the dangers inherent in so judging, the theologian must become an instrument of the Divine Judgement against a distorted world.

So far as they can grasp it in the light of their own questions, Paul's listeners are willing to accept this two-fold answer. But Paul then speaks of a third thing which they are not able to bear. They either reject it immediately, or they postpone the decision to reject or accept it. He speaks of a Man Whom God has destined to be the Judgement and the Life of the world. That is the third and final part of the theological answer. For we are real theologians when we state that Jesus is the Christ, and that it is in Him that the Logos of theology is manifest.

But we are only theologians when we interpret this paradox, this stumbling-block for idealism and realism, for the weak and the strong, for both pagans and Jews. As theologians, we must interpret that paradox, and not throw paradoxical phrases at the minds of the people. We must not preserve or produce artificial stumbling-blocks, miracle-stories, legends, myths, and other sophisticated paradoxical talk. We must not distort, by ecclesiastical and theological arrogance, that great cosmic paradox that there is victory over death within the world of death itself. We must not impose the heavy burden of wrong stumbling-blocks upon those who ask us questions. But neither must we empty the true paradox of its power. For true theological existence is the witnessing to Him Whose yoke is easy and Whose burden is light, to Him Who is the true paradox.

Tillich's sermon is clearly written, and is generally easy to understand. The first paragraph sets out a theme which is characteristic of Tillich: that human culture raises certain "ultimate questions," which the Christian faith is in a position to engage and answer. Although Tillich would later frame and answer these questions in existentialist terms, he adopts a much more open-ended attitude in this sermon. Note how Tillich suggests, following both Martin Luther and John Calvin, that culture degenerates into idolatry if its searching is not anchored to the Christian revelation. Note also his intriguing suggestion that "genuine atheism is not humanly possible." How does he arrive at this conclusion? Do you think he is right?

Later in the sermon, we find a second major theme of Tillich's theology – the idea of "paradox." As the passage makes clear, Jesus of Nazareth is one such paradox. Tillich holds that such paradoxes hold the key to theological insight, in that they force us to revise and review existing ways of thinking. How does he develop this point in the final sentences of this extract?

1.7   C. S. Lewis on myths in theology

One of the most important debates in modern theology has to do with how Christianity relates to other religions. This raises some important questions about the nature of divine revelation, and how other religions are understood to relate to this. One of the most interesting discussions of this question comes from the Oxford literary critic and novelist C. S. Lewis (1898–1963). Lewis held that Christianity takes the structural form of a myth (a word that Lewis uses to mean a grand account of things, or a "metanarrative"). Yet it differs from all other such myths, because it is the *real* myth, to which all other myths only approximate. In this extract, taken from a paper entitled "Is Theology Poetry?," delivered to the Socratic Club at Oxford in 1945, Lewis sets out why occasional similarities between Christianity and other religions is to be expected, on the basis of the overarching nature of the Christian view of reality.

There are, however, two other lines of thought which might lead us to call Theology a mere poetry, and these I must now consider. In the first place, it certainly contains elements similar to those which we find in many early, and even savage, religions. And those elements in the early religions may now seem to us to be poetical. The question here is rather complicated. We now regard the death and return of Balder as a poetical idea, a myth. We are invited to infer thence that the death and resurrection of Christ is a poetical idea, a myth. But we are not really starting with the datum "Both are poetical" and thence arguing "Therefore both are false." Part of the poetical aroma which hangs about Balder is, I believe, due to the fact that we have already come to disbelieve in him. So that disbelief, not poetical experience, is the real starting point of the argument. But this is perhaps an over-subtlety, certainly a subtlety, and I will leave it on one side.

What light is really thrown on the truth or falsehood of Christian Theology by the occurrence of similar ideas in Pagan religion? I think the answer was very well given a fortnight ago by Mr Brown. Supposing, for purposes of argument, that Christianity is true, then it could avoid all coincidence with other religions only on the supposition that all other religions are one hundred per cent erroneous. To which, you remember, Professor Price replied by agreeing with Mr Brown and saying: Yes. From these resemblances you may conclude not "so much the worse for the Christians" but "so much the better for the Pagans." The truth is that the resemblances tell nothing either for or against the truth of Christian Theology. If you start from the assumption that the Theology is false, the resemblances are quite consistent with that assumption. One would expect creatures of the same sort, faced with the same universe, to make the same false guess more than once. But if you start with the assumption that the Theology is true, the resemblances fit in equally well. Theology, while saying that a special illumination has been vouchsafed to Christians and (earlier) to Jews, also says that there is some divine illumination vouchsafed to all men. The Divine light, we are told, "lighteneth every man." We should, therefore, expect to find in the imagination of great Pagan teachers and myth-makers some glimpse of that theme which we believe to be the very plot of the whole cosmic story – the theme of incarnation, death and rebirth. And the differences between the Pagan Christs (Balder, Osiris, etc.) and the Christ Himself is much what we should expect to find. The Pagan stories are all about someone dying and rising, either every year, or else nobody knows where and nobody knows when. The Christian story is about a historical personage, whose execution can be dated pretty accurately, under a named Roman magistrate, and with whom the society that He founded is in a continuous relation down to the present day. It is not the difference between falsehood and truth. It is the difference between a real event on the one hand and dim dreams or premonitions of that same event on the other. It is like watching something come gradually into focus: first it hangs in the clouds of myth and ritual, vast and vague, then it condenses, grows hard and in a sense small, as a historical event in first-century Palestine. This gradual focusing goes on even inside the Christian tradition itself. The earliest stratum of the Old Testament contains many truths in a form which I take to be legendary, or even mythical – hanging in the clouds: but gradually the truth condenses, becomes more and more historical. From things like Noah's Ark or the sun standing still upon Ajalon, you come down to the court memoirs of King David. Finally you reach the New Testament and history reigns supreme, and the Truth is incarnate. And "incarnate" is here more than a metaphor. It is not an accidental resemblance that what, from the point of view of being, is stated in the form "God became Man," should involve, from the point of view of human knowledge, the statement "Myth became Fact." The essential meaning of all things came down from the "heaven" of myth to the "earth" of history. In so doing, it partly emptied itself of its glory, as Christ emptied Himself of His glory to be Man. That is the real explanation of the fact that Theology, far from defeating its rivals by a superior poetry is, in a superficial but quite real sense, less poetical than they. That is why the New Testament is, in the same sense, less poetical than the Old. Have you not often felt in Church, if the first lesson is some great passage, that the second lesson is somehow small by comparison – almost, if one might say so, humdrum? So it is and so it must be. This is the humiliation of myth into fact, of God into Man: what is everywhere and always, imageless and ineffable, only to be glimpsed in dream and symbol and the acted poetry of ritual, becomes small, solid – no bigger than a man who can lie asleep in a rowing boat on the Lake of Galilee.

Lewis' argument in this passage is that, throughout its history, humanity has developed myths which can be seen as glimpsing something of the true situation. (The word "myth" is being used in a technical sense here, and does not mean "something untrue." Perhaps the idea of a "narrated worldview" expresses Lewis' approach best.) These myths can therefore be seen as approximations to a greater truth. So the question then arises: which of these myths is best? Which corresponds most closely to reality? Lewis argues that the Christian story or "myth" is to be seen as the reality to which all myths bear witness, however partially and inadequately. The incarnation, Lewis suggests, can be understood as "myth become fact."

Read the passage carefully, and try to assemble the various elements of Lewis' argument. How does Lewis account for similarities between Christianity and other religions? What does he mean by his intriguing phrase "the humiliation of myth into fact"? And how does this lead into his cryptic final statement about Jesus of Nazareth?

1.8   John Paul II on faith and reason

One of the finest essays on the relation of faith and reason was published in 1998. The encyclical letter *Fides et Ratio* ("Faith and Reason") was issued by Pope John Paul II (1920–2005), formerly the Polish cardinal Karol Józef Wojtyła. (An "encyclical" letter is a letter that is widely distributed – in this case, to all the bishops of the Catholic church.) In this letter, John Paul II explores the significance of the universal human drive to make sense of things, which underlies both philosophy and theology. He affirms the importance of reason, while protesting against excessively optimistic accounts of what it can achieve unaided. So how, he asks, does this universal human quest for truth and wisdom relate to the truths of the Christian faith? How can reflection on the world of nature lead into the presence of God?

The approach adopted by *Fides et Ratio* is classic, honoring the genuine human quest for wisdom, while insisting that this reaches its climax and goal in the person of Jesus Christ. Although wounded and partially blinded by sin, the human mind has not lost its innate longing to pursue meaning, or its ability to know the truth. John Paul II thus argues the case for a philosophy that is capable of transcending empirical data in order to attain something absolute, ultimate, and foundational – which the Christian faith declares to have been disclosed, once and for all, in Jesus of Nazareth.

"Wisdom knows all and understands all" (Wisdom 9:11)

16. Sacred Scripture indicates with remarkably clear cues how deeply related are the knowledge conferred by faith and the knowledge conferred by reason; and it is in the Wisdom literature that this relationship is addressed most explicitly. What is striking about these biblical texts, if they are read without prejudice, is that they embody not only the faith of Israel, but also the treasury of cultures and civilizations which have long vanished. As if by special design, the voices of Egypt and Mesopotamia sound again and certain features common to the cultures of the ancient Near East come to life in these pages which are so singularly rich in deep intuition.

It is no accident that, when the sacred author comes to describe the wise man, he portrays him as one who loves and seeks the truth: "Happy the man who meditates on wisdom and reasons intelligently, who reflects in his heart on her ways and ponders her secrets. He pursues her like a hunter and lies in wait on her paths. He peers through her windows and listens at her doors. He camps near her house and fastens his tent-peg to her walls; he pitches his tent near her and so finds an excellent resting-place; he places his children under her protection and lodges under her boughs; by her he is sheltered from the heat and he dwells in the shade of her glory" (Sirach 14:20–27).

For the inspired writer, as we see, the desire for knowledge is characteristic of all people. Intelligence enables everyone, believer and nonbeliever, to reach "the deep waters" of knowledge (cf. Proverbs 20:5). It is true that ancient Israel did not come to knowledge of the world and its phenomena by way of abstraction, as did the Greek philosopher or the Egyptian sage. Still less did the good Israelite understand knowledge in the way of the modern world which tends more to distinguish different kinds of knowing. Nonetheless, the biblical world has made its own distinctive contribution to the theory of knowledge.

What is distinctive in the biblical text is the conviction that there is a profound and indissoluble unity between the knowledge of reason and the knowledge of faith. The world and all that happens within it, including history and the fate of peoples, are realities to be observed, analysed and assessed with all the resources of reason, but without faith ever being foreign to the process. Faith intervenes not to abolish reason's autonomy nor to reduce its scope for action, but solely to bring the human being to understand that in these events it is the God of Israel who acts. Thus the world and the events of history cannot be understood in depth without professing faith in the God who is at work in them. Faith sharpens the inner eye, opening the mind to discover in the flux of events the workings of Providence. Here the words of the Book of Proverbs are pertinent: "The human mind plans the way, but the Lord directs the steps" (Proverbs 16:9). This is to say that with the light of reason human beings can know which path to take, but they can follow that path to its end, quickly and unhindered, only if with a rightly tuned spirit they search for it within the horizon of faith. Therefore, reason and faith cannot be separated without diminishing the capacity of men and women to know themselves, the world and God in an appropriate way.

17. There is thus no reason for competition of any kind between reason and faith: each contains the other, and each has its own scope for action. Again the Book of Proverbs points in this direction when it exclaims: "It is the glory of God to conceal things, but the glory of kings is to search things out" (Proverbs 25:2). In their respective worlds, God and the human being are set within a unique relationship. In God

there lies the origin of all things, in him is found the fullness of the mystery, and in this his glory consists; to men and women there falls the task of exploring truth with their reason, and in this their nobility consists. The Psalmist adds one final piece to this mosaic when he says in prayer: "How deep to me are your thoughts, O God! How vast is the sum of them! If I try to count them, they are more than the sand. If I come to the end, I am still with you" (Psalm 139:17–18). The desire for knowledge is so great and it works in such a way that the human heart, despite its experience of insurmountable limitation, yearns for the infinite riches which lie beyond, knowing that there is to be found the satisfying answer to every question as yet unanswered.

Read the passage carefully, and try to identify the thread of argument that runs through it. How is a connection established between the general quest for wisdom and the Christian revelation?

Make a list of all the biblical works that are cited in this passage. You ought to be able to find six passages that are either explicitly cited, or referred to. All are taken from the Old Testament. These are: Psalms; Proverbs; Sirach (also known as Ecclesiasticus); and the Book of Wisdom (which Protestants treat as part of the Apocrypha, in that it was not originally written in Hebrew). Interestingly, these four books belong to the genre usually known as "wisdom literature," both celebrating and illustrating the human longing to make sense of the world.

Much of what is stated in this section of the document can be summarized in its terse declaration that "faith sharpens the inner eye." Locate this statement, and examine its context. What do you think John Paul II meant by this? And how does it illuminate the relation of faith and reason?

CHAPTER 2

God

Theology is "talk about God." So what sort of ideas about God have been explored by Christian theology? Limits on space mean that we can only look at some of the most interesting aspects of the many discussions within Christian theology concerning the nature, attributes, and character of God.

During the patristic period, much attention was given to distinguishing the Christian God from rival conceptions of divinity, particularly within the Greek culture of the eastern Mediterranean area. The great Egyptian city of Alexandria, for example, was home to a wide variety of religions with an astonishingly diverse range of understandings of what the word "god" meant. Some clarification was clearly needed, if the God worshipped by Christians was not to be confused with its pagan alternatives. How could the "God and Father of our Lord Jesus Christ" (Ephesians 1:3) be distinguished from more generic notions of divinity, or from the various gods of late classical culture?

In more recent years, other questions have become increasingly important. Christian theology has tended to use predominantly male language when referring to God – for example, think of the way in which the Lord's Prayer begins with the words "Our Father." The rise of feminism has seen considerable reflection on whether this implies that God is male – and,

Theology: The Basic Readings, Third Edition. Edited by Alister E. McGrath.
Editorial material and organization © Alister E. McGrath.
Published 2018 by John Wiley & Sons Ltd.

if not, how this can be expressed more appropriately in the language and terminology used to refer to God.

A further area of debate concerns whether God may be said to suffer. Most discussions of this question during the patristic and medieval periods took the position that God was immune from experiencing suffering. If God was believed to be perfect, it was argued, surely that perfection would be compromised if God experienced something so degrading as suffering. However, the question was reopened in the twentieth century, partly in response to the vast human sufferings of the world wars of that age. How, many asked, could God not be affected by such suffering? Surely God had to be impacted in some way by the pain of his creation?

In this chapter, we shall survey a range of Christian explorations of the nature and character of God, beginning with an attempt from the first centuries of the Christian church to distinguish the "God and Father of our Lord Jesus Christ" from other ideas of God.

2.1   Athenagoras of Athens on the Christian God

One of the more intriguing ironies of history is that the first Christians were widely accused of being "atheists" by their pagan critics – not because they denied the existence of a god, but because they challenged the validity of the pagan religious system of the late classical world. The Christian refusal to observe the state religious conventions marked them out as troublemakers and potential revolutionaries – something that the Roman authorities were not prepared to tolerate. Roman political stability often depended on conformity to the "imperial cult" – treating the emperor as a divine figure, something that Christians were not prepared to do, believing it compromised their commitment to God.

The imperial cult became so influential in the major cities of the eastern Roman empire in the late first century that it was inevitable that some form of confrontation would take place between the secular authorities and Christian "atheists." One of the most frequently cited pieces of evidence here is the famous letter of Pliny the Younger to Trajan, dating from about 112. In this letter, Pliny the Younger comments on the growing number of Christians who refused to worship the image of the Roman emperor. Although Pliny reports that he found nothing more sinister than "a depraved and extravagant superstition," it is clear from his letter that Christianity was suspect on account of its refusal to worship the emperor, which suggested that it was bent on overthrowing the existing social order.

In this defense of the Christian faith against pagan criticisms, written in Greek around 177 and addressed to the Roman emperors Marcus Aurelius Antonius and Lucius Aurelius Commodus, the second-century writer Athenagoras of Athens sets out the main features of the gospel in a lucid and reasoned manner. The early Christians were accused of atheism on account of their refusal to worship the emperor. In this extract, in which Athenagoras explains what Christians believe about God, important anticipations of later thinking on the Trinity can be detected.

First of all, let us consider the allegation that we are atheists (I will meet the charges one by one, that we may not be ridiculed for having no answer to give to those who make them). The Athenians had good reason to judge Diagoras guilty of atheism. To start with, he spread the Orphic doctrine, published the mysteries of Eleusis and of the Cabiri, and even chopped up a wooden statue of Hercules so that he could boil his turnips. But he went further than that, and actually publicly declared that there was no God at all! But surely it is ludicrous to describe us as "atheists," when we distinguish God from matter, and teach that matter is one thing and God another, and that they are separated by a wide interval (for that the Deity is uncreated and eternal, to be beheld by the understanding and reason alone, while matter is created and perishable.) [...] But, since our doctrine acknowledges one God, the Maker of this universe, who is himself uncreated (for that which is does not come to be, but that which is not) but has made all things by the Logos which is from him, we are treated unreasonably in both respects, when we are both defamed and persecuted. [...]

We are not atheists, therefore, in that we acknowledge one God, who is uncreated, eternal, invisible, impassible, incomprehensible, illimitable, who is apprehended by understanding and reason, who is surrounded by light, and beauty, and spirit, and power ineffable, by whom the universe has been created through His Logos, and set in order, and is kept in being. I think I have made this clear. (I say "his Logos," for we acknowledge also a Son of God.) Nor should anyone think that it is ridiculous that God should have a Son. For though the poets, in their fictions, represent the gods as no better than human beings, our way of thinking is not the same as theirs, concerning either God the Father or the Son. But the Son of God is the Logos of the Father, in idea and in operation. All things were made by him after his pattern, since the Father and the Son being one. And, the Son being in the Father and the Father in the Son, in oneness and power of spirit, the understanding and reason of the Father is the Son of God.

But if, in your outstanding intelligence, it occurs to you to inquire what is meant by the Son, I will state briefly that he is the first product of the Father, not as having been brought into existence (for from the beginning, God, who is the eternal mind, had the Logos in himself, being from eternity instinct with Logos); but inasmuch as He came forth to be the idea and energizing power of all material things, which lay like a nature without attributes, and an inactive earth, the weightier elements being mixed up with the lighter. The prophetic Spirit also agrees with our statements. "The Lord," it says, "made me, the beginning of His ways to His works." The Holy Spirit himself also, which operates in the prophets, we assert to be an outpouring from God, flowing from Him, and returning back again like a beam of the sun.

Who, then, would not be astonished to hear men who speak of God the Father, and of God the Son, and of the Holy Spirit, and who declare both their power in union and their distinction in order, called atheists? Nor is our teaching in what relates to the divine nature confined to these points; but we recognize also a multitude of angels and ministers, whom God the Maker and Framer of the world distributed and appointed to their several posts by his Logos, to occupy themselves about the elements, and the heavens, and the world, and the things in it, and the goodly ordering of them all.

As noted above, early Christian writers were often branded as atheists by their critics within the secular imperial establishment, because they either denied the gods of the classical Roman pantheon, or refused to conform to the imperial cult which had become particularly well established in the eastern regions of the Roman empire. Part of the task of the first Christian apologists was thus to rebut the charge of atheism.

Yet the rejection of the charge of atheist was often combined with an explanation of the nature of Christian belief. It must be remembered that Christianity was still being oppressed at this time, so that most Christian meetings took place in secret. There was little way that the Roman imperial public could gain an informed understanding of what Christians believed, other than through the writings of Christians who were prepared to take seriously the concerns of secular culture, such as Athenagoras.

Read the passage carefully. What are the characteristics of Athenagoras' teaching about the nature of God? How do you think that this would help him refute the charge of atheism? What are the building blocks of his concept of God? It is important to note how an implicitly trinitarian idea of God can be seen in this passage, even though Athenagoras does not weave its elements together to yield a more developed form of this doctrine.

2.2   Thomas Aquinas on analogies of God

Talking about God involves using words. So how does this work? How can words be used to refer to God? This question, along with many others, is considered in the works of the great medieval scholastic theologian Thomas Aquinas (ca. 1225–75). Of those works, the greatest is generally agreed to be his *Summa Theologiae* ("The Totality of Theology"), written during the years 1265–74, when he was based at the University of Paris. This work is widely regarded as a landmark in Christian theology, and is one of the most widely used and widely cited theological sources.

One of the issues which Aquinas discusses in his *Summa Theologiae* is whether human language that is used to refer to God – as in the phrases "God is righteous" or "God is wise" – bears any relation to the same words, when used to refer to human beings – for example, in the phrase "Socrates is righteous" or "Solomon is wise." The basic idea that Aquinas explores is that these words are used *analogously* in these different contexts. Although they are used with different meanings, there is a clear relationship between them, reflecting in part the fact that the created order bears the likeness of its creator. The way in which the word refers to God is similar to, but not identical with, the way it refers to earthly objects.

Basing himself on Paul's statement (Romans 1:20) that "the invisible things of God are made known by those things that are made," Aquinas argues that there is an analogy between God the creator and the creation – between the invisible things of God, and the visible things of the world. This basic idea provides a theological gateway from what we see in this world, and what lies beyond it. On account of it having been created by God, the physical world is able to point beyond itself, and – providing it is correctly interpreted – point to God.

We can distinguish two kinds of analogical uses of words. First, there is the case of one word being used of several things because each of them has some proportion to another. Thus we use the word "healthy" in relation to both a diet and a complexion because each of these has some order and proportion to "health" in an animal, the former as its cause, the latter as its symptom. Second, there is the case of the same word used because of some proportion – just as "healthy" is used in relation to both the diet and the animal because the diet is the cause of the health in the animal.

In this way some words are used neither univocally nor purely equivocally of God and creatures, but analogically. We cannot speak of God at all except on the basis of creatures, and so whatever is said of both God and creatures is said in virtue of a certain order that creatures have in relation to God as their source and cause in which all their perfections pre-exist.

This way of using words lies somewhere between pure equivocation and simple univocity. The word is used neither in the same sense, as in the case of univocation, nor in totally different senses, as with equivocation. The several senses of a word which is used analogically signify different relations to something, just as "health" in a complexion means a symptom of health and in a diet means a cause of that health. [...]

All words used metaphorically in relation to God apply primarily to creatures and secondarily to God. When used in relation to God they signify merely a certain likeness between God and the creature. When we speak of a meadow as "smiling," we only mean that it is seen at its best when it flowers, just as people are seen at their best when they smile, according to a similarity of proportion between them. In the same way, if we speak of God as a "lion," we only mean that he is mighty in his deeds, like a lion. It is thus clear that, when something is said in relation to God, its meaning is to be determined on the basis of the meaning it has when used in relation to creatures.

This is also the case for words that are not used metaphorically, if they were simply used, as some have supposed, to express God's causality. If, for example, "God is good" meant the same as "God is the cause of goodness in creatures," the word "good," as applied to God, would have contained within its meaning the goodness of the creature. "Good" would thus apply primarily to creatures and secondarily to God.

But it has already been shown that words of this sort are said of God not just causally, but also essentially. When we say "God is good" or "God is wise," we do not simply mean that God causes wisdom or goodness, but that these perfections pre-exist supremely in God. We conclude, therefore, that from the point of view of what the word means it is used primarily of God and derivatively of creatures, for what the word means – the perfection it signifies – flows from God to the creature. But from the point of view of our use of the word we apply it first to creatures because we know them first. That, as we have mentioned already, is why it has a way of signifying what is appropriate to creatures.

In this major analysis of the way in which the created order mirrors its creator, Aquinas points out that speaking about God involves using words that normally apply to things in the everyday world. So how do these two different uses relate to each other? Aquinas draws a distinction between the "univocal" use of a word (where the word means exactly the same thing in every context) and the "equivocal" use (where the same word is used, but with different meanings). Thus the word "bat" is used *univocally* when it is used to refer to a horseshoe bat and a long-eared bat, in that the same word is being used to refer to nocturnal flying animals in each case. But the word "bat" is used *equivocally* when the same word is used to refer to both a nocturnal flying animal, and a piece of wood used to strike a ball in baseball or cricket. The word may be the same, but the meaning is quite different.

In this important passage, Aquinas argues that words cannot be used univocally to refer both to God and to humanity. Thus the word "wise" does not mean the same in the statements "God is wise" and "Solomon is wise." The gulf between God and humanity is too great for the word to mean the same. Yet the word is not used equivocally, as if it referred to something totally different. There is a relation between its use to refer to God and its use in human contexts. The word "wise" is used *analogously*, to mean that divine wisdom is not identical to, nor totally different from, human wisdom. There is "an analogy, that is, a certain proportion, between them."

2.3   Jürgen Moltmann on the suffering of God

Early Christian writers were virtually unanimous: God could not share in the suffering of the world. To be perfect is to be unchanging and self-sufficient. It is therefore impossible for such a perfect being to be affected or changed by anything outside itself. And since God is a perfect being, it was argued that he could not be affected by the pain and suffering of the world.

Now an obvious objection to this position might be raised, based on the doctrine of the incarnation. Since Jesus Christ was God incarnate – truly divine and truly human – it would therefore follow that God suffered in Christ. If Jesus Christ is God, at least in some sense of the word, and Jesus suffered, then it would seem that, in some way, God suffered as well. Not so, declared most of the patristic writers, deeply influenced by the pagan idea of the "impassibility" of God. Christ suffered only in his human nature. His divine nature was not affected in this way. God thus did not experience human suffering, and remained unaffected by the pain of the world.

This view was challenged in the twentieth century by a number of writers, including the German Protestant theologian Jürgen Moltmann (born 1926), formerly professor of systematic theology at the University of Tübingen. His book *The Crucified God* (1972) broke new ground, by insisting that a God who could not suffer was a God who could not be said to love. For Moltmann, the crucifixion of Jesus Christ was to be seen as the supreme moment of God's sharing in the suffering of his world. In this extract, taken from an essay written around this time, Moltmann sets out the case for affirming God's capacity and willingness to suffer.

If God were really incapable of suffering, he would also be as incapable of loving as the God of Aristotle, who was loved by all, but could not love. Whoever is capable of love is also capable of suffering, because he is open to the suffering that love brings with it, although he is always able to surmount that suffering because of love. God does not suffer, like his creature, because his being is incomplete. He loves from the fullness of his being and suffers because of his full and free love. […]

Christians have to speak about God in the presence of Jesus' abandonment by God on the cross, which can provide the only complete justification of their theology. The cross is either the Christian end of all theology or it is the beginning of a specifically Christian theology. When theologians speak about God on the cross of Christ, this inevitably becomes a trinitarian debate about the "story of God" which is quite distinct from all monotheism, polytheism or pantheism. The central position occupied by the crucified Christ is the specifically Christian element in the history of the world and the doctrine of the Trinity is the specifically Christian element in the doctrine of God. Both are very closely connected. It is not the bare trinitarian formulas in the New Testament, but the constant testimony of the cross which provides the basis for Christian faith in the Trinity. The most concise expression of the Trinity is God's action on the cross, in which God allowed the Son to sacrifice himself through the Spirit (B. Steffen). [...]

Paul introduced a new meaning into the term *paredokein* when he presented Jesus' abandonment by God not in the historical context of his life, but in the eschatological context of faith. God "did not spare his own Son, but gave him up for us all; will he not also give us all things with him?" (Romans 8:32). In the historical abandonment of the crucified Christ by the Father, Paul perceived the eschatological abandonment or "giving up" of the Son by the Father for the sake of "ungodly" men who had abandoned and been abandoned by God. In stressing that God had given up "his own Son," Paul extended the abandonment of the Son to the Father, although not in the same way, as the Patripassian heretics had done, insisting that the Son's sufferings could be predicated of the Father. In the Pauline view, Jesus suffered death abandoned by God. The Father, on the other hand, suffered the death of his Son in the pain of his love. The Son was "given up" by the Father and the Father suffered his abandonment from the Son. Kazoh Kitamori has called this "the pain of God."

The death of the Son is different from this "pain of God" the Father, and for this reason it is not possible to speak, as the Theopaschites did, of the "death of God." If we are to understand the story of Jesus' death abandoned by God as an event taking place between the Father and the Son, we must speak in terms of the Trinity and leave the universal concept of God aside, at least to begin with. In Galatians 2:20, the word *paredokein* appears with Christ as the subject: "... the Son of God, who loved me and gave himself for me." According to this statement, then, it is not only the Father who gives the Son up, but the Son who gives himself up. This indicates that Jesus' will and that of the Father were the same at the point where Jesus was abandoned on the cross and they were completely separated. Paul himself interpreted Christ's being abandoned by God as love, and the same interpretation is found in John (John 3:16). The author of 1 John regarded this event of love on the cross as the very existence of God himself; "God is love" (1 John 4:16). This is why it was possible at a later period to speak, with reference to the cross, of *homoousia*, the Son and the Father being of one substance. In the cross, Jesus and his God are in the deepest sense separated by the Son's abandonment by the Father, yet at the same time they are in the most intimate sense united in this abandonment or "giving up." This is because this "giving up" proceeds from the event of the cross that takes place between the Father who abandons and the Son who is abandoned, and this "giving up" is none other than the Holy Spirit.

The ideas which are set out in this passage, and more fully in *The Crucified God*, have been highly influential. According to Moltmann, both the Father and the Son suffer – but they experience that suffering in different manners. The Son suffers the pain and death of the cross; the Father gives up and suffers the loss of the Son. Although both Father and Son are involved in the cross, their involvement is not *identical* but *distinct*.

The emphasis upon "love" is also of importance. Central to Moltmann's argument is that the notion of love implies suffering. Can God be said to "love" without being said to "suffer"? For Moltmann, the answer is emphatically negative. "Whoever is capable of love is also capable of suffering." Locate this passage within the text. What does Moltmann mean by this? And how does it relate to his argument?

2.4   Hans Urs von Balthasar on the glory of God

What does it mean to speak of God's "glory"? And in what way is this glory reflected in nature, when seen as God's creation? It is a theme that is explored in one of the more familiar verses of the Old Testament: "The heavens declare the glory of the Lord" (Psalm 19:1). This verse has often served as the basis of a natural theology, offering a defense and an explanation of how the glory of God can be mediated to humanity through the natural order.

The idea of "glory" is difficult to put into words. The Hebrew word for glory (*khavod*) literally means "weight." It points to God being distinct from the created order, possessing qualities which set him utterly apart from nature. Perhaps the most famous discussion of this point is found in the writings of Rudolf Otto, especially his landmark work *The Holy* (1917). Otto uses the Latin phrase *mysterium tremendum* to refer to the qualities of the human encounter with the divine, and argues that this experience has three elements: awfulness (that is, inspiring awe, a sort of profound unease), being overwhelmed (inspiring a feeling of humility), and energy (creating an impression of immense vigor).

The twentieth-century theologian who is most associated with the exploration of the theme of the glory of God is the Swiss Catholic writer Hans Urs von Balthasar (1905–88). A prolific writer, von Balthasar never held a formal university teaching position. His masterpiece is generally regarded as being his *Glory of the Lord: A Theological Aesthetics* (1961–9), occupying seven volumes in English translation. Our extract is taken from this work.

The passage begins by making brief reference to Otto's account of "the holy," before departing from it. God, for von Balthasar, is an *adorandum* – something or someone that is to be adored and worshipped. This is the insight that sets any discussion of the glory of God in its proper perspective.

> The God of the Bible is neither a *tremendum* nor a *fascinosum*, but first of all an *adorandum*. He is and remains the unutterable first origin from which everything that exists, everything that is good and full of grace, comes forth – he is the Father who gives only good gifts (Luke 11:13). But, as the one who lives and is free, he is present in his creatures and gifts in such a way that he distances himself from them in order to leave them a space of freedom. Therefore his power, divinity, wisdom and radiant majesty fill the universe, and can be perceived by intellectual beings (Romans 1:19, 20, 23; 1 Corinthians 1:21); yet, at the same time,

they permit the freedom to recognise God's majestic freedom or not (Romans 1:21). As the "holy one," God makes known especially his divinity in its supramundane character separated from the world; as the "glorious one," he makes known both his "being present" in the world and, united to this, his sovereign superiority to the world. It is precisely this interplay of the immanence of God's power and wisdom in all that exists in the world, and his transcendence over the creatures (as the free creator who remains free), who thereby receive a space for their own existence and freedom, that is the foundation of the biblical *doxa*, and precisely this free elevation above what is not God gives God again the freedom to reveal himself in his free divinity personally – in the "Word" – to what is not God. Thus the distinction here is not one between a ground and what it grounds (for a ground can express itself completely in what is based upon it), but rather one between free creation (as the setting-free of existence that is other than God) and the free gift of God (who is the foundation of its being) to the free creature. Theology has termed this the distinction between the "natural" and the "supernatural"; it is never wholly reducible.

As was suggested above, one may call the immanence of God's divinity in the world his "sovereignty" or "majesty"; one may term his permanent free elevation above the world his "sublimity" or "dignity," to which "honour" and adoration are due; and one may finally term the free turning of his personal divinity to the creature his "glory" in the strongest sense. This glory can further take on ascending stages in the dispensation of salvation, from God's address, which in him will always be creatively active (*dabar* as word and deed), through the creation of his image (*eikon, homoioma*) which takes root in the created order, to the definitive expression (*charakter*) of his invisible "face" (*panim*) in the visible face of Christ.

There is a succession of variations between the majesty of the creator in the circle of his creatures, and the sublimity of his elevation above them which leaves him fully free to express himself to them; this makes it possible to subsume everything under the same cipher of *doxa*. Besides this, at every stage there is an interpenetration (*circumincessio*) of the various aspects or "properties" of God, which are not separable but can certainly be distinguished from one another, and must be so separated. We have already seen how God's holiness is distinct from his glory, although this too (in his free "sublimity") points to God's inability to be mingled with the created world. Glory and power are close to each other; and not only the "eternal power" (Romans 1:20) that displays itself in the corruptible creatures of time, but also – and much more so – God's far more astonishing power to give comprehensible and appropriate expression to the utter otherness of his being in his supernatural "word"-revelation for the world. This means that, without ceasing to be the one who is unfathomable, he can cross over the boundaries of the human "search" for God "in the hope that they might feel after him and find him" (Acts 17:27), and can establish a valid and finally definitive word concerning himself. This power that dwells in the glory is most clearly seen where God's revelation takes account of, and overcomes, man's guilty turning-away, which had led to the "loss of *doxa* for all sinners" (Romans 3:23): this he does through the superior power of his grace (Romans 5:15, 17, 20f.), but in such a way that this power of grace is displayed in the event of the Cross as the sheer momentum of the judgement over sin.

Von Balthasar is not the easiest of writers for those who are new to studying theology, and makes considerable demands of his readers. The extract is studded with Greek, Latin, and Hebrew words, including *dabar* (Hebrew for "word") and *doxa* (Greek for "glory"). Nevertheless, most readers will find that they can follow von Balthasar's line of thought on the second reading. Read the text through slowly, trying to summarize his thought. A central theme of the passage is that God's inexpressible glory is somehow manifested in the natural order.

You may find it helpful to read the biblical account of Paul's famous sermon at the Areopagus (Acts 17:22–31), which von Balthasar mentions in this passage. This sermon is traditionally interpreted to represent an early attempt to correlate some elements of the Christian gospel with themes of classical culture. What use does von Balthasar make of this?

2.5   Elizabeth A. Johnson on female analogies for God

Christian theology has traditionally used male language and imagery to refer to God – for example, in its appeal to fathers, shepherds, and kings as analogues of God. This has caused difficulty for some in recent years, as it could be taken to imply that Christianity is a religion of a male god which privileges males. In fact, to speak of God as father is to say that the role of the father in ancient Israel allows us insights into the nature of God. It is not to say that God *is* a male human being. Neither male nor female gender identity is to be attributed to God. Gender identity is actually something that is encountered within the created order. It may originate from God; this does not, however, mean that this corresponds directly to any such polarity within the creator.

In an attempt to bring out the fact that God is not male, a number of recent writers have explored the idea of God as "mother" (which brings out the female aspects of God), or as "friend" (which brings out the more gender-neutral aspects of God). Elizabeth Johnson (born 1941), a Catholic professor of systematic theology at Fordham University, New York, has been a particularly significant contributor to this discussion, especially in her landmark publication *She Who Is: The Mystery of God in Feminist Theological Discourse* (1992). We shall consider some aspects of her approach in the following extract from this work.

Although drawing their predominant speech about God from the pool of male images, the biblical, early theological, and medieval mystical traditions also use female images of the divine without embarrassment or explanation. The images and personifications are not considered feminine aspects or features of the divine, to be interpreted in dualistic tension with masculine dimensions or traits, but rather they are representations of the fullness of God in creating, redeeming, and calling the world to eschatological shalom.

Ancient religions that spoke of deity in both male and female symbols may also be helpful in clarifying the thrust of this third approach. As evidenced in psalms and prayers, male and female deities were not stereotyped according to later ideas of what was properly masculine and feminine, but each represented a diversity of divine activities and attributes. In them "gender division is not yet the primary metaphor for imaging the dialectics of human existence," nor is the idea of gender complementarity present in the ancient myths. Rather, male and female enjoy broad and equivalent powers. A goddess such as Ishtar, for example, is addressed by devotees as a source of divine power and sovereignty embodied in female form, and praised as a deity who performs the divine works of dividing heaven from earth, setting captives free, waging war, establishing peace, administering justice, exercising judgment, and enlightening human beings with truth, along with presiding over birth, healing the sick, and nurturing the little ones. When a god such as Hocus is addressed, he is credited with similar functions. Both male and female are powerful in the private and public spheres.

The point for our interest is that the female deity is not the expression of the feminine dimension of the divine, but the expression of the fullness of divine power and care shown in a female image. A striking example of the same intuition is given in Luke's Gospel in the parallel parables of the shepherd looking for his lost sheep and the homemaker looking for her lost coin (Luke 15:4–10). In both stories someone vigorously seeks what is lost and rejoices with others when it is found. Neither story discloses anything about God that the other hides. Using traditional men's and women's work, both parables orient the hearer to God's redeeming action in images that are equivalently male and female. The woman with the coin image, while not frequently portrayed in Christian art due largely to the androcentric nature of the traditioning process, is essentially as legitimate a reference to God as is the shepherd with his sheep. Conversely, God spoken of in this way cannot be used to validate role stereotyping wherein the major redeeming work in the world is done by men to the exclusion or marginalization of women.

The mystery of God transcends all images but can be spoken about equally well and poorly in concepts taken from male or female reality. The approach advocated here proceeds with the insight that only if God is so named, only if the full reality of women as well as men enters into the symbolization of God along with symbols from the natural world, can the idolatrous fixation on one image be broken and the truth of the mystery of God, in tandem with the liberation of all human beings and the whole earth, emerge for our time.

Options
The linguistic options which guide this study, made with the judgment that they are appropriate and necessary, converge into speech about God using female metaphors that intend to designate the whole of divine mystery. Theoretically I endorse the ideal of language for God in male

and female terms used equivalently, as well as the use of cosmic and metaphysical symbols. In actual fact, however, male and female images simply have not been nor are they even now equivalent. Female religious symbols of the divine are underdeveloped, peripheral, considered secondarily if at all in Christian language and the practice it continues to shape, much like women through whose image they point to God. In my judgment, extended theological speaking about God in female images, or long draughts of this new wine, are a condition for the very possibility of equivalent imaging of God in religious speech. This book's choice to use mainly female symbolism for God, let me state clearly, is not intended as a strategy of subtraction, still less of reversal. Rather, it is an investigation of a suppressed world directed ultimately toward the design of a new whole. Shaping this kind of speech is not an end in itself but must be received as an essential element in reordering an unjust and deficiently religious situation. Until a strong measure of undervalued female symbolism is introduced and used with ease, equivalent imaging of God male and female, which I myself have advocated and still hold to be a goal, remains an abstraction, expressive of an ideal but unrealizable in actual life.

Johnson's exploration of her theme is clear and easily grasped. The perhaps puzzling use of the term "eschatological shalom" at the end of the first paragraph needs comment. "Shalom" is the Hebrew word for "peace"; "eschatological" refers to the Christian hope, especially the hope of the final restoration and renewal of all things at the end of history. The phrase thus designates the final, redeemed state of creation, when all has been restored to what God intended – when things are again what they are meant to be.

You will still find it helpful to summarize Johnson's approach in your own words, identifying the core elements of her arguments. What point does she make by noting the complementarity of two parables found in Luke 15? (You may find it helpful to get a New Testament, and read the passages she has in mind.) And what point does she make with reference to the goddess Ishtar? Finally, how do you evaluate her assessment of the options open to Christian theology, especially through her proposal for an enhanced use of female imagery for God?

2.6   Sarah Coakley on vulnerability and God

Traditional Christian language about God has placed emphasis on the divine omnipotence. Many theological and liturgical writings affirm that God is the all-powerful ruler of the universe, who deserves to be worshipped and adored by humanity on account of what God has done, and who God is. This emphasis on the divine omnipotence raises a number of issues, perhaps most importantly how an all-powerful, good God can allow suffering and pain in the world.

Yet another concern needs to be noted alongside this classic conundrum of Christian theology. If Christian ethics is partly about the imitation of God, how are we to understand the exercise of power within society, and especially within the church? It is an especially important issue for feminist writers, but has a relevance far beyond this sphere.

In a reflective essay first published in 1996, the Cambridge theologian Sarah Coakley (born 1951) reflects on how the notion of vulnerability in human relationships can be affirmed and informed in the light of the Christian vision of God. Her thoughtful analysis touches on many themes of theological importance – including the way in which a Christian understanding of God is shaped by the life and death of Jesus of Nazareth, and how our understanding of prayer is strongly influenced by our notion of God.

It is no secret why "vulnerability" has been such a taboo subject in Christian feminist writing up till now. The (rightful) concentration in the literature on the profound, and continuing, damage to women from sexual and physical abuse, even in "Christian" families and churches, and on the seeming legitimation of this by men otherwise committed to disciplined religious practice and the rhetoric of cruciform redemption, shows what a perilous path we are treading here. An undiscriminating adulation of "vulnerability" might appear to condone, or even invite, such evils. I do not in any way underestimate these difficulties [...] what I am suggesting is that there is another, and longer-term, danger to Christian feminism in the *repression* of all forms of "vulnerability," and in a concomitant failure to confront issues of fragility, suffering or "self-emptying" except in terms of victimology. And that is ultimately the failure to embrace a feminist reconceptualizing of the power of the cross and resurrection. Only, I suggest, by facing – and giving new expression to – the paradoxes of "losing one's life in order to save it" can feminists hope to construct a vision of the Christic "self" that transcends the gender stereotypes we are seeking to up-end.

But what can I mean by this? I know of no better way to express it than by reflection on the practice of prayer, and especially wordless prayer or "contemplation." This is to take a few leaps beyond the notion of *kenōsis* as a speculative christological theory about the incarnate life of Jesus; but if the majority of New Testament commentators are correct, then the "hymn" of Philippians 2 was, from the start, an invitation to enter into Christ's extended life in the church, not just to speculate dispassionately on his nature. The "spiritual" extension of Christic *kenōsis*, then [...], involves an ascetical commitment of some subtlety, a regular and willed *practice* of ceding and responding to the divine. The rhythm of this *askēsis* is already inscribed ritually and symbolically in the sacraments of baptism and eucharist; but in prayer (especially the defenceless prayer of silent waiting on God) it is "internalized" over time in a peculiarly demanding and transformative fashion. If I am asked, then, what Christian feminism must do to avoid emulating the very forms of "worldly" power we criticize in "masculinism," I point to this *askēsis*. It might be objected [...] that such a danger is not one confronted by women less fortunate, less affluent and less "powerful" than such as me. But I do wonder about this. Foucault has shown us that we all wield "power" in *some* area, however insignificant it may appear to the outside world (power over our children, our aged dependants, even our domestic animals). If "abusive" human power is thus always potentially within our grasp, how can we best approach the healing resources of a non-abusive divine power? How can we hope to invite and channel it, if not by a patient opening of the self to its transformation?

What I have elsewhere called the "paradox of power and vulnerability" is uniquely focused in this act of silent waiting on the divine in prayer. This is because we can only be properly "empowered" here if we cease to set the agenda, if we "make space" for God to be God. Prayer which makes this "space" may take a variety of forms, and should not be conceived in an élitist way; indeed, the debarring of "ordinary" Christians from "contemplation" has been one of the most sophisticated – and spiritually mischievous – ways of keeping lay women (and men) from exercising religious influence in the western church. Such prayer may use a repeated phrase to ward off distractions, or be wholly silent; it may be simple Quaker attentiveness, or take a charismatic expression (such as the use of quiet rhythmic "tongues"). What is sure, however, is that engaging in any such regular and repeated "waiting on the divine" will involve great personal commitment and (apparently) great personal risk; to put it in psychological terms, the dangers of a too-sudden uprush of material from the unconscious, too immediate a contact of the thus disarmed self with God, are not inconsiderable. [...] But whilst risky, this practice is profoundly transformative, "empowering" in a mysterious "Christic" sense; for it is a feature of the *special* "self-effacement" of this gentle space-making – this yielding to divine power which is no worldly power – that it marks one's willed engagement in the pattern of cross and resurrection, one's deeper rooting and grafting into the "body of Christ." [...]

If, then, these traditions of Christian "contemplation" are to be trusted, this rather special form of "vulnerability" is not an invitation to be battered; nor is its silence a silenc*ing*. (If anything, it builds one in the courage to give prophetic voice.) By choosing to "make space" in this way, one "practises" the "presence of God" – the subtle but enabling presence of a God who neither shouts nor forces, let alone "obliterates." No one can *make* one "contemplate" (though the grace of God invites it); but it is the simplest thing in the world not to "contemplate," to turn away from that grace. Thus the "vulnerability" that is its human condition is not about asking for unnecessary and unjust suffering, nor is it a "self-abnegation." On the contrary, this special "self-emptying" is the place of the self's transformation and expansion into God.

Read the passage carefully, and try to summarize the argument. It is clear that one major concern lying behind the passage is a suspicion of how power is acquired and exercised – note, for example, her allusion to Michel Foucault, a leading postmodern observer of power relationships. What reasons does she give for her belief that feminism has generally avoided discussion of vulnerability?

Now read the passage again, and try to answer these two questions. First, what insights does Coakley derive from the famous "hymn" of Philippians 2:5–11 (you might like to read this before answering this question)? Second, how does Coakley's discussion of prayer and "waiting on God" depend on her vision of the nature of God?

CHAPTER 3

Creation

The present collection of readings is loosely structured around the Apostles' Creed, an early statement of Christian beliefs that continues to be widely used within the churches. Its opening declaration affirms belief in a God who is "creator of heaven and earth." So what does this mean? How are we to make sense of this notion of God "creating" the world? And what are its implications for how we respond to that world?

Christian theology has developed a rich imagery to express its fundamental belief that the hand of God can be discerned as lying behind the world. Many theologians have compared God's work of creation as being analogous to that of a builder or master-craftsman, whose wisdom is evident in the resulting structure. Others have suggested that the world can be compared to a work of art, in which the character of the artist is expressed in what has been created. More recently, partly in response to Darwinian theories of biological evolution, some theologians have followed some leads in patristic writers – such as Augustine of Hippo – and begun to understand creation in terms of a divinely directed process of bringing the world into being, rather than as a single action which instantaneously brought everything into existence in its present form.

The doctrine of creation is not limited to the natural order, but extends to include humanity itself. One of the most fundamental Christian insights into human nature is that it bears the "image of God."

Theology: The Basic Readings, Third Edition. Edited by Alister E. McGrath.
Editorial material and organization © Alister E. McGrath.
Published 2018 by John Wiley & Sons Ltd.

For some theologians, this affirms that human reason has the capacity to make sense of the world, and begin to find its way home to God. For others, it has to do with the human ability to relate to God.

The readings assembled in this chapter explore a number of aspects of the doctrine of creation. What is the status of humanity within creation? In what way, and to what extent, does God's creation have the capacity to disclose God? Why is there evil present in the world, when God is meant to have made things "good"? We shall turn immediately to the first such reading, drawn from the high noon of the Renaissance, which offers a controversial assessment of the place of humanity within nature.

3.1   Giovanni Pico della Mirandola on human nature

One of the most intriguing discussions within Christian theology is the extent to which God can be said to delegate creative authority or capacity to humanity. The great Oxford literary scholar and novelist J. R. R. Tolkien (1892–1973) held that God inspired humanity to create works of art, which in some way reflected the glory of God, even in a fragmented or dulled manner. He expressed this in his notion of the "sub-creator," which views the artist in this view as an active participant in the creative process. Though artists may refract the light of truth that shines from the creator, they can still be regarded as agents of that act of creation.

Another debate has concerned whether humanity was created with a definite, fixed identity – or whether it was endowed with the capacity to emerge, and develop new forms of identity. This issue began to become of particular importance in early modern Europe, as the movement widely known as the "Renaissance" gained momentum.

Giovanni Pico della Mirandola (1463–94), one of the leading voices of the Italian Renaissance, delivered his "oration on the dignity of humanity" in 1486 at the precocious age of 24. This "manifesto of the Renaissance," written in a highly polished and elegant Latin style, represents a significant development of the traditional Christian doctrine of creation. Humanity is here depicted as a creature with the capacity to determine its own identity, rather than being obliged to receive this in any given fixed form. As God's creature, humanity has a dynamic, not a static, identity. Pico della Mirandola argues that humanity possesses no determinate image, and depicts it as being urged by its creator to pursue its own perfection.

Historically, this is an important text. The ideas of this oration proved to be enormously influential in the late Renaissance, and can be seen as setting the scene for the Enlightenment assertion of human autonomy in the face of God. Pico della Mirandola's approach to the doctrine of creation seems to leave open the possibility that humanity may decide to develop in ways that make it ultimately independent of God – a leading theme of the Enlightenment of the eighteenth century.

Now God the Father, the supreme Architect, had already constructed this cosmic home that we see, the most noble temple of His godhead, by the laws of His mysterious wisdom. He adorned the region above the heavens with minds, he populated the heavenly spheres with eternal souls, and he filled the excrementary and filthy parts of the lower world with a multitude of animals of every kind. But, when this work was finished, the Craftsman wished that there might be someone to admire the plan of so great a work, to love its beauty, and to wonder at its grandeur. Therefore, when everything was done (as Moses and Timaeus bear witness), he finally gave thought to the creation of humanity. But there was nothing among his archetypes from which he could fashion a new creation, nor was there in his treasure houses anything that he could bestow on his new son as an inheritance, nor was there a seat in all the world from where this son might contemplate this universe. Everything was now complete: everything had been assigned to the highest, the middle, and the lowest orders.

Yet it was not in the nature of the power of the Father to fail in this last act of creation; nor was it in the nature of that supreme Wisdom to hesitate through lack of counsel in so crucial a matter; nor, finally, was it in the nature of his beneficent love to compel the creature destined to praise the divine generosity in all other things to find it wanting in himself.

At last the best of artisans ordained that this creature, to whom he could give nothing that was distinctively his own, should have a share in the particular endowment of every other creature. Taking humanity, therefore – this creature of indeterminate image – he set him in the middle of the world and spoke to him:

> We have given you, Adam, neither a fixed dwelling place, nor a form that is yours alone, nor any function that is peculiar to you alone. This is so that you may have and possess whatever dwelling place, form, and functions that you yourself may desire, according to your longing and judgment. The nature of all other beings is limited and constrained within the bounds of laws prescribed by us. You are constrained by no limits, and shall determine the limits of your nature for yourself, in accordance with your own free will, in whose hand we have placed you.
>
> We have set you at the center of the world, in order that you may more easily observe whatever is in the world. We have made you neither of heaven nor of earth, neither mortal nor immortal, in order that you may, as the free and proud shaper of your own being, fashion yourself in whatever form you may prefer. It will be in your power to descend to the lower orders of animals; it will also be in your power to rise again to the higher orders, whose life is divine.

This elegant, occasionally flamboyant, piece of rhetoric sets out the Renaissance vision of human nature, drawing on multiple sources, including the Old Testament and Plato (note the references to "Moses and Timaeus," the latter being one of Plato's dialogues that deals with the concept of creation). It includes many Christian elements, most notably the idea of humanity as representing the height of creation, alone possessing the capacity to admire, understand, and revere the created order, and hence its creator. Yet the oration also opens up a new way of thinking about the location of humanity within the created order. Pico della Mirandola insists that humanity is not assigned to any particular location or assigned any specific function within creation. It is the privilege and responsibility of humanity to determine its own place and function, through the proper exercise of its freedom and intelligence. Humanity can thus descend to the level of animals, or rise to the level of God.

Read the passage carefully, and try to summarize its argument. Note in particular the ideas found in God's address to Adam. How "Christian" do you think it is? What fundamental motivation does Pico della Mirandola give for the creation of humanity? And for God's desire that humanity should choose its own future?

A fundamental theme of this oration is that humanity must determine its own identity. How does Pico della Mirandola lay the foundations for this doctrine? What might the implications of this be? In particular, can you see ways in which Pico della Mirandola's understanding of human nature might come into conflict with more traditional Christian views on this matter?

3.2   Jonathan Edwards on the beauty of creation

Many theologians have argued that, since God created the natural world, it is to be expected that something of the wisdom, beauty, and rationality of God can be discerned within nature. As we noted earlier, the great medieval theologian Thomas Aquinas used his theory of analogy to allow a connection to be established between the creator and the creation: the latter offered analogies of the former. Similar ideas were commonplace at the time. For example, Aquinas' near-contemporary Bonaventure (1217–74) developed a similar approach, arguing that aspects of the physical world could be seen as "the shadows, echoes and pictures, the vestiges, images and manifestations" of their creator.

This idea was developed further in the writings of Jonathan Edwards (1703–58), widely regarded as America's greatest theologian. Edwards was a Puritan preacher and theologian who was caught up in the "Great Awakening," a religious revival that swept through much of New England in the eighteenth century. His writings can be seen both as a classic statement of Puritan ideals, and as a considered response to the new intellectual challenges emerging from the rationalism of the Enlightenment.

Edwards extended the classic Puritan scheme for making sense of the Bible, and applied it to the natural order. His justification for doing so was that both could be regarded as "books" written by God, in which something of the divine nature and purpose could be identified. Edwards took the traditional idea of a "type," regularly used in interpreting the Old Testament, and applied it to nature.

What is a type? Edwards accepts a definition that was widely recognized in the New England Puritanism of his day: "A type is some outward or sensible thing ordained of God under the Old Testament, to represent and hold forth something of Christ in the New." For example, the crossing of the Red Sea could be seen as a "type" of redemption through Christ.

Yet an idea that was originally developed to establish connections between events or institutions of the Old Testament and the person of Christ was given a new application by Edwards. For Edwards, the Bible allowed and encouraged Christians to interpret nature in two ways: first, by providing knowledge of the great mysteries of faith; and second, by "actually making application of the signs and types in the book of nature as representations of those spiritual mysteries." The entire created order can thus, when rightly interpreted, point toward God.

The text that we shall study is usually known as *The Images of Divine Things*. It was never intended for publication, consisting of a collection of

Edwards' notes and jottings, now on deposit at Yale University Library. Edwards develops the idea that God can be known, to a limited extent, through the created order. In common with earlier Protestant writers, such as John Calvin, Edwards regards nature as echoing what may be found in Scripture, while maintaining the greater clarity and authority of the latter.

57. It is very fit and becoming of God who is infinitely wise, so to order things that there should be a voice of His in His works, instructing those that behold him and painting forth and shewing divine mysteries and things more immediately appertaining to Himself and His spiritual kingdom. The works of God are but a kind of voice or language of God to instruct intelligent beings in things pertaining to Himself. And why should we not think that he would teach and instruct by His works in this way as well as in others, viz., by representing divine things by His works and so painting them forth, especially since we know that God hath so much delighted in this way of instruction. [...]

70. If we look on these shadows of divine things as the voice of God purposely by them teaching us these and those spiritual and divine things, to show of what excellent advantage it will be, how agreeably and clearly it will tend to convey instruction to our minds, and to impress things on the mind and to affect the mind, by that we may, as it were, have God speaking to us. Wherever we are, and whatever we are about, we may see divine things excellently represented and held forth. And it will abundantly tend to confirm the Scriptures, for there is an excellent agreement between these things and the Holy Scripture. [...]

156. The book of Scripture is the interpreter of the book of nature in two ways, viz., by declaring to us those spiritual mysteries that are indeed signified and typified in the constitution of the natural world; and secondly, in actually making application of the signs and types in the book of nature as representations of those spiritual mysteries in many instances. [...]

211. The immense magnificence of the visible world in inconceivable vastness, the incomprehensible height of the heavens, etc., is but a type of the infinite magnificence, height and glory of God's world in the spiritual world: the most incomprehensible expression of His power, wisdom, holiness and love in what is wrought and brought to pass in the world, and the exceeding greatness of the moral and natural good, the light, knowledge, holiness and happiness which shall be

communicated to it, and therefore to that magnificence of the world, height of heaven. These things are often compared in such expressions: Thy mercy is great above the heavens, thy truth reacheth; thou hast for thy glory above the heavens, etc.

It is important to appreciate that our extract consists of four disconnected jottings, so that there is no coherent line of argument joining them together. What unites them is their common interest in how something of God, especially God's beauty, may be known through nature. The passage is best approached on a paragraph by paragraph basis, rather than as a whole.

Let's begin with paragraph 156, which sets out the fundamental theological principle underlying Edwards' approach. Set this out in your own words, perhaps allowing the introduction to this reading to help you appreciate the point. By stressing the congruence between the "book of nature" and the "book of Scripture," Edwards was attempting to show how a "religion of nature" could only find its fulfillment in the Christian gospel. This was an important challenge to the emerging "religion of nature" associated with the Enlightenment, which saw nature as having no transcendent dimension. Edwards insists that the natural is a sign of the transcendent.

Now move on to paragraph 57. Why does Edwards seem to think that God would choose to allow his works to witness to him in this way? What is the fundamental point being made in this paragraph? What implications does this have for natural theology, and especially the study of nature through the natural sciences?

Now move on to paragraph 70. What are the consequences of referring to various aspects of the created order as "shadows of divine things"? How does this develop the argument of the previous paragraph?

Finally, read through the last paragraph (211). Notice how Edwards seems to suggest that the physical vastness of the world helps people appreciate the glory of God. How do you think Edwards' approach would affect the way in which he appreciated nature?

3.3   William Paley on the contrivance of nature

The general enterprise of trying to prove God's existence from nature is often referred to as "natural theology." One of the most remarkable works of "natural theology" was penned in 1802 by the English churchman William Paley (1743–1805). Its full title gives an excellent indication of what Paley believed could be discovered by intelligent reflection on nature: *Natural Theology: or, Evidences of the Existence and Attributes of the Deity, Collected from the Appearances of Nature.*

Paley was deeply impressed by the scientific achievements of Isaac Newton, especially his demonstration of the regularity of nature during the late seventeenth century. The new discipline of "celestial mechanics" was widely seen as endorsing the notion of God creating the universe in a rational and ordered manner. The phrase "the mechanical universe" was often used in the eighteenth century to stress the regularity of the world. It seemed increasingly clear to many that the entire universe could be thought of as a complex mechanism, operating according to regular and understandable principles.

For Paley, the Newtonian image of the world as a mechanism immediately suggested the metaphor of a clock or watch. So if the world was like a watch, who was it who had constructed its intricate mechanism? Who designed it? And who made it? Paley's conclusion was clear: "The marks of design are too strong to be got over. Design must have had a designer. That designer must have been a person. That person is GOD."

One of Paley's most significant arguments is that mechanism implies "contrivance" – that is, design and construction for a specific purpose. Writing against the backdrop of the emerging Industrial Revolution, Paley sought to exploit the apologetic potential of the growing interest in machinery – such as "watches, telescopes, stocking–mills, and steam engines" – within England's literate classes.

Paley's approach involves the demonstration that the natural world is "contrived" – that is, that it is intelligently *designed* and *constructed*. At the time, England was experiencing the Industrial Revolution, in which machinery was coming to play an increasingly important role in industry. Paley argues that only someone who is mad would suggest that such complex mechanical technology came into being by purposeless chance. Mechanism presupposes contrivance – that is to say, a sense of purpose and an ability to design and fabricate. Both the human body in particular, and the world in general, could be seen as mechanisms which had been designed and constructed in such a manner as to achieve harmony of both means and ends. It must be stressed that Paley is not suggesting that there exists an analogy between human mechanical devices and nature. The force of his argument rests on an identity: nature *is* a mechanism, and hence was intelligently designed.

In crossing a heath, suppose I pitched my foot against a *stone*, and were asked how the stone came to be there: I might possibly answer, that, for any thing I knew to the contrary, it had lain there for ever; nor would it perhaps be very easy to show the absurdity of this answer. But suppose I had found a *watch* upon the ground, and it should be inquired how the watch happened to be in that place; I should hardly think of the answer which I had before given – that, for any thing I knew, the watch might have always been there. Yet why should not this answer serve for the watch as well as for the stone? Why is it not as admissible in the second case, as in the first? For this reason, and for no other, viz. that, when we come to inspect the watch, we perceive (what we could not discover in the stone) that its several parts are framed and put together for a purpose, *e.g.* that they are so formed and adjusted as to produce motion, and that motion so regulated as to point out the hour of the day; that, if the different parts had been differently shaped from what they are, of a different size from what they are, or placed after any other manner, or in any other order, than that in which they are placed, either no motion at all would have been carried on in the machine, or none which would have answered the use that is now served by it. To reckon up a few of the plainest of these parts, and of their offices, all tending to one result: We see a cylindrical box containing a coiled elastic spring, which by its endeavour to relax itself, turns round the box. We next observe a flexible chain (artificially wrought for the sake of flexure) communicating the action of the spring from the box to the fusee. We then find a series of wheels, the teeth of which catch in, and apply to, each other, conducting the motion from the fusee to the balance, and from the balance to the pointer: and at the same time, by the size and shape of those wheels, so regulating that motion, as to terminate in causing an index, by an equable and measured progression, to pass over a given space in a given time. We take notice that the wheels are made of brass in order to keep them from rust; the springs of steel, no other metal being so elastic; that over the face of the watch there is placed a glass, a material employed in no other part of the work, but in the room of which, if there had been any other than a transparent substance, the hour could not be seen without opening the case. This mechanism being observed (it requires indeed an examination of the instrument, and perhaps some previous knowledge of the subject, to perceive and understand it; but being once, as we have said, observed and understood), the inference we think is inevitable, that the watch must have had a maker: that there must have existed, at some time, and at some place or other, an artificer or artificers who formed it for the purpose which we find it actually to answer: who comprehended its construction, and designed its use.

The passage is easy to understand, apart from some aspects of the technical description of the mechanism of a watch. For example, a "fusee" is a watch wheel which counterbalances the tension of the watch spring. But it is not necessary to have a detailed grasp of late-eighteenth-century clock mechanisms to understand Paley's point. Everything in nature seems to fit together remarkably well – as if it had been designed.

Begin by summarizing the ways in which Paley makes the analogy of the watch. In what way does the finding of a watch on a heath differ from the finding of a stone in the same place? What distinguishes the watch from the stone, causing it to stand out as unusual? How much is Paley's argument shaped by the new interest in mechanical things resulting from the Industrial Revolution?

Paley's argument was very influential. But it had its critics. The Scottish geologist and theologian Hugh Millar (1802–56) argued that machines could be ugly. To compare God to a piece of machinery might indeed help people understand that God had designed the world. But what if the machine was ugly? How do you think Paley might respond to such a criticism?

More seriously, the evolutionary theory of Charles Darwin, set out in his *Origin of Species* (1859), suggested that the appearance of design that Paley saw in nature had come about through natural processes, over a very long period of time. How do you think Paley's approach might be adapted in the light of this criticism?

3.4   John Henry Newman on natural religion

John Henry Newman (1801–90) is widely regarded as the most important English theologian of the nineteenth century. In 1828, Newman was
appointed vicar of the University Church of St Mary, Oxford, remaining
in this position until 1843. He resigned in order to be received into the
Catholic church, eventually being created a cardinal in 1879.

Our reading is taken from *An Essay in Aid of a Grammar of Assent* (1870),
dealing with the question of "natural religion," and how this can prepare
the human heart and mind for the fuller revelation of God associated with
Christianity.

To understand Newman at this point, we need to appreciate that he was
writing against the background of a growing crisis of faith in Victorian
England. Increasing skepticism about the reliability of the Bible was causing many to question the foundations of their faith. Newman sought to
show how Christian faith could be believed with certainty, even though its
fundamental themes could not always be proved rationally. For Newman,
a converging series of probabilities may establish a truth quite conclusively
and irrefutably.

In making his cumulative case for the Christian faith, Newman explores
what he terms "natural religion." By this, Newman means "the knowledge of God, of His Will, and of our duties towards Him" which can be
ascertained by reflection on nature. Newman argues that there are "three
main channels which Nature furnishes for our acquiring this knowledge,
viz. our own minds, the voice of mankind, and the course of the world,
that is, of human life and human affairs." Our extract concerns the third
of these channels, which is clearly linked with the doctrine of creation.

Now we come to the third natural informant on the subject of Religion; I mean the system and the course of the world. This established
order of things, in which we find ourselves, if it has a Creator, must
surely speak of His will in its broad outlines and its main issues. This
principle being laid down as certain, when we come to apply it to things
as they are, our first feeling is one of surprise and (I may say) of dismay,
that His control of this living world is so indirect, and His action so
obscure. This is the first lesson that we gain from the course of human
affairs. What strikes the mind so forcibly and so painfully is, His absence
(if I may so speak) from His own world. It is a silence that speaks. It is as
if others had got possession of His work. Why does not He, our Maker
and Ruler, give us some immediate knowledge of Himself? Why does

He not write His Moral Nature in large letters upon the face of history, and bring the blind, tumultuous rush of its events into a celestial, hierarchical order? Why does He not grant us in the structure of society at least so much of a revelation of Himself as the religions of the heathen attempt to supply? Why from the beginning of time has no one uniform steady light guided all families of the earth, and all individual men, how to please Him? Why is it possible without absurdity to deny His will, His attributes, His existence? Why does He not walk with us one by one, as He is said to have walked with His chosen men of old time? We both see and know each other; why, if we cannot have the sight of Him, have we not at least the knowledge? On the contrary, He is specially "a Hidden God;" and with our best efforts we can only glean from the surface of the world some faint and fragmentary views of Him. I see only a choice of alternatives in explanation of so critical a fact: – either there is no Creator, or He has disowned His creatures. Are then the dim shadows of His Presence in the affairs of men but a fancy of our own, or, on the other hand, has He hid His face and the light of His countenance, because we have in some special way dishonoured Him? My true informant, my burdened conscience, gives me at once the true answer to each of these antagonist questions: – it pronounces without any misgiving that God exists: – and it pronounces quite as surely that I am alienated from Him; that "His hand is not shortened, but that our iniquities have divided between us and our God." Thus it solves the world's mystery, and sees in that mystery only a confirmation of its own original teaching.

Let us pass on to another great fact of experience, bearing on Religion, which confirms this testimony both of conscience and of the forms of worship which prevail among mankind; – I mean, the amount of suffering, bodily and mental, which is our portion in this life. Not only is the Creator far off, but some being of malignant nature seems, as I have said, to have got hold of us, and to be making us his sport. Let us say there are a thousand millions of men on the earth at this time; who can weigh and measure the aggregate of pain which this one generation has endured and will endure from birth to death? Then add to this all the pain which has fallen and will fall upon our race through centuries past and to come. Is there not then some great gulf fixed between us and the good God? Here again the testimony of the system of nature is more than corroborated by those popular traditions about the unseen state, which are found in mythologies and superstitions, ancient and modern; for those traditions speak, not only of present misery, but of pain and evil hereafter, and even without end. But this dreadful addition is not necessary for the conclusion which I am here wishing to draw. The real mystery is, not that evil should never have an end, but that it should ever have had a beginning. Even a universal restitution could not undo what had been, or account for evil being the necessary condition of good. How are we to explain it, the existence of God being taken for granted, except by saying that another will, besides His, has had a part in the disposition of His work, that there is a quarrel without remedy, a chronic alienation, between God and man?

Read the passage through carefully. Note how the tone of the work is quite different from what we find in Paley, who seems optimistic and simplistic in the light of Newman's more cautious and reflective analysis.

The first section deals with the ambiguity of nature, leading Newman to conclude that "either there is no Creator, or He has disowned His creatures." Locate this statement. What does Newman mean by this? How does he reach this conclusion? And how does he use this as a way of pointing to the truths of Christianity?

The second section deals with the problem of pain and suffering. Newman regards the existence of pain as both obvious and significant. Where Paley tried to minimize their importance, Newman interprets their existence as implying that "there is a quarrel without remedy, a chronic alienation, between God and man." Locate this statement. What does Newman mean by this? And how does he see it as establishing a case for revealed religion?

3.5   G. K. Chesterton on the doctrine of creation

One of the most fundamental themes of the Christian doctrine of creation is that the natural order is not divine. It originates from God, and, as we have been exploring in recent readings, can be said to bear the imprint of God's nature. So what difference does this idea make? If God is declared to be distinct from nature, what are its implications?

It is a question that has been explored by many theologians. One of the clearest discussions of this point is found in the writings of the amateur theologian and journalist G. K. Chesterton (1874–1936). In his influential work *Orthodoxy* (1908), Chesterton offered a witty and elegant defense of the Christian faith, including an incisive analysis of the doctrine of creation, exploring the point that we have just raised.

Christianity came into the world firstly in order to assert with violence that a man had not only to look inwards, but to look outwards, to behold with astonishment and enthusiasm a divine company and a divine captain. The only fun of being a Christian was that a man was not left alone with the Inner Light, but definitely recognized an outer light, fair as the sun, clear as the moon, terrible as an army with banners.

All the same, it will be as well if Jones does not worship the sun and moon. If he does, there is a tendency for him to imitate them; to say, that because the sun burns insects alive, he may burn insects alive. He thinks that because the sun gives people sun-stroke, he may give his neighbour measles. He thinks that because the moon is said to drive men mad, he may drive his wife mad. This ugly side of mere external optimism had also shown itself in the ancient world. About the time when the Stoic idealism had begun to show the weaknesses of pessimism, the old nature worship of the ancients had begun to show the enormous weaknesses of optimism. Nature worship is natural enough while the society is young, or, in other words, Pantheism is all right as long as it is the worship of Pan. But Nature has another side which experience and sin are not slow in finding out, and it is no flippancy to say of the god Pan that he soon showed the cloven hoof. The only objection to Natural Religion is that somehow it always becomes unnatural. A man loves Nature in the morning for her innocence and amiability, and at nightfall, if he is loving her still, it is for her darkness and her cruelty. He washes at dawn in clear water as did the Wise Man of the Stoics, yet, somehow at the dark end of the day, he is bathing in hot bull's blood, as did Julian the Apostate.

[…] In this dilemma (the same as ours) Christianity suddenly stepped in and offered a singular answer, which the world eventually accepted as *the* answer. It was the answer then, and I think it is the answer now.

This answer was like the slash of a sword; it sundered; it did not in any sense sentimentally unite. Briefly, it divided God from the cosmos. That transcendence and distinctness of the deity which some Christians now want to remove from Christianity, was really the only reason why any one wanted to be a Christian. […] And the root phrase for all Christian theism was this, that God was a creator, as an artist is a creator. A poet is so separate from his poem that he himself speaks of it as a little thing he has "thrown off." Even in giving it forth he has flung it away. This principle that all creation and procreation is a breaking off is at least as consistent through the cosmos as the evolutionary principle that all growth is a branching out. A woman loses a child even in having a child. All creation is separation. Birth is as solemn a parting as death.

It was the prime philosophic principle of Christianity that this divorce in the divine act of making (such as severs the poet from the poem or the mother from the new-born child) was the true description of the act whereby the absolute energy made the world. According to most philosophers, God in making the world enslaved it. According to Christianity, in making it, He set it free. God had written, not so much a poem, but rather a play; a play He had planned as perfect, but which had necessarily been left to human actors and stage-managers, who had since made a great mess of it. […]

And then followed an experience impossible to describe. It was as if I had been blundering about since my birth with two huge and unmanageable machines, of different shapes and without apparent connection – the world and the Christian tradition. I had found this hole in the world: the fact that one must somehow find a way of loving the world without trusting it; somehow one must love the world without being worldly. I found this projecting feature of Christian theology, like a sort of hard spike, the dogmatic insistence that God was personal, and had made a world separate from Himself. The spike of dogma fitted exactly into the hole in the world – it had evidently been meant to go there – and then the strange thing began to happen. When once these two parts of the two machines had come together, one after another, all the other parts fitted and fell in with an eerie exactitude. I could hear bolt after bolt over all the machinery falling into its place with a kind of click of relief. Having got one part right, all the other parts were repeating that rectitude, as clock after clock strikes noon. Instinct after instinct was answered by doctrine after doctrine. [...] Even those dim and shapeless monsters of notions which I have not been able to describe, much less defend, stepped quietly into their places like colossal caryatides of the creed. The fancy that the cosmos was not vast and void, but small and cosy, had a fulfilled significance now, for anything that is a work of art must be small in the sight of the artist; to God the stars might be only small and dear, like diamonds. And my haunting instinct that somehow good was not merely a tool to be used, but a relic to be guarded, like the goods from Crusoe's ship – even that had been the wild whisper of something originally wise, for, according to Christianity, we were indeed the survivors of a wreck, the crew of a golden ship that had gone down before the beginning of the world.

The passage is very clear, and needs little in the way of comment. The core of Chesterton's argument can be summarized in the following statement: "God was a creator, as an artist is a creator." Locate this in the text. What does Chesterton mean by this? Try to identify the main points of comparison that he regards as helpful and important.

Chesterton's analysis is laced with memorable aphorisms – such as "one must somehow find a way of loving the world without trusting it." What do you think he means by this? And how does his analysis of the doctrine of creation bring him to this conclusion?

3.6   Dorothy L. Sayers on creation and evil

How can a good creator allow evil to exist in the world? Where can evil come from, if the creator is declared to be fundamentally good? One answer to this question was developed by Dorothy L. Sayers (1893–1957), perhaps best known as the creator of the fictional detective Lord Peter Wimsey. Yet Sayers was a theologian of no small merit, and penned some religiously significant works, including *The Mind of the Maker* (1941).

One of the most interesting themes Sayers develops in this important work is the parallel between God's action of creation, and the processes which lead an artist to produce a work of art – such as an author writing a book. (There is an interesting parallel with G. K. Chesterton's analysis in the previous reading.) God and humanity, she suggests, share both "the desire and the ability to make things." In much the same way as theology is "thinking God's thoughts after Him," so art is "doing God's deeds after Him." If this is so, the process of producing a work of art from an original idea can be seen as analogous to the divine act of creation *ex nihilo* – from nothing. "It is the artist who, more than other men, is able to create something out of nothing."

So how might this analogy be explored? In *The Mind of the Maker*, Sayers proposes and explores the analogy between a human creator – such as herself, as a writer of novels and plays – and the divine work of creation. She suggests that such an enterprise must be considered to be trinitarian, in that any human creation of significance involves Idea, Energy, and Power. The original idea leads to a process of writing and the "incarnation" of that idea as a material object; and then to a process of reading, hearing, and understanding which creates its effect upon the audience. In developing this approach, Sayers sets out her imaginative exploration of how the idea of evil might arise in God's creation.

> Shakespeare writes *Hamlet*. That act *of* creation enriches the world with a new category of Being, namely: *Hamlet*. But simultaneously it enriches the world with a new category of Not-Being, namely: Not-Hamlet. Everything other than *Hamlet*, to the farthest bounds of the universe, acquires in addition to its former characteristics, the characteristic of being Not-Hamlet; the whole of the past immediately and automatically becomes Not-Hamlet.
>
> Now, in a sense, it is true to say that the past was Not-Hamlet before *Hamlet* was created or thought-of; it is true, but it is meaningless, since apart from *Hamlet* there is no meaning that we can possibly attach to

the term Not-Hamlet. Doubtless there is an event, X, in the future, by reference to which we may say that we are at present in a category of Not-X, but until X occurs, the category of Not-X is without reality. Only X can give reality to Not-X; that is to say, Not-Being depends for its reality upon Being. In this way we may faintly see how the creation of Time may be said automatically to create a time when Time was not, and how the Being of God can be said to create a Not-Being that is not God. The bung-hole is as real as the barrel, but its reality is contingent upon the reality of the barrel.

Arguing along these lines, we may make an attempt to tackle the definition of Evil as the deprivation or the negation of the Good. If Evil belongs to the category of Not-Being, then two things follow. First: the reality of Evil is contingent upon the reality of Good; and secondly, the Good, by merely occurring, automatically and inevitably creates its corresponding Evil. In this sense, therefore, God, Creator of all things, creates Evil as well as Good, because the creation of a category of Good necessarily creates a category of Not-Good. From this point of view, those who say that God is "beyond Good and Evil" are perfectly right: He transcends both, because both are included within His Being. But the Evil has no reality except in relation to His Good; and this is what is meant by saying that Evil is negation or deprivation of Good.

But we have not quite finished with our Hamlet example. So long as Not-Being remains negative and inactive, it produces no particular effects, harmful or otherwise. But if Not-Hamlet becomes associated with consciousness and will, we get something which is not merely Not-Hamlet: we get Anti-Hamlet. Some one has become aware of his Not-Hamletness, and this awareness becomes a centre of will and of activity. The creative will, free and active like God, is able to will Not-Being into Being, and thus produce an Evil which is no longer negative but positive. This, according to the ancient myth of the Fall, is what happened to Men. They desired to be "as gods, knowing good and evil." God, according to St. Thomas Aquinas, knows Evil "by simple intelligence" – that is, in the category of Not-Being. But men, not being pure intelligences, but created within a space-time framework, could not "know" Evil as Not-Being – they could only "know" it by experience; that is, by associating their wills with it and so calling it into active Being. Thus the Fall has been described as the "fall into self-consciousness," and also as the "fall into self-will." And we may see why the Manichaeans were to some extent justified in connecting Evil with Matter; not that Matter itself is Evil, but that it is the medium in which active Evil is experienced.

Once more, our literary analogy may be used to illustrate this distinction between Evil known by pure intelligence and Evil known by experience.

Our perfect writer is in the act of composing a work – let us call it the perfect poem. At a particular point in this creative act he selects the "right" word for a particular place in the poem. There is only the one word that is "dead right" in that place for the perfect expression of the Idea. The very act of choosing that one "right" word, automatically and necessarily makes every other word in the dictionary a "wrong" word. The "wrongness" is not inherent in the words themselves – each of them may be a "right" word in another place – their "wrongness" is contingent upon the "rightness" of the chosen word. It is the poet who has created the "wrongness" in the act of creating the "rightness." In making a good which did not exist before he has simultaneously made an evil which did not exist before. Nor was there any way by which he could possibly make the Good without making the Evil as well.

Read the passage carefully. Try to summarize its first paragraph, which is of particular importance here. What precisely is the point that Sayers makes in relation to *Hamlet*? And how is it developed in later paragraphs? (You need to make sure you are absolutely clear about the difference between "Not-Hamlet" and "Anti-Hamlet.") So how does this relate to God's creation of the world?

Note Sayers' intriguing conclusion: that God cannot "make the Good without making the Evil as well." How does she get to that conclusion? Do you think it is right? And what are its implications?

3.7 John Polkinghorne on creation and science

John Polkinghorne (born 1930) was professor of mathematical physics at the University of Cambridge from 1968 to 1979, when he resigned his chair to study theology so that he could serve as a priest in the Church of England. He was ordained in 1982. He subsequently served as dean of chapel at Trinity Hall, Cambridge, from 1986 to 1988, when he became president of Queens' College, Cambridge. One of Polkinghorne's major theological interests is the relation of the natural sciences and Christian theology. In dealing with this theme, Polkinghorne regularly explores the way in which scientific and theological views on the origins of the universe interact with each other.

The extract for consideration is taken from his 1994 work *The Faith of a Physicist*, in which he sought to apply scientific habits of thought to the core themes of Christian belief. After outlining scientific views on the origins of the universe, Polkinghorne turns to consider how these can inform or challenge Christian theology.

Such, in outline, is the story that science tells us about the history of the world. There are some speculations (particularly in very early cosmology) and some ignorances (particularly in relation to the origins of life), but there seems to me to be every reason to take seriously the broad sweep of what we are told. Theological discourse on the doctrine of creation must be consonant with that account.

Of course, the first thing to say about that discourse is that theology is concerned with ontological origin and not with temporal beginning. The idea of creation has no special stake in a datable start to the universe. If Hawking is right, and quantum effects mean that the cosmos as we know it is like a kind of fuzzy space-time egg, without a single point at which it all began, that is scientifically very interesting, but theologically insignificant. [...]

An important implication of the Christian doctrine of creation is that it clearly distinguishes the created order from its creator. Barth says that "creation is that freely willed and executed positing of reality distinct from God." Burrell says, "what is at issue here is a clean discrimination of creation from emanation, of intentional activity from necessary bringing forth." Emanationism pictures the world as arising in a kind of panentheistic way, as the divine being's fruitfulness inevitably spills over into a multiplicity of consequences. In its view, the world is at the hem of deity.

Christian theology, on the contrary, sees the world as a consequence of a free act of divine decision and is separate from deity. The universe's incoherent contingency is conventionally and vividly expressed in the idea of creation *ex nihilo*. Nothing else existed (such as the brute matter and the forms of the classical Greek scheme of things) either to prompt or to constrain the divine creative act. The divine will alone is the source of created being. [...] God's decision was freely made. This concept can be held to have played an important part in the ideological undergirding of modern science, for it implied both that the world was rational and also that the nature of its rationality depended on the choice of its Creator, so that one must look to see what actual form it had taken.

It is sometimes said that creation *ex nihilo* is just the sort of metaphysical speculation which got grafted on to biblical ideas when Christianity expanded into the late Hellenic world. It is certainly true that it is possible to give a natural exegesis of Genesis 1 which falls short of the explicit articulation of this concept. But I agree with Keith Ward that the doctrine is implicit in the clear claim that all depends on God's will ("and God said, 'let there be...'"). [...]

The doctrine safeguards the fundamental theological intuition that creation is separate from its creator, that he has made ontological room for something other than himself. Moltmann says, "it is only God's withdrawal into himself which gives that *nihil* the space in which God becomes creatively active." On the other hand, [A. N.] Whitehead rejected the doctrine because he did not want God to play so absolute a role. Whitehead said that God "is not *before* all creation but *with* all creation." In their account of process theology, [J. B.] Cobb and [D. R.] Griffin tell us that it "rejects the notion of *creatio ex nihilo*, if that means creation out of absolute nothingness... Process theology affirms instead a doctrine of creation out of chaos" – which is certainly an exegetically possible view of what is involved in Genesis's reference to that which was "without form and void" (*tohu wabohu* in Gen. 1.2). But once again I feel that process theology's diminished view of divine power does not allow God to be God.

[...]

To hold a doctrine of creation *ex nihilo* is to hold that all that is depends, now and always, on the freely exercised will of God. It is certainly not to believe that God started things off by manipulating a curious kind of stuff called "nothing." There is no contradiction in holding at the same time a doctrine of *creatio continua*, which affirms a continuing creative interaction of God with the world he holds in being. The two are respectively the transcendent and the immanent poles of divine creativity.

The passage sets out a number of themes which have become trademarks of Polkinghorne's approach – such as his insistence that the doctrine of creation is about theological reflection, not chronological analysis. Science can clarify how and when the universe came into being; this, however, is not of particular theological significance. Polkinghorne also affirms the importance of the idea of creation "from nothing" (Latin: *ex nihilo*), holding that this represents a reasonable interpretation of the Genesis creation account.

There are many points for discussion here. Why do you think Polkinghorne dislikes the view of process theology? And why does he espouse *creatio continua* – the notion that creation does not simply designate a fixed moment in the past, but refers to an ongoing process?

CHAPTER 4

Jesus

Jesus of Nazareth plays a central role in Christian theology. As even a cursory survey of the history of theology makes clear, Christians have always insisted that there was something special, something qualitatively different about Jesus, which sets him apart from religious teachers or thinkers. But what is special about him? These questions are addressed in the area of Christian theology traditionally known as *Christology*. The beginnings of an answer lie in the fact that Jesus of Nazareth is seen by Christians as being far more than the founder of their religion. Jesus is not merely the historical point of departure for the Christian faith; he is part of its content.

The early church wrestled long and hard with the biblical texts to try to work out the best way of making sense of the identity and significance of Jesus. Various approaches were explored, often to be rejected as inadequate. By the fourth century, a consensus can be seen emerging, based on the concept of *incarnation*. This term, based on Latin terms meaning "in the flesh," refers to the idea that, in Christ, God took human nature upon himself, in order to redeem it. This basic position was formulated in the "doctrine of the two natures of Christ," which was set out by the Council of Chalcedon in 451: that Jesus Christ was "perfect in divinity and humanity, truly God and truly human."

Theology: The Basic Readings, Third Edition. Edited by Alister E. McGrath.
Editorial material and organization © Alister E. McGrath.
Published 2018 by John Wiley & Sons Ltd.

This represents a landmark in Christian theology in general, and especially its understanding of the person and identity of Christ. Although there were some significant debates within Christian theology over how best to make sense of this approach, it was generally regarded as definitive.

We begin our explorations of how theologians have engaged with these questions by considering Athanasius of Alexandria's classic statements on the reasons for the incarnation.

4.1   Athanasius of Alexandria on the incarnation

One of the most important works of fourth-century theology is the treatise *On the Incarnation*, by Athanasius of Alexandria (ca. 293–373). In this
work, probably written around 318 (though some scholars argue for a
much later date), Athanasius set out to offer a defense and explanation of
the doctrine of the incarnation, particularly in the light of various criticisms of the idea that had become influential around that time.

Athanasius' basic argument is that humanity required redemption, and
that only God is able to bring that redemption. God, and God alone, can
break the power of sin, and bring us to eternal life. An essential feature
of being a creature is that one requires to be redeemed. No creature can
save another creature. Only the creator can redeem the creation. Having
emphasized that it is God alone who can save, Athanasius then observes
that both the New Testament and the Christian liturgical tradition alike
regard Jesus Christ as Savior. *Yet only God can save.* So how are we to make
sense of this?

The only possible solution, Athanasius argues, is to accept that Jesus is
God incarnate. If Jesus Christ was only a human being, he would not have
the ability to redeem humanity. In the section of this major treatise that
is here extracted for study, Athanasius sets the incarnation in the context
of God's overall purpose of salvation. His argument involves the human
need for knowledge of God, and thence for salvation by God. In each
case, the incarnation plays a critical role. Jesus Christ makes God known,
and makes salvation possible.

Athanasius' argument hinges on the fact that Jesus is God incarnate.
Because Jesus is God, Jesus is able to reveal God – not simply disclose
truths about God, but make him known personally. And because Jesus is
God, he is able to do something that only God can do – effect the salvation
of humanity.

When Almighty God was creating humanity through his Word, he realized that, on account of limitations of their nature, they could not by
themselves have any knowledge of their creator. He therefore took pity
on them, and did not leave them lacking any knowledge of himself, in
case their existence should prove purposeless. For of what use is existence to the creature if it cannot know its creator? How could humanity be reasonable beings if they had no knowledge of the Word and
Reason of the Father, through whom they had received their being?
They would be no better than animals, having no knowledge except

of earthly things. So why should God have made humanity at all, if he had not intended them to know him? [...]

God knew the limitations of humanity. Although the grace of being made in God's Image was sufficient to give them knowledge of the Word – and, through him, of the Father – as a safeguard against their neglect of this grace, God also provided the works of creation as means by which the creator might be known. [...] Three ways lay open to humanity, by which they might obtain the knowledge of God. They could look up into the immensity of heaven, and by pondering the harmony of creation come to know its Ruler, the Word of the Father, whose all-ruling providence makes the Father known to all. Or, if this was beyond them, they could converse with the saints, and through them learn to know God, the creator of all things, the Father of Christ, and to recognize the worship of idols as the denial of truth, full of impiety. Or else, in the third place, they could cease from indifference and lead a good life simply by knowing the Law. For the Law was not given only for the Jews. Nor was it only for their sake that God sent the prophets (though it was to the Jews that they were sent and by the Jews that they were persecuted). The Law and the prophets were a sacred school of the knowledge of God and the conduct of the spiritual life for the whole world.

So great, indeed, were the goodness and the love of God. Yet humanity, overwhelmed by the pleasures of the moment and by the frauds and illusions of evil spirits, did not lift up their heads towards the truth. [...] What, then, was God to do? What else could he possibly do, being God, but renew his Image in humanity, so that they might once more come to know him? And how could this be done, other than by the coming of the very Image Himself – our Savior Jesus Christ? Humanity could not do this for themselves, for they are only made after the Image. Nor could angels have done it, for they are not the images of God. The Word of God came in his own Person, because it was he alone, the Image of the Father, who could recreate humanity made after the Image. In order to effect this re-creation, however, he first had to eliminate death and corruption. Therefore he assumed a human body, in order that in it death might once for all be destroyed, and that humanity might be renewed according to the Image. Here is an illustration to prove this.

You know what happens when a portrait that has been painted onto a panel becomes obliterated through external stains. The artist does not throw away the panel. Rather, the subject of the portrait has to come and sit for it again, so that his likeness can be drawn again on the same material. It was the same with the all-holy Son of God. He, the Image of the Father, came and dwelled in our midst, in order that he might renew humanity, which was made after Himself, and seek out his lost sheep, just as he says in the Gospel: "I came to seek and to save that which was lost" (Luke 19:10). This also explains his saying to the Jews: "Unless someone is born all over again" (John 3:3). He was not referring to someone's natural birth from his mother here, as they thought, but to the re-birth and recreation of the soul in the Image of God.

The passage is relatively easy to follow. Begin by reading the first paragraph. What is Athanasius saying here? What understanding of human nature is he advocating? One of the basic themes here is that, without knowledge of their creator, humanity lacks any awareness of their purpose or true identity. For this reason, God chooses to make himself known to them. But what form does that knowledge take?

Read the next paragraph. Athanasius here sets out a series of ways in which humanity could know God. Summarize and assess these in your own words. In what way do you think Athanasius sees the incarnation as the culmination of these? Note how the creation and the law are seen as witnesses to Christ.

Finally, summarize the point Athanasius makes with reference to the image of the stained panel. How does this illuminate his understanding of what Christ needed to do for human nature? How central is the role of the image of God to this argument? You might like to find and read Colossians 1:15, and note its statement about Christ as the "image of the invisible God." How does this theme express itself in this passage?

4.2 Leo the Great on the two natures of Christ

Unlike the eastern church, the church in the west never became embroiled in complex and subtle Christological debates, such as the great Arian debate of the fourth century. The major theological debates in the west, many of which were associated with Augustine of Hippo, mainly concerned the doctrines of the church and grace, rather than the person of Christ.

The "Tome of Leo" is one of the few Christological documents of major importance to emerge within the Latin-speaking church. This document takes the form of letter, written in Latin by Pope Leo I (died 461) to Flavian, patriarch of Constantinople, on June 13, 449. It adopts a strongly conciliatory approach to the somewhat fractious debates over this question within the church, aiming to identify what was absolutely *essential* to the orthodox Christological positions, and what was open to negotiation or discussion. The document was well received, especially by the Council of Chalcedon (451), which recognized it as a classic statement of Christological orthodoxy.

The "Tome of Leo" is widely regarded as a landmark of positive theological synthesis at a time dominated by polemical works and considerations, and offers a reliable summary of the prevailing Christological consensus within the Latin church in the early fifth century.

Christ was born God of God, Almighty of Almighty, co-eternal of eternal; not later in time, not inferior in power, not different in glory, not divided in essence. The same only-begotten, eternal Son of the eternal Father was born of the Holy Spirit and the Virgin Mary. But this birth in time has taken nothing from, and added nothing to, that divine eternal nativity, but has bestowed itself wholly on the restoration of humanity, which had been deceived: that it might overcome death and by its own virtue overthrow the devil who had the power of death. For we could not overcome the author of sin and death, unless he had taken our nature and made it his own, whom sin could not defile nor death retain, since he was conceived of the Holy Spirit, in the womb of his Virgin Mother, whose virginity remained entire in his birth as in his conception. [...]

Thus the properties of each [i.e., the divine and human] nature and substance were preserved in their totality, and came together to form one person. Humility was assumed by majesty, weakness by strength, mortality by eternity; and to pay the debt that we had incurred, an inviolable nature was united to a nature that can suffer. And so, to fulfill the conditions of our healing, the human being Jesus Christ, one and the same mediator between God and humanity, was able to die in respect of the one, yet unable to die in respect of the other. Thus there was born true God in the entire and perfect nature of true humanity, complete in his own properties, complete in ours. By "ours" we mean those things which the Creator formed in us at the beginning, which he assumed in order to restore; for in the Savior there was no trace of the properties which the deceiver brought in, and which humanity, being deceived, allowed to enter. Christ did not become partaker of our sins because he entered into fellowship with human infirmities. He assumed the form of a servant without the stain of sin, making the human properties greater, but not detracting from the divine. For that "emptying of himself," by which the invisible God chose to become visible, and the Creator and Lord of all willed to be a mortal, was an inclination of compassion, not a failure of power.

Accordingly, the one who created humanity, while remaining in the form of God, was made a human being in the form of a servant. Each nature preserves its own characteristics without diminution, so that the form of a servant does not detract from the form of God. Now the devil boasted that humanity, deceived by his guile, had been deprived of the divine gifts and, stripped of the power of immortality, had incurred the stern sentence of death; that he himself had found some consolation in his plight from having a companion in sin. He boasted too that God, because justice required it, had changed his purpose in respect of humanity, which God had created in such honor. Therefore there was need for a dispensation by which God might carry out God's own hidden plan, that the unchangeable God, whose will cannot be deprived of its own mercy, might accomplish the first design of God's affection towards us by a more secret mystery; and that humanity, driven into sin by the devil's wicked craftiness, should not perish contrary to the purpose of God.

The Son of God therefore came down from his throne in heaven without withdrawing from his Father's glory, and entered this world, born after a new order, by a new mode of birth. After a new order, inasmuch as he is invisible in his own nature, and he became visible in ours. [...] From his mother the Lord took nature, not sin. Jesus Christ was born from a virgin's womb, by a miraculous birth. And yet his nature is not on that account unlike ours, for he that is true God is also truly human. There is no unreality in this unity since the humility of the manhood and the majesty of the deity exist in reciprocity. For just as the divinity is not changed by his compassion, so the humanity is not swallowed up by his dignity. Each nature performs its proper functions in communion with the other; the Word performs what pertains to the Word, the flesh what pertains to the flesh.

You will find the following questions helpful in interacting with this important text. First, consider this question: why did God become a human being? Leo's letter gives a clear account of the rationality of the incarnation. Try to summarize in your own words the fundamental elements of his argument. What does Leo mean when he speaks of the incarnation representing "an inclination of compassion, not a failure of power," on God's part?

Next, you should locate this statement within the text: "The properties of each nature and substance were preserved in their totality." (Note my gloss, explaining that this refers to the divine and human nature and substance.) So what does Leo mean by this statement? And why do you think that it is so important for him?

4.3   Martin Kähler on the "Jesus of history"

One of the most interesting nineteenth-century works dealing with the significance of Jesus of Nazareth was *The So-Called Historical Jesus and the Historic, Biblical Christ*, which appeared in 1892. The work, written by the German theologian Martin Kähler (1835–1912), was only 45 pages long, and represented an expansion of a lecture he had earlier given on the same theme. Kähler set out to criticize and reject the basic ideas of the "life of Jesus" movement, which held that faith must be based on Jesus of Nazareth, as based on objective historical scholarship, not the "Christ of faith."

Kähler's work may be regarded as an attempt to establish a secure basis for faith in the midst of the crisis which he perceived to be developing in the final decade of the century. If Jesus of Nazareth is a distant historical figure, how can we have faith in him? How can we be sure that we are not basing our faith on a historical error or misjudgment? How can Jesus Christ be the authentic basis and content of Christian faith, when historical science can never establish certain knowledge concerning the historical Jesus? In this extract from this work, Kähler argued that it is the "Christ who is preached" rather than the "historical Jesus" which is of decisive importance to Christian faith.

"Christ is Lord." Neither flesh nor blood can attain, sustain, or impart this certainty. Jesus himself said this to Peter after his confession (Matthew 16:17). He said it again as he reproached the unbelieving Jews (John 6:43–4). It was confirmed by Peter's denial in the outer court of the High Priest; later, it was said by Paul to his congregations in full expectation that they would assent to it (1 Corinthians 12:3). Yet, wherever this certainty has arisen and exercised influence, it has clearly been linked to another conviction – that Jesus is the crucified, risen, and living Lord.

And when we ask at what point in their discussions the historians deal with this certainty, we find that they do not begin with the much disputed and disconnected final narratives of the evangelists, but with the experience of Paul. They determine the constant faith of the early church, to the extent that they can, on the basis of the testimonies and traces left by those early witnesses. The risen Lord is not the historical Jesus behind the Gospels, but the Christ of the apostolic preaching, of the entire New Testament. And if this Lord is called "Christ" (Messiah), it is to confess his historical mission, or as we say today, his vocation, or as our forebears said, meaning the same thing, his "threefold office," that is to say: to confess his unique, supra-historical significance for the whole of humanity.

Christians became certain that Jesus was the Messiah, the Christ, in total opposition to public opinion, not just in relation to the idea of the Messiah (that is, the way the Messiah was understood and what one expected of him), but also with regard to the person of this Jesus of Nazareth. This was as true then as it is today. When Christians tried to make the Messiahship of Jesus credible in their sermons and then in the letters and Gospels, they always made use of two kinds of evidence: personal testimony to his resurrection, based on experience, and the witness of the Scriptures. As the living Lord, he was for them the Messiah of the Old Covenant.

And so we speak of the historic Christ of the Bible. The historical Jesus, as we see him in his earthly ministry, certainly did not win from his disciples a faith capable of witnessing to him, but only a very precarious commitment, easily prone to panic and betrayal. It is clear that they were all born again, like Peter, into a living hope only through the resurrection of Jesus from the dead (1 Peter 1:3) and that they needed the gift of the Spirit to "bring to remembrance" what Jesus had said, before they were able to understand what he had already given them and to grasp what they had been unable to bear (John 14:26; 16:12, 13). It is clear that they did not subsequently go out into the world to make Jesus the head of a "school" by propagating his teachings, but to witness to his person and his eternal significance for every person, in the same way that it is certain that his first followers could understand his person and mission, his deeds and his word as the offer of God's grace and faithfulness only after he appeared to them in his state of fulfillment – in which he was himself the fruit and the eternal bearer of his own work of universal and lasting significance, a work (to be exact) whose most difficult and decisive part was the *end* of the historical Jesus. Even though we once knew the Messiah according to the flesh, now we no longer see him in this way (2 Corinthians 5:16).

This is the first characteristic of his influence, that he won faith from his disciples. And the second characteristic is, and continues to be, that this faith was confessed. His promise depends upon this (Romans 10:9–10), as does our own decision of faith and the history of Christianity. The real Christ, that is, the influential Christ, with whom millions in history have had fellowship in a childlike faith, along with the great witnesses of faith as they struggled, gained, triumphed, and proclaimed for this relationship – the real Christ is the preached Christ. The preached Christ, however, is precisely the one who is believed in. He is the Jesus whom the eyes of faith see in every step he takes and through every syllable he utters – the Jesus whose image we impress upon our minds because we both would and do have fellowship with him, as the ascended and living one. From the features of that portrait, which has deeply impressed itself upon the memory of his own people, the person of our living Savior, the person of the Word incarnate, of God revealed, gazes upon us.

First, try to summarize the argument of the passage. You will find it helpful to remember that Kähler is arguing against those who insist that historical scholarship can disclose an authentic picture of Jesus, and that this picture is significantly different from the traditional Christian understanding of Jesus.

"The risen Lord is not the historical Jesus behind the Gospels, but the Christ of the apostolic preaching, of the entire New Testament." Locate this passage within the text. What does Kähler mean by this? In what sense is the "preached Christ" the real Christ? You may find it helpful to appreciate that Kähler is arguing that we do not need to have access to every historical detail about Jesus of Nazareth. The important thing, he suggests, is that a reliable interpretation of the significance of Jesus is passed down to us. It is grounded in history, but is passed on to us without the full historical context. Kähler uses the phrase "the preached Christ" to mean "the perceived significance of Christ" or "the interpretation of the importance of Christ to humanity." It is this, he argues, not a collection of historical facts, that is transmitted to us by the New Testament.

4.4   George Tyrrell on modern views of Jesus

In the year of his death, the English Catholic modernist writer George
Tyrrell (1861–1909) wrote a lively and remarkably insightful account of
the views of Jesus of Nazareth that were gaining ground in liberal Protestantism, on account of the revisionist ideas of writers such as the New
Testament scholar Wilhelm Bousset (1865–1923), and especially the histo-
rian Adolf von Harnack (1851–1930). In his *Essence of Christianity* (1901),
Harnack argued for an understanding of the Christian faith which saw
Jesus primarily as a religious and ethical teacher. Jesus was not himself
part of the gospel message; that development, Harnack argued, took place
when Christianity was transplanted from Palestine to the Greek-speaking
world.

This view was criticized by many, including the Catholic writer Alfred
Loisy (1857–1940), who was excommunicated in 1908. Tyrrell's response
to Harnack represents an important evaluation of the weaknesses of
the liberal Protestant understanding of Jesus from a modernist Catholic
perspective. The term "modernist" was first used to refer to a school of
Roman Catholic theologians operating toward the end of the nineteenth
century, which adopted a positive attitude toward radical biblical criticism,
and stressed the ethical, rather than the more theological, dimensions of
faith. Tyrrell might therefore be expected to be sympathetic to Harnack,
making his criticisms of his position all the more interesting and
significant.

The Jesus of the school of critics, represented today by Harnack and
Bousset, was a Divine Man because He was full of the Spirit of God; full
of Righteousness. He came (it is assumed rather than proved) at a time
when the Jews were full of apocalyptic expectations as to the coming
of the Messiah, who was to avenge them of their enemies and establish
a more or less miraculous and material Kingdom of God upon earth.
He Himself seems to have shared this view in a spiritual form, translating it from material to ethical terms. As destined by a Divine vocation
to inaugurate a reign of Righteousness, a Kingship of God over men's
hearts and consciences, He felt Himself to be the true, because the spiritual, Messiah. With difficulty He trained a few of His followers to this
conception of the Kingdom and the Christ. He went about doing good
(even working cures which He supposed to be miraculous) and teaching goodness. The essence of His Gospel was the Fatherhood of God
and the Brotherhood of man; or else the two great Commandments of

the law – the love of God and of one's neighbour; or else the Kingdom of God that is within us. True, these were platitudes of contemporary Jewish piety, and even of pagan philosophy. But Jesus drove them home to the heart by the force of personal example and greatness of character – above all, by dying for His friends and for these ethical principles. Of course He was, to some extent, of His time. He believed in miracles, in diabolic possession; above all, He believed in the immediate end of the world; and a great deal of His ethics, coloured by that belief, was the ethics of a crisis. But these were but accidents of His central idea and interest, in regard to which we may say He was essentially modern, so far as our rediscovery of the equation *Religion* = *Righteousness* is modern, not to say Western and Teutonic.

For this almost miraculous modernity the first century was not prepared. No sooner was the Light of the World kindled than it was put under a bushel. The Pearl of Great Price fell into the dustheap of Catholicism, not without the wise permission of Providence, desirous to preserve it till the day when Germany should rediscover it and separate it from its useful but deplorable accretions. Thus between Christ and early Catholicism there is not a bridge but a chasm. Christianity did not cross the bridge; it fell into the chasm and remained there, stunned, for nineteen centuries. The explanation of this sudden fall – more sudden because they have pushed Catholicism back to the threshold of the Apostolic age – is the crux of Liberal Protestant critics. […]

It was to the credit of their hearts, if to the prejudice of their scientific indifference, that these critics were more or less avowedly actuated by apologetic interests. They desired to strip Jesus of His medieval regalia, and to make Him acceptable to a generation that had lost faith in the miraculous and any conception of another life that was not merely a complement, sanction and justification of this life. They wanted to bring Jesus into the nineteenth century as the Incarnation of its ideal of Divine Righteousness, i.e. of all the highest principles and aspirations that ensure the healthy progress of civilization. They wanted to acquit Him of that exclusive and earthscorning otherworldliness, which had led men to look on His religion as the foe of progress and energy, and which came from confusing the accidental form with the essential substance of His Gospel. With eyes thus preoccupied they could only find the German in the Jew; a moralist in a visionary; a professor in a prophet; the nineteenth century in the first; the natural in the supernatural. Christ was the ideal man; the Kingdom of Heaven, the ideal humanity. As the rationalistic presupposition had strained out, as spurious, the miraculous elements of the Gospel, so the moralistic presupposition strained out everything but modern morality. That alone was the substance, the essence, of Christianity – *das Wesen des Christentums*. If God remained, it was only the God of moralism and rationalism – the correlative of the Brotherhood of man; not the God of Moses, of Abraham, Isaac and Jacob; of David and the prophets.

[...] [Yet] here the Liberal Protestant critics failed no less than the positively anti-Christian critics. Their hypothesis was an article of faith, not an instrument of inquiry. If they have been beaten off the field we need not, perhaps, set it down to the severer detachment of their conquerors, but to the stricter application of that critical method which they invoked. [...] The Christ that Harnack sees, looking back through nineteen centuries of Catholic darkness, is only the reflection of a Liberal Protestant face, seen at the bottom of a deep well.

This critique of the development of the "quest for the historical Jesus" mingles wit and wisdom. Tyrrell exposes some of the more difficult assumptions that underlay the movement, most notably its concept of the early corruption of a "primitive gospel" at the hands of the early church. Note that the German phrase *das Wesen des Christentums* (which means "the essence of Christianity") refers to the original German title of Harnack's publication of 1901.

On the basis of your reading of this passage, what is Tyrrell's most fundamental criticism of the liberal Protestant quest for the historical Jesus?

Now find the following citation: "The Pearl of Great Price fell into the dustheap of Catholicism, not without the wise permission of Providence, desirous to preserve it till the day when Germany should rediscover it and separate it from its useful but deplorable accretions." What is the point being made here?

Adolf von Harnack had argued that the simple gospel of Jesus had become complicated and muddled through the Hellenistic assumptions of the early church; Tyrrell argues that Harnack introduces just as many distortions and confusions through his own attempt to reconstruct the "historical Jesus." Our passage ends with this statement. "The Christ that Harnack sees, looking back through nineteen centuries of Catholic darkness, is only the reflection of a Liberal Protestant face, seen at the bottom of a deep well." What does Tyrrell mean by this? How does he reach this significant conclusion?

4.5   Austin Farrer on the incarnation and suffering

What relevance does the idea of the incarnation have to Christian living? In particular, what does it have to say to those who are experiencing pain and suffering? Austin Farrer (1904–68), one of the most interesting philosophical theologians of the twentieth century, had much to say about this question in his well-received book *Love Almighty and Ills Unlimited* (1962). Farrer's theme in this book was how one could make intellectual sense of the existence of suffering in the world. In addressing this question, he comes to explore the question of the relevance of Jesus of Nazareth to human pain.

Farrer begins by setting out the Christian hope in terms of the second coming of Christ, noting its importance as a statement of the future elimination of suffering. However, his attention soon turns to Christ's first coming – to the incarnation.

> It was the primitive faith that the Son of Man should come on clouds, and every eye should see him; even the eye that clay had sealed, or flame reduced to ashes. And it was held that he would not be seen in solitary splendour, but accompanied by ten thousand holy ones, and king among the saints. What had been hidden – the life of Christ in mankind – would now be revealed; in an aureole of glory they would see the *Corpus Mysticum*, both Head and members. Our first Christian predecessors, persecuted and despised by the world, dwelt naturally upon the reversal of empire which that confrontation would represent. They saw the princes and the mighty wailing and deeply mourning for their error, when the Church, the mystical Christ whom they had pierced, was throned in the sky; when they were found to have been wounding the only power ultimately worth conciliating, or able at last to kill and make alive. Yet however just the picture of guilty terror, the mercy of God is not measured by the anticipations of human fear; they pray that the mountains may fall on them, and the hills cover them, but the everlasting Shepherd takes into his flock all hearts that have been tender to him in any of his disguises; who have fed the hungry, clothed the naked, or succoured the miserable. [...]
>
> In essence it must seem that the two-sided fact of last judgement and ultimate salvation lies in a confrontation with the Supreme Being. But, as we have already insisted, to meet God, it is not enough that we should die. God, out of his invisible omnipresence, must gather himself to meet us in a form we can recognise. And how he will do this, Christians are

not left to conjecture; they know. God revealed himself in the human body of Jesus, and in that same person he will visit us again. But in what form, through the pages of gospel story, does the Godhead already stand revealed?

If we have two lanterns, in one of which a light burns, while the other is unilluminated, we see the difference immediately. But as between Christ, in whom the Godhead shone, and John the Baptist, in whom it did not, there was no such visible difference. Christ was not a mystical saint so incandescent with the graces of contemplation that he must be acknowledged a person of Godhead; and it is indeed scarcely intelligible how any holy incandescence should evidence such a fact to the eyes of sinful men. Christ shone in his transfiguration, but it was a single episode, and it was not the basis of the gospel. The divine life which radiated through him took effect in words, deeds, and sufferings; a saving action developed in discourse, and in mutual dealing with friends or enemies; more especially with friends. The Christ of the Gospels can only be known through what he did, and in the doing of it. And how shall the Christ of Advent be known, but through what he has done, and the possession of it? If Christ's glory and Godhead were at first manifest in his saving of men, and in the men he saved, how shall these things be manifest at last, but in the men he has saved, and in their being at one with him?

To put the point a little more philosophically. We speak of the incarnation of the Godhead, his taking of human flesh. Such a fashion of speech emphasises the height of the miracle, and the depth of the condescension: God brings an animal nature into personal identity with himself. But the flesh is not the point of union; the divine action does not fuse with the throbbing of Jesus' pulses; it fuses with the movement of his mind. And mind in man is a cultural or social fact.

It cannot arise in isolation, and it has its natural being in mutual discourse. God could not become incarnate in a human vacuum, and neither can he remain incarnate so. How justly, then, are Christians called the members of Christ! It is not only that they cannot find their perfection, except by subordination to such a head. It is just as much that he cannot live as a human person, without his person being extended and expressed in such members as these. What we are saying has nothing to do with the heresy, or rather, the blasphemy, which declares us men to be necessary for the completion of the life of God. No; God need never have created us, nor, having created us, need he have redeemed us, nor, perhaps, need he have redeemed us by becoming incarnate in us. But since he has been pleased to become incarnate, he needs the stuff and the embodiment which are involved in a true incarnation; that is, he needs the mystical Church, with which he will appear on the Last Day.

This is a significant passage, in terms of Farrer's approach to the incarnation, and of his use of it. To begin with, read the first paragraph. Try to summarize this in your own words. What comfort, according to Farrer, does the hope of the second coming of Christ in glory bring to believers? You might like to read Matthew 24:30, a biblical text which clearly lies behind some of Farrer's reflections here.

Farrer has an interest in linking the incarnation and the doctrine of the church. He does this through the idea of the *corpus mysticum* – the "mystical body" of believers, with Christ as their head. To use a phrase from the Church of England's *Book of Common Prayer* (1662), well-known to Farrer, this "mystical body" is "the blessed company of all faithful people" who are "heirs through hope of [God's] everlasting kingdom." Why does Farrer think this connection has relevance to the problem of suffering? What hope does it offer?

Now move on to the next two paragraphs. What point is Farrer making through his comparison of Jesus and John the Baptist? Why does he appeal to the transfiguration of Christ as an event of such importance? You may find it helpful to read a gospel account of the transfiguration in reflecting on this – for example, see Luke 9:28–36. Why do you think Farrer draws our attention to Christ's sufferings in this paragraph?

Now turn to the final paragraph, which you should read carefully. What is the point that Farrer makes here? Note his emphasis on God's decision to become incarnate. Why is this so important to him?

4.6   Morna D. Hooker on Chalcedon and the New Testament

One of the recurrent themes in contemporary debates about the theological significance of Jesus of Nazareth is whether the approach set out at the Council of Chalcedon (451) can be justified on the basis of the New Testament. There is no doubt that the Council itself believed that it had identified the most reliable and authentic way of making sense of the complex witness to Jesus of Nazareth in the New Testament. But that was back in 451. What about now? Do we need to revise and review Chalcedon's approach? How do we account for the philosophically complex language of Chalcedon, when compared with the simple statements of the New Testament?

In this essay, the New Testament scholar Morna Hooker (born 1931), who served as Lady Margaret Professor of Divinity at the University of Cambridge from 1976 to 1996, concedes "the great gulf between the thought-world" of the New Testament and that of Chalcedon. She points to three reasons which help explain why the language of Chalcedon is so different from that of the New Testament, while at the same time arguing that the Chalcedonian way of thinking about the identity of Christ was "an inevitable development."

First of all, Chalcedon was primarily intended as a bastion against heresy. Definition was necessary in order to make quite clear which heretical views were being excluded. In the days of the New Testament, on the other hand, Christianity was itself the heresy. This is something which is frequently forgotten by exegetes, who tend to read back later situations into the New Testament and suppose that our writers were defending the true Christian gospel against this or that heresy. But for most of the time they were not; they were propagating a message which was itself heretical, and were still in the process of working out its significance. The orthodoxy was Judaism; the Christian sect was trying to work out its position *vis-à-vis* the parent body and to reconcile faith in Jesus as God's Messiah with the conviction that God was indeed the God who had revealed himself to his people in the past. What our writers say about Christ has to be seen in this context. By the time of the Chalcedonian Council, the statements which had once been heresy had become orthodoxy, and were therefore handled in a completely different way.

Secondly, our New Testament writers were primarily concerned to describe the activity of God: he had acted, he had redeemed his people. They used a great variety of imagery – anything and everything available to them – in order to describe this activity; it was natural to them to employ narrative and metaphor. Their concern was not to offer definitions of the being of God or the being of Christ. The nature of God is known by what he does: many of the most important New Testament christological passages are hymns extolling God for what he has done through Christ. This is what is meant by describing New Testament christology as "functional" rather than as "ontological"; it seems to me to be a valid distinction. Nor is this simply an aberration on the part of our New Testament writers: it is part of the biblical tradition. Nowhere in the Old Testament does one find God being spoken of in terms of pure being: even in Deutero-Isaiah, where the description of God is at its most majestic, God is still celebrated as the one who acts. He is the God who reveals himself to his people and acts on their behalf, "the God of Abraham, Isaac and Jacob," the "Lord your God, who brought you out of the land of Egypt" (Exodus 3:6; 20:2). But by the time of Chalcedon things had changed radically; after four centuries in which Christians had grown accustomed to the idea of a divine Father and a divine Son and were used to speaking of them as peers, the Fathers of the Church approached the questions of christology in a very different way. What had been for our New Testament authors helpful images used to describe their experience of God have now become doctrines which themselves need to be defined and analysed.

Thirdly, leading on from there, our New Testament authors write from within a Jewish context and not a Greek philosophical one. One hesitates these days to make contrasts between Greek and Hebrew language, but in spite of the pitfalls involved in easy contrasts it is still true to say that there are differences in outlook. Paul, for example, could never have spoken of Christ as "consisting of a reasonable soul and a body." He speaks of man as *sōma psuchikon*, and the contrasts he uses are not between God and man, but between spirit and flesh. The debate at Chalcedon makes no sense to those accustomed to think in Jewish terms. Most important of all, the issues were quite different: our New Testament authors were wrestling with the question: "How do our new beliefs about Christ relate to what we have always believed about God – about the creation of the universe, his election of Israel, and his promises to his people?" Their concern was to show that it was the same God who had been at work in the past who was now at work in Christ, and that his new work in Christ was the fulfilment of everything that had gone before: hence the importance of showing his superiority to Moses.

The idea of an incarnate God is, we suggest, foreign to Jewish thinking. Remember the prayer of Solomon: "Will God indeed dwell on the earth? Behold, heaven and the highest heaven cannot contain thee" (1 Kings 8:27). To be sure, the Shekinah dwelt on earth, but the Shekinah was a particular manifestation of God's universal presence, and like other manifestations (angels, wisdom, the Spirit, the Word) was a way of speaking of God's self-revelation. Again, individuals were accorded divine honours: Moses, in particular, was said by Philo, elaborating Exodus 7:1, to have been given the name of god and king (e.g. *Mos. i.* 158; *De som. 2.* 189). Ezekiel the Tragedian relates a dream of Moses, in which he is enthroned by God on his own throne and given the emblems of rule – symbols of his future authority over men (68–89); the passage is reminiscent of that in 1 Enoch 45, where it is said that the Elect One (i.e. the Son of man) will sit on God's throne of glory. In these passages and others, five men share in divine honour because they are given divine authority, but this does not mean that they are themselves "divine" beings: rather their authority and honour are manifestations of the fact that God is revealing his power and purpose through them.

Before we begin to engage with the passage, a few points of clarification are in order. The term "Deutero-Isaiah" is a scholarly way of referring to Isaiah 40–55. The Greek phrase *sōma psuchikon*, used by Paul at 1 Corinthians 15:44, means "spiritual body."

Hooker is clearly interested in understanding the transition from the New Testament ways of speaking about Jesus Christ to the more elaborate approach, heavily influenced by Greek philosophy, found in the Council of Chalcedon. Some argue that this means that Chalcedon represented a distortion of the New Testament. Hooker, however, rejects this, seeing the transition as representing a change in *emphasis* and a change in *context*. In particular, she notes the biblical emphasis on the *actions of God*, which is converted to an emphasis on the *identity of Christ* as a result of the church's shift from a Jewish to a Greek context.

Summarize in your own words the three points that Hooker makes in this passage. How do you assess her argument? What does she mean by "functional" and "ontological" approaches to Christology? How is this related to her point about a shift in emphasis from actions to being?

Hooker argues that the idea of incarnation is foreign to Jewish thinking. How might this help us understand the fact that it took the church something like three hundred years to confirm that this was the best way of explaining the significance of Jesus Christ?

4.7   N. T. Wright on Jesus and the identity of God

The question of how Jesus of Nazareth relates to the God of Israel has been the subject of much discussion in both New Testament scholarship and systematic theology. Many believed that Adolf von Harnack was right when he argued that the language of the Council of Chalcedon represented a philosophical distortion of the simple ideas of the New Testament. Jesus did not think of himself as being God; he simply understood himself as the messenger or herald of the coming "kingdom of God."

Others have taken a different perspective, arguing that the New Testament itself points to a pattern of self-identification with God on the part of Jesus. Both the words and the deeds of Jesus of Nazareth show him to have understood himself as one who in some way saw himself as acting as and for God. An excellent example of a modern writer who takes this view is the New Testament scholar N. T. ("Tom") Wright (born 1948), currently professor of New Testament and early Christianity at the University of St Andrews, Scotland. Wright is the author of a multi-volume work aiming to understand the emergence of Christian views of the person and significance of Jesus of Nazareth by engaging with the historical context within which they emerged. In this 1998 article, Wright explores how appreciating the Jewish context of Jesus' ministry enables us to understand his view of his relationship with God.

The question of "Jesus and God" is a huge and difficult matter. [...] What we should be asking is: never mind what would count in our culture, how would a first century Jew have approached and thought about these matters?

There is some evidence – cryptic, difficult to interpret, but evidence none the less – that some first century Jews had already started to explore the meaning of certain texts, not least Daniel 7, which spoke of Israel's God sharing his throne with another (something expressly denied, of course, in Isaiah 42–8). These were not simply bits of speculative theology. They belonged, as more or less everything did at that period, to the whirling world of politics and pressure groups, of agendas and ambitions, all bent on discovering how Israel's God would bring in the kingdom and how best to speed the process on its way. To say that someone would share God's throne was to say that, through this one, Israel's God would win the great decisive victory. This is what, after all, the great Rabbi Akiba seems to have believed about bar-Kochba.

And Jesus seems to have believed it about himself. The language was deeply coded, but the symbolic action was not. He was coming to Zion, doing what YHWH had promised to do. He explained his action with riddles all pointing in the same direction. Recognize this, and you start to see it all over the place, especially in parables and actions whose other layers have preoccupied us. Why, after all, does Jesus tell a story about a yearning father in order to account for his own behavior? It is this that also accounts for his sovereign attitude to Torah, his speaking on behalf of Wisdom, and his announcement of forgiveness of sins. By themselves none of these would be conclusive. Even if they are allowed to stand as words and actions of Jesus, they remain cryptic. But predicate them of the same young man who is then on his way to Jerusalem to confront the powers that be with the message and the action of the kingdom of God and who tells stories as he does which are best interpreted as stories of YHWH returning to Zion, then you have reached, I believe, the deep heart of Jesus' own sense of vocation. He believed himself called to do and be what in the scriptures only Israel's God did and was.

Or suppose we approach the matter from another angle, vital and central but, remarkably enough, frequently overlooked. Jesus' actions during the last week of his life focused on the Temple. Judaism had two great incarnational symbols, Temple and Torah: Jesus seems to have believed it was his vocation to upstage the one and outflank the other. Judaism spoke of the presence of her God in her midst, in the pillar of cloud and fire, in the Presence ("Shekinah") in the Temple. Jesus acted and spoke as if he thought he were a one-man counter-temple movement. So, too, Judaism believed in a God who was not only high-and-mighty, but also compassionate and caring, tending his flock like a shepherd, gathering the lambs in his arms. Jesus used just that God-image, more than once, to explain his own actions. Judaism believed that her God would triumph over the powers of evil, within Israel as well as outside. Jesus spoke of his own coming vindication, after his meeting the Beast in mortal combat. Jesus, too, used the language of the Father sending the Son. The so-called Parable of the Wicked Tenants could just as well be the Parable of the Son Sent at Last. His awareness, in faith, of the one he called Abba, Father, sustained him in his messianic vocation to Israel and enabled him to act as his Father's personal agent to her. So we could go on. Approach the incarnation from this angle, and it is no category mistake, but the appropriate climax of creation. Wisdom, God's blueprint for humans, at last herself becomes human. The Shekinah glory turns out to have a human face.

What are we therefore saying about the earthly Jesus? In Jesus himself, I suggest we see the biblical portrait of YHWH come to life: the loving God, rolling up his sleeves (Isaiah 52:10) to do in person the job that no one else could do, the creator God giving new life, the God who works through his created world and supremely through his human creatures, the faithful God dwelling in the midst of his people, the stern and tender God relentlessly opposed to all that destroys or distorts the good creation, and especially human beings, but recklessly loving all those in need and distress. "He shall feed his flock like a shepherd; he shall carry the lambs in his arms; and gently lead those that are with young" (Isaiah 40:11). It is the Old Testament portrait of YHWH, but it fits Jesus like a glove.

Before we begin to engage with the passage, a few points of clarification are in order. "YHWH" is a way of representing the "tetragrammaton" – the four Hebrew letters that are traditionally used to refer to the God of Israel. These are sometimes represented as "Yahweh," and are more commonly translated as "the Lord God." The word "Torah" is a technical term, meaning "the Jewish law." "Shekinah" is another Jewish technical term, referring to the presence or dwelling-place of God. Shimon bar-Kochba (the name means "son of a star") was the leader of a Jewish revolt against occupying Roman forces during the period 135–132 BC, who was believed by some (including Rabbi Akiba) to be the Messiah.

Now read the passage carefully. Note how Wright insists on understanding Jesus within his Jewish context. List the points that he makes, and note how he interprets them within that context. One of Wright's most important statements in this passage is that Jesus "believed himself called to do and be what in the scriptures only Israel's God did and was." Find this statement, and try to identify the examples Wright offers in support of it. How persuasive do you find his approach?

CHAPTER 5

Salvation

A major section of Christian theology considers the nature of salvation, and how this is achieved. Christian understandings of salvation are linked, in different ways, to the death of Christ on the cross, which is widely regarded as constituting the basis of salvation. The area of theology that deals with the nature and basis of salvation is often referred to as "soteriology" (from the Greek term *soteria*, "salvation"). In many English-language theological textbooks, this is referred to as "theories of the atonement" – the word "atonement" having come to mean something like "understandings of the meaning of the death of Christ."

The origins of the English word "atonement" can be traced back to 1526, when the English writer William Tyndale (ca. 1494–1536) was confronted with the task of translating the New Testament into English. There was, at that time, no English word which meant "reconciliation." Tyndale thus had to invent such a word – "at-one-ment." This word soon came to bear the developed meaning "the benefits which Jesus Christ brings to believers through his death upon the cross." This unfamiliar word is rarely used in modern English. Theologians now generally prefer to speak of this field as "the doctrine of the work of Christ."

In this collection of readings, we shall explore a number of ways of understanding how salvation is linked with the death of Christ. Some of these approaches emphasize that salvation is to be understood as victory

Theology: The Basic Readings, Third Edition. Edited by Alister E. McGrath.
Editorial material and organization © Alister E. McGrath.
Published 2018 by John Wiley & Sons Ltd.

over sin and death. Others place the emphasis upon the forgiveness of sins, or the purging of moral guilt. Some stress the transformation of the believer as a result of the impact of Christ's death, especially in disclosing the love of God. Others speak of Christ's death as a sacrifice. Many hold that all these elements ought to be incorporated into a holistic view of salvation, and are reluctant to commit themselves to any one specific way of understanding the cross. A further issue that has received particular attention in more recent theological debate has been the redemptive value of suffering.

We begin our exploration of this theme by turning to consider a major discussion of redemption, dating from the patristic period.

5.1   Rufinus of Aquileia on Christ's death as a victory

In his commentary on the Apostles' Creed, which dates from around the year 400, Rufinus of Aquileia (ca. 345–410) sets out an approach to Christ's death which emphasizes that it represents a victory over death and sin. Rufinus develops what is widely seen as a classic statement of the "mousetrap" or "fish-hook" theory of the atonement, which held that Christ's death on the cross was an elaborate trap laid for Satan. Satan, it was argued, held humanity so securely captive that God was unable to liberate them by any legitimate means, and thus resorted to divine deception. The humanity of Christ was the bait, and his divinity the hook. Unaware of Christ's divinity, Satan was trapped through his humanity. The highly questionable morality of this theory was the subject of intense criticism by many medieval writers, but its unquestionable dramatic force made it a great favorite in popular preaching. It is widely encountered in popular accounts of theology, such as the great York Mystery Plays.

Rufinus opens his discussion by citing a phrase from the Apostles' Creed, and then offering a commentary on it.

> *He was crucified under Pontius Pilate and was buried: He descended into hell.* The Apostle Paul teaches us that we ought to have "the eyes of our understanding enlightened" in order that we might "understand what is the height and breadth and depth" (Ephesians 3:18). "The height and breadth and depth" is a description of the cross. The part which is fixed in the earth he calls the "depth," that which is erected upon the earth and reaches upward is the "height," and that which is spread out to the right hand and to the left is the "breadth." Now since there are so many kinds of death by which human beings depart this life, why does the Apostle wish us to have our understanding enlightened so as to know the reason why the cross was chosen in preference to any of them for the death of the Saviour?
>
> We must know that that Cross was a triumph – a signal trophy. A triumph is a token of victory over an enemy. Now Christ, when He came, brought three kingdoms into subjection under his authority. For this is what the Apostle means when he affirms that "at the name of Jesus every knee should bow, of things in heaven, and things on earth, and things under the earth" (Philippians 2:10). He conquered all of these by his death, in which he was lifted up in the air, and subdued the powers of the air, so that he might make a display of his victory over these supernatural and celestial powers. [...]

But perhaps some may be alarmed at hearing us speak of the death of the one whom we earlier said that he is everlasting with God the Father, begotten of the Father's substance, and one with God the Father in dominion, majesty, and eternity. But there is no need to be alarmed, O faithful hearer. In due course, you will see the one of whose death you hear restored to immortality, as the death to which he submitted would destroy death. For the object of the mystery of the incarnation that we expounded earlier was that the divine virtue of the Son of God might be like a kind of hook hidden beneath the form of human flesh. As the Apostle Paul said, he was "found in the form of a human being" (Philippians 2:5), so that he might lure on the prince of this world to a contest; that the Son might offer him his human flesh as a bait and that the divinity which lay underneath might catch him and hold him fast with its hook, through the shedding of his sinless blood. For he alone who knows no stain of sin has destroyed the sins of all – at least, of all those who have marked the door-posts of their faith with His blood. Then, just as a fish when it seizes a baited hook not only fails to drag off the bait but is itself dragged out of the water to serve as food for others; so he that had the power of death seized the body of Jesus in death, unaware of the hook of divinity which lay hidden inside. Having swallowed it, he was immediately caught. The gates of hell were broken, and he was, as it were, drawn up from the pit, to become food for others.

The Prophet Ezekiel long ago foretold this event using this same image, saying, "I will draw you out with my hook, and stretch you out upon the earth: the plains shall be filled with you, and I will set all the birds of the air over you, and I will satisfy all the beasts of the earth with you" (Ezekiel 29:5). The prophet David also says, "You have broken the heads of the great dragon, You have given him to be meat to the people of Ethiopia" (Psalm 74:13). And Job in a similar way speaks about the same mystery, for he says in the person of the Lord speaking to him, "Will you draw forth the dragon with a hook, and will you put your bit in his nostrils?" (Job 41:2).

It is therefore with no loss of, or damage to, his divine nature that Christ suffers in the flesh. His divine nature through the flesh descended into death, so that by the infirmity of that flesh he might effect salvation. Christ was not held prisoner according to the law of mortality, but so that, through this resurrection, he might throw open the gates of death. It is as if a king were to proceed to a prison, and to go in and open the doors, undo the fetters, and smash the chains, bars, and bolts into pieces. He would then bring forth and set at liberty the prisoners, and restore those who are sitting in darkness and in the shadow of death to light and life. The king, therefore, can rightly be said to have been in prison – but not under the same condition as the prisoners who were detained there. They were in prison to be punished; he was there to free them from punishment.

Although the imagery of the passage may seem somewhat strange to some modern readers, the argument is relatively easy to follow. Rufinus begins by citing the section of the Apostles' Creed which refers to the death of Christ, and links this with a symbolical reference to the cross. He then insists that the cross is to be understood as a victory, using the technical term "triumph" – a reference to the great victory parades held in Rome, at which conquering armies celebrated their victory over defeated enemies by displaying captured trophies. For Rufinus, Christ's death on the cross represents a victory over three kingdoms, each of which he subdued. What are they? And what point does Rufinus make by listing them?

The central section deals with the image of Christ's death being like a bait to entrap a large fish. Set out, in your own words, the mechanics of how this "fish-hook" theory of the atonement works. According to Rufinus, what was the bait? And what was the hook? Does this approach seem entirely moral to you? And what point does he make through asking us to imagine Christ entering hell, and setting its occupants free?

5.2   Maximus the Confessor on the economy of salvation

Maximus the Confessor – also known as Maximus of Constantinople – (ca. 580–662) is widely regarded as one of the most significant Greek Christian writers, whose ideas continue to play an important role in modern Greek and Russian Orthodox theology. He is often thought of as the last great Christian Neoplatonist, and is particularly valued for his writings on the incarnation. Maximus' writings are often quite difficult to understand, making it difficult to identify short passages suitable for study. However, his responses to a number of questions raised by his colleague Thalassius of Caesarea are relatively accessible.

Our extract, taken from this correspondence with Thalassius, deals with the place of the incarnation in history. More specifically, it engages with a question that is usually framed in terms of the notion of the "economy of salvation." This term, which seems to have been introduced in the second century by Irenaeus of Lyons, refers to the internal logic and chronological ordering of God's work of salvation in human history. The basic idea is suggested by a statement in Paul's letter to the Galatians: "But when the fullness of time had come, God sent his Son, born of a woman, born under the law" (Galatians 4:4). Maximus here explains why God chose to become incarnate at this specific stage in human history, and how events prior to this can be seen as leading up to this. He uses the term "dividing the ages" to clarify the historical location of the incarnation.

In this passage, Maximus speaks of salvation particularly in terms of divinization – that is, the process of salvation is understood to result in human beings becoming divine. This approach is based on a number of texts in the New Testament, especially 2 Peter 1:4, which speaks of the believer becoming "a partaker of the divine nature." Maximus presents this as the perfection of humanity, and sees this as the climax of the entire "economy of salvation." From the outset, the passage establishes a theological link between the incarnation of the Word of God and the divinization of humanity.

> The one who brought all of creation into existence, visible and invisible, according to the sole decision of prompting of his will, beyond all the ages and the very creation of all things that were created, had a supreme goodness of the will toward them. This was that he should be united, without change, with the nature of humanity, without change, through a true union of existence, so that he himself would become a human

being, as he himself knows, and he would make humanity divine on account of this union with him. He therefore divided the ages wisely, and allocated one part of them to the work of his becoming a human being, and the other to the work of making humanity divine.

Of the ages that were appointed to the work of his becoming a human being, the last part has come to us, when the divine intention was fulfilled by actuality of the incarnation, which is exactly what the divine apostle studied; in the actual incarnation of God and Word he saw the fulfillment of this divine intention of God to become a human being. For this reason, he says that the end of ages has come to us (1 Corinthians 10:11). Obviously, he does not mean by this that all the ages ended with us, but rather that the part of them which was appointed to the work of God becoming a human being has had its proper end according to the intention of God.

Since, then, the ages appointed to the work of God becoming a human being have come to fulfillment in us, and since God worked truly to complete his perfect incarnation, we should accept that the ages to come are appointed to the work of the mystical and ineffable deification of humanity, when God will reveal the supreme wealth of his goodness upon us (Ephesians 2:7), having worked perfectly to make us worthy of such deification. Because, if he himself has completed the mystical work of the incarnation, having become like us in all manners except for sin, and having descended even to the lowest parts of the earth, where the tyranny of sin had expelled and exiled humanity, it is certain that the mystical work of the deification of humanity will also be completed in every respect, except obviously in the single respect of our identity of essence with him.

The basic theme of this passage is the divine preparation for the redemption of humanity through the incarnation. Maximus argues that Christ's incarnation must be understood to be the ultimate purpose of history because it restores the original equilibrium between God and humanity which was destroyed by Adam's fall. If Christ is not fully God and fully man, argues Maximus, salvation is impossible. The passage sets out an understanding of the economy of salvation which proposes the incarnation happening in the fullness of time, followed by a period allocated to the divinization of humanity as a result of the incarnation.

You will find it helpful to summarize Maximus' argument in your own words, especially the way in which he understands the relationship of incarnation and redemption, and especially the theological link between the incarnation of the Word of God, and the process of "making humanity divine." In what way does Maximus seem to offer a commentary on Galatians 4:4?

Find this quotation in the text: "He therefore divided the ages wisely, and allocated one part of them to the work of his becoming a human being, and the other to the work of making humanity divine." What does Maximus mean by this? You might find it interesting to compare his approach here with the argument we considered earlier in Athanasius' classic work *On the Incarnation of the Word* (4.1).

5.3   Anselm of Canterbury on satisfaction for sin

How can God forgive sin, without compromising the divine justice? And how can this forgiveness be connected with the death of Christ? A landmark discussion of this issue is found in the writings of Anselm, archbishop of Canterbury (ca. 1033–1109). In his *Why God Became Man*, originally written in Latin in 1098, Anselm sets out his understanding of the link between forgiveness and the death of Christ. The treatise takes the form of a dialogue between Anselm and his colleague Boso. While occasionally asking useful questions, Boso's contribution to the treatise is generally minimal, being limited to bland comments such as "it would certainly seem so."

The argument of this treatise is quite complex, and can be summarized as follows.

1. God created humanity in a state of original righteousness, with the objective of bringing humanity to a state of eternal blessedness.
2. That state of eternal blessedness is contingent upon human obedience to God. However, through sin, humanity is unable to achieve this necessary obedience, which appears to frustrate God's purpose in creating humanity in the first place.
3. In that it is impossible for God's purposes to be frustrated, there must be some means by which the situation can be remedied. However, the situation can only be remedied if a *satisfaction* is made for sin. In other words, something has to be done, by which the offense caused by human sin can be purged.
4. There is no way in which humanity can provide this necessary satisfaction. It lacks the resources which are needed. However, God possesses the resources needed to provide the required satisfaction.
5. A "God-man" would possess both the *ability* (as God) and the *obligation* (as a human being) to pay the required satisfaction. Therefore the incarnation takes place, in order that the required satisfaction may be made, and humanity redeemed.

The section of this work that has been extracted for study focuses on Anselm's insistence that humanity has an obligation to offer God an infinite satisfaction, which only God can meet. Therefore a God-man would have both the ability (as God) and the obligation (as a human) to pay this satisfaction, and thus obtain forgiveness of sins. Anselm has just finished arguing that, on account of sin, humanity has forfeited its hopes to salvation. So might there be a remedy for this situation? Anselm picks up the discussion at this point.

Anselm. Now for these reasons, we can see that God will either complete what he has begun with regard to human nature, or else that there was no point in creating so elevated a nature, capable of such great good. Now if we understand that God has created nothing more valuable than this rational existence, which is capable of enjoying him, it would seem completely alien to his nature to suppose that he would allow it to be extinguished.

Boso. No reasonable person could think otherwise.

Anselm. Therefore is it necessary for God to perfect in human nature what he has already begun. But this, as we have already said, cannot be accomplished save by a complete neutralization of sin, which sinners cannot achieve for themselves.

Boso. I now understand why God had to complete what he had begun, rather than allow a frustration of his intentions. […]

Anselm. But this cannot take place, unless the price paid to God for the sin of humanity is something greater than all the universe apart from God.

Boso. So it would seem.

Anselm. Moreover, it is necessary that anyone who can give God something more valuable than all things possessed by God must be greater than everyone but God himself.

Boso. I cannot deny it.

Anselm. Therefore no one other than God can make this satisfaction.

Boso. So it would seem.

Anselm. But only a human being ought to do this, otherwise it is not humanity that makes the satisfaction.

Boso. Nothing seems more just.

Anselm. So if it is necessary, as it seems, that the heavenly kingdom be made up of human beings; and this cannot take place unless this satisfaction is made; and that no one other than God can make and no one other than humanity ought to make, it is necessary for the God-man to make it.

Boso. Now blessed be God! We have made a great discovery with regard to our question.

Anselm. Now we must explore how God can become man. The divine and human natures cannot change, so that the divine should become human or the human become divine. Nor can they be so mixed up together in such a way that a third nature results, which is neither totally divine nor totally human. For, assuming that it is possible for either to be changed into the other, it would in that case be only God and not humanity, or only humanity and not God. Or, if they were so mixed together that a third nature resulted from the combination of the two (as from two animals, a male and a female of different species, a third is produced, which does not preserve entire the species of either parent, but has a mixed nature derived from both), it would be neither God nor humanity. Therefore the God-man, whom we require to possess a nature that is both human and divine, cannot be produced by a change from one into the other, nor by an imperfect mixing of both to give a third nature. Either these things cannot take place, or, if they could, they would be of no relevance to our purposes. Furthermore, if these two complete natures are said to be joined together in such a way that one could be divine while the other is human, and yet that which is divine is not the same as that which is human, it is impossible for both to do the work that is necessary to be accomplished. For God will not do it, because he has no debt to pay; and humanity will not do it, because it cannot. Therefore, in order that the God-man may achieve this, it is necessary that the same being should be perfect God and perfect human, in order to make this atonement. For he cannot and ought not to do it, unless he really is God and human. And since it is necessary that the God-man preserve the completeness of each nature, it is no less necessary that these two natures be united together in one person, just as a body and a reasonable soul exist together in every human being. Otherwise, it would be impossible that the same being should really be God-human.

Boso. All that you say is satisfactory to me.

The passage is very straightforward, and is easily understood once the basic structure of Anselm's argument is appreciated. You will find it helpful to try and summarize this in your own words, disregarding Boso's somewhat uninteresting interjections. Notice how, early in the passage, Anselm assumes that it is beyond dispute that God would ever abandon humanity, once it had fallen into sin. Why do you think he believes this to be so obvious?

Anselm introduces the term "satisfaction," and this requires a little explanation. A "satisfaction" is what is required to restore the situation to what it had been before. It involves rectification of the situation, and compensation for any offense. For Anselm, human sin has caused God offense, and requires to be "satisfied" – that is, for an appropriate penalty to be paid. And since God is infinite, an infinite satisfaction is required – which humanity, being finite, cannot hope to pay. How does Anselm resolve this dilemma by proposing a "God-man"?

5.4   F. D. E. Schleiermacher on Christ as redeemer

In the second edition of his *Christian Faith* (1834), the important German liberal Protestant theologian F. D. E. Schleiermacher (1768–1834) set out an account of Christ's work as redeemer which emphasized the role of Jesus as the founder of the Christian community. Aware of recent rationalist challenges to traditional Christian teachings concerning the work of Christ, Schleiermacher tried to give an account of the work of Christ which avoided concepts and values which were objectionable to the Enlightenment. It was not necessary to invoke "magical" understandings of Christ to understand his powerful appeal to humanity, or his ability to change people's lives. The model of Christ as a charismatic community leader seemed to offer Schleiermacher a perfectly acceptable way of explaining the significance of Jesus, which avoided allegedly "irrational" approaches to the atonement.

> An analogy to this relation may be pointed out in a sphere which is universally familiar. As contrasted with the condition of things existing before there was any law, the civil community within a defined area is a higher vital potency. Let us now suppose that some person for the first time combines a naturally cohesive group into a civil community (legend tells of such cases in plenty); what happens is that the idea of the state first comes to consciousness in him, and takes possession of his personality as its immediate dwelling-place. Then he assumes the rest into the living fellowship of the idea. He does so by making them clearly conscious of the unsatisfactoriness of their present condition by effective speech. The power remains with the founder of forming in them the idea which is the innermost principle of his own life, and of assuming them into the fellowship of that life. The result is, not only that there arises among them a new corporate life, in complete contrast to the old, but also that each of them becomes in themselves new persons – that is to say, citizens. And everything resulting from this is the corporate life – developing variously with the process of time, yet remaining essentially the same – of this idea which emerged at that particular point of time, but was always predestined in the nature of that particular racial stock. The analogy might be pushed even further, to points of which we shall speak later. But even this presentation of it will seem mystical to those who admit only a meagre and inferior conception of the civic state.

Let us be content, then, that our view of the matter should be called mystical in this sense; naturally everything to be derived from this main point will be called mystical too. But just as this mystical view can substantiate its claim to be the original one, so too it claims to be the true mean between two others, of which I shall call the one the magical way, and the other the empirical. The former admits, of course, that the activity of Christ is redemptive, but denies that the communication of His perfection is dependent on the founding of a community; it results, they maintain, from His immediate influence upon the individual: and for this some take the written word to be a necessary means, others do not. The latter show themselves the more consistent, but the more completely they cut themselves loose from everything originating in the community the more obvious becomes the magical character of their view. This magical character lies in an influence not mediated by anything natural, yet attributed to a person. This is completely at variance with the maxim everywhere underlying our presentation, that the beginning of the Kingdom of God is a supernatural thing, which, however, becomes natural as soon as it emerges into manifestation; for this other view makes every significant moment a supernatural one. Further, this view is completely separatist in type, for it makes the corporate life a purely accidental thing; and it comes very near being docetic as well. For if Christ exerted influence in any such way as this – as a person, it is true, but only as a heavenly person without earthly presence, though in a truly personal way – then it would have been possible for Him to work in just the same way at any time, and His real personal appearance in history was only a superfluous adjunct. But those who likewise assume an immediate personal influence, but mediate it through the word and the fellowship, are less magical only if they attribute to these the power of evoking a mood in which the individual becomes susceptible to that personal influence. They are more magical still, if these natural elements have the power of disposing Christ to exert His influence; for then their efficacy is exactly like that attributed to magic spells. The contrary empirical view also, it is true, admits a redemptive activity on the part of Christ, but one which is held to consist only in bringing about an increasing perfection in us; and this cannot properly occur otherwise than in the forms of teaching and example. These forms are general; there is nothing distinctive in them. Even suppose it admitted that Christ is distinguished from others who contribute in the same way to our improvement, by the pure perfection of His teaching and His example, yet if all that is achieved in us is something imperfect, there remains nothing but to forgo the idea of redemption in the proper sense – that is, as the removal of sin – and, in view of the consciousness of sin still remaining even in our growing perfection, to pacify ourselves with a general appeal to the divine compassion. Now, teaching and example effect no more than such a growing perfection, and this appeal to the divine compassion occurs even apart from Christ. It must therefore be admitted that His appearance, in so far as intended to be something special, would in that case be in vain. At most it might be said that by His teaching He brought people to the point of giving up the effort, previously universal, to offer God substitutes for the perfection they lacked. But since the uselessness of this effort can be demonstrated, already in our natural intelligence we have the divine certainty of this, and had no need to obtain it elsewhere. And probably this view is chiefly to blame for the claim of philosophy to set itself above faith and to treat faith as merely a transitional stage. But we cannot rest satisfied with the consciousness of growing perfection, for that belongs just as much to the consciousness of sin as to that of grace, and hence cannot contain what is peculiarly Christian. But, for the Christian, nothing belongs to the consciousness of grace unless it is traced to the Redeemer as its cause, and therefore it must always be a different thing in His case from what it is in the case of others – naturally, since it is bound up with something else, namely, the peculiar redemptive activity of Christ.

Schleiermacher locates the significance of Jesus of Nazareth in terms of the impact which he has upon the church, or "community of faith." In this passage, Schleiermacher suggests that Jesus of Nazareth relates to the church in much the same way as a charismatic leader relates to his or her people. Note in particular the emphasis placed upon the role of the community, and the criticism of the traditional language of "satisfaction" (see the previous reading), which Schleiermacher here refers to as "magical." What difficulties does Schleiermacher note with what he terms the "magical" understanding of the work of Christ? And how does he resolve these problems?

5.5   Bernard Lonergan on the rationality of salvation

Can human reason make sense of redemption? As we noted earlier, Anselm of Canterbury certainly believed so, setting out what he regarded as an excellent argument for the necessity of redemption through Christ's death on the cross. Others have been slightly more cautious in their evaluation of this possibility.

In an important discussion of this question, the distinguished Canadian Jesuit theologian Bernard J. F. Lonergan (1904–84) suggested a more modest approach. The passage here reprinted is an extract taken from a lecture given in 1958 at the Thomas More Institute, Montreal, on the general topic of "redemption." Lonergan here considers the question of how we may be said to "understand" redemption, and offers five points of reflection on this theme. Although Lonergan clearly believes that it is possible both to speak of the "rationality" of atonement and to identify some of its features, he is critical of any attempt to "prove" the necessity of the atonement by a deductive argument.

1. Not a Necessity
The first point to be noted is that, while the redemption is an intelligibility, it is not to be thought of as a necessity.

The early Protestants, the orthodox Lutherans and the orthodox Calvinists, mainly the thinkers who succeeded the first Reformers, flatly affirmed that God in his justice could not possibly forgive the sins of mankind, unless Christ became man and suffered and died. Calvin had even gone further. He was not content with the sufferings that Christ endured at the hands of the soldiers and of Pilate, but also required that the phrase in the creed "He descended into hell" be taken to mean that Christ also suffered the punishment of the damned.

The doctrine – not Calvin's, but the doctrine – that suffering is a necessary condition limiting God's goodness can in some way be attributed to St Anselm. He frequently seems to be offering a theory that would explain why Christ's suffering and death were necessary. On the other hand, he also qualifies what he means by necessary. And it requires very nuanced interpretive efforts to determine what precisely St Anselm thought. As a matter of fact, his thinking, at the end of the eleventh century, was prior to any developed systematic distinction between philosophy and theology or any systematic attempt at determining the precise nature of theological thinking and the intelligibility that theology can grasp. [...]

2. A Dynamic Intelligibility

In the second place, that intelligibility is not static but dynamic, not a matter of deductive but rather of dialectical thought. Its fundamental element is a reversal of roles. In the book of Genesis, we read that God said to Adam when forbidding him to eat of the fruit of the tree, "On whatever day thou eatest thereof, thou shalt die" (Genesis 2:17). Death is presented in the book of Genesis, and in the book of Wisdom, as the penalty for sin. The same doctrine is repeated by St Paul in Romans 5:12: "By one man sin entered into the world, and by sin death." And again in chapter 6, verse 23, "The wages of sin are death." Yet death is not simply and solely the wages of sin. It is by the death of Christ that we are saved. And our salvation through the death of Christ is reaffirmed continuously throughout the New Testament. As St Paul says in 1 Corinthians 15:21, "A man has brought us death, and a man should bring us resurrection from the dead; just as all have died with Adam, so with Christ all will be brought to life." The theme of death and resurrection takes many forms and is constantly returning in St Paul. And the meaning of that recurrence is that death is swallowed up in victory (the words in 1 Corinthians 15:54), that what was the consequence of sin became the means of salvation. […]

3. An Incarnate Intelligibility

Again, the intelligibility to be reached in considering the redemption is not an abstract but an incarnate intelligibility. It exploits all the subtle relations that hold between body and mind, between flesh and spirit. Christ crucified is a symbol of endless meaning, and it is not merely a symbol but also a real death. It is again in the concrete, in the flesh of Christ, in his blood, and in his death that punishment is transfigured into satisfaction. And as you no doubt are aware, the notion of punishment is an extremely difficult notion to philosophize upon. The notion of the satisfaction of Christ contains all those difficulties and the transformation of them. […]

4. A Complex Intelligibility

Again, the redemption is not a simple but a complex intelligibility; and I use the word "complex" in the sense that the mathematician speaks of "complex numbers." The mathematician uses not only rational but also irrational numbers, not only real numbers but also imaginary numbers. And everything goes well, provided he does not mix them up, provided he does not consider that they are all numbers in exactly the same sense and manner. Similarly with regard to the redemption, we must not think of it as something that will fall into a single intelligible pattern. [...]

5. A Multiple Intelligibility

Finally, the intelligibility to be reached in the consideration of the redemption is not a single but a multiple intelligibility. It is not something that is going to be fitted into some single formula, some neat reason. St Anselm's *Cur Deus homo?* does illustrate the tendency to try to reduce everything to a single formula. But it was followed by a much less celebrated work about a century and a half later, about the beginning of the first quarter of the thirteenth century, by William of Auvergne, Bishop of Paris, the title of which was not *Cur Deus homo?* (why a God-man?) but *De causis cur Deus homo* (on the causes or the reasons why God was made man). What William wanted to put forward was that the redemption is not a matter of some single reason but of many reasons. [...]

Such, then, are the general characteristics, the precautions that one must take, I think, in seeking a total view of the redemption. There is an intelligibility to be grasped, but that intelligibility is not a necessity. It is an expression of what God thought wise, what God thought good, and that is intelligible, but it is not an expression of what simply had to be. It is like an empirical law, not a mathematical necessity.

While Lonergan insists that we may legitimately speak about the redemption as being "intelligible," he criticizes attempts to reduce the complexity of redemption to a single theological principle. Summarize, in your own words, the five points that Lonergan makes. How do you react to each of them? And what does Lonergan mean by contrasting deductive and dialectical approaches to redemption?

Note that Lonergan is particularly critical of the approach introduced by Anselm of Canterbury. (Note that Lonergan uses the Latin title (*Cur Deus homo*) of Anselm's work *Why God Became Man*, which we considered earlier in this chapter.) At what points does Lonergan engage with Anselm? What issues does he raise? Do you think he is right? Lonergan clearly believes that Anselm reduces the mystery of atonement to one theological formula. While affirming the intelligibility of redemption, he insists that it is to be approached, not as a mathematical or logical truth, but as an empirical law. What does he mean by the statement that redemption is "like an empirical law, not a mathematical necessity"?

5.6   Colin Gunton on the language of salvation

What is the status of the language that theology uses when discussing salvation? In an important discussion of this matter, the British theologian Colin E. Gunton (1941–2003) drew attention to the importance of metaphors in theories of the atonement. A proper appreciation of the *status* of the language used in relation to the cross of Christ is fundamental to a correct understanding of its meaning. In his work *The Actuality of Atonement* (1988), which has the significant subtitle *A Study of Metaphor, Rationality and the Christian Tradition*, Gunton called for a recovery of the patterns of divine action that were implied by the biblical images of salvation – the ways in which they "create ways both of speaking of God and of realising his action in the world." Gunton here hints at the importance of Richard Boyd's work on metaphor, especially his leading idea (noted elsewhere in *The Actuality of Atonement*) that metaphor offers "epistemic access" to the world.

The emphasis on divine action is significant. Gunton was concerned that the approach to theological metaphors developed in works such as Sallie McFague's *Metaphorical Theology: Models of God in Religious Language* (1983) was somewhat abstract. An alternative was clearly called for. Gunton suggests that the correct starting point is not an analysis of language in general, followed by an attempt to apply such theories to the New Testament. Rather, he argues, we should begin with the New Testament itself, attempting to understand how its language works and is used.

> We have seen that the metaphorical use of language is the heart of the way in which we come to speak of our world, approaching it as we do indirectly in the hope that by forcing changes in our language it will enable us to come to a measure of understanding of its structures. What is the case with our language of the world in general is even more characteristic of theological language. Because we are not able to speak of the action and being of God independently of the metaphors in which it is first expressed, we must begin with the language and move from there to a discussion of how the language has worked – or failed to work – and may still work as a way of articulating how the action of God may be conceived to take place here and now. Before, however, we move to the first main stage of the enquiry, some clarificatory points remain to be made.
>
> First: to discuss together the doctrine of the atonement and the nature of theological language brings considerable advantages. Many

treatments of the matter of theological language discuss the nature of analogy, symbolism and metaphor at great length and in general, and then show how their work bears upon theological language. The outcome is a tendency to abstraction; for example, to yet more discussions of the meaning of the term Father when it is used of God (e.g. McFague 1983). Such abstraction carries the danger that certain expectations or presuppositions will be taken into the discussion and prevent the theological meaning from speaking for itself. By contrast, to begin with the concrete relationships expressed in the New Testament metaphors, is to centre attention on the way in which theological language actually has been and, perhaps, should or may be used now.

Second, there is an overwhelming case for holding that traditional atonement metaphor is particularly well suited to show that language takes shape in a kind of conversation. We have seen that according to Boyd's account it is scarcely an exaggeration to say that the world forces new meanings upon words. Language is not just the tool of the user, to be employed at will, but a subtle instrument whose meaning is in part the gift of the (indwelt) world to which it seeks to refer. That is true in science, as we have seen: the world gives itself to be understood in the sense that its perceived and experimentally revealed structures demand of us changes in our language. Metaphor, as we have seen, is a major way in which those changes are achieved as our language is moulded to fit the causal structures of reality. A fortiori is this true of the relationship of human beings to God in the light of the atonement, whose very centre is the historical action of God for and among those who had placed themselves outside the covenant relationship. Our language is remoulded as we are. If the fact of atonement takes its shape from the initiative of God, to be true to it our language must take a metaphorical shape corresponding to the changes brought about by the incarnation, cross and resurrection of Jesus.

Third, however, it must not be supposed that certain images or forms of language are in some way forced upon the theologian by a bolt from the blue, in contradiction of all other experience. The biblical words upon which theology has drawn are themselves often metaphors, changes of language imposed upon the users by changes of personal situation and understanding. The language that is adopted already belongs in a context, and that context is not only a specific tradition – although it certainly is that – but the tradition as it makes variations on almost universal features of human thought and speculation. To take the example which will form the framework for a later chapter, Greeks and

Hebrews alike had concepts of the justice or righteousness of God, because concern with the rights and wrongs of life on earth animated not only the prophets, priests and wise of Israel but also Greek philosophers and artists. Yet the way the concept was understood was particular to the traditions within which they lived and thought. Christian talk of the righteousness of God is shaped by that of Israel as it comes to a climax in the cross of Jesus. [...]

The fourth point is perhaps the most important theologically, and takes up a theme from earlier in the chapter. It was here suggested that the creation of metaphorical language, particularly in theology, is partly at least at the initiative of that to which the language refers. If this is so, may it not be that, far from the metaphors being mainly or simply projections from standard to theological use, the reverse is true, in the sense that the theological use operates normatively and so alters the meaning of the word in its world? Here is real sacrifice, victory and justice, so that what we thought the words meant is shown to be inadequate and in need of reshaping by that to which the language refers.

And so our enquiry is established. In the next three chapters we shall look at three ways in which the story of Jesus can – or must – be understood to create ways both of speaking of God and of realising his action in the world. In each case, we shall ask whether they are viable ways of speaking about the life, death and resurrection of Jesus as redemption, atonement.

Begin by summarizing the four points that Gunton makes in this passage. Why do you think he places such importance on the relational aspects of Christian faith? Notice also his emphasis on how novelty forces linguistic change. When something happens that stands outside the experience of a community, they are forced to take one of two options – forge new words to describe this event, or adapt older words. Which of these approaches seems to underlie Gunton's analysis at this point?

Gunton engages briefly with Sallie McFague's work *Metaphorical Theology* (1983), which emphasized the importance of metaphor in theology. How would you summarize Gunton's attitude to the theological use of metaphors, as seen in this extract?

5.7   Rosemary Radford Ruether on suffering and redemption

The New Testament establishes a connection between the suffering and death of Christ on the cross and redemption. This link has been developed within Christian theology, as it reflects on the New Testament material. The redemptive suffering of Christ has been interpreted in a wide range of ways within the theological tradition – for example, in classic Protestant thought, as the basis of the merit of Christ, which is transferred to believers through faith. Others, uneasy about the mechanical and impersonal aspects of this approach, have stressed how the suffering of Christ has a powerful emotional and exemplary impact on believers, transforming their view of the world and energizing their commitment to Christ.

These debates are important, but they do not exhaust the questions that modern theology has engaged concerning the redemptive suffering of Christ. The leading feminist theologian Rosemary Radford Ruether (born 1936) has been particularly concerned to explore some of the wider questions that arise from Christ's suffering on the cross, some of which have particular relevance for women. In her *Introducing Redemption in Christian Feminism* (1998), Ruether explored how the traditional understanding of Christ's suffering brought together the notion of "deserved suffering for guilt" and the promise of "becoming a Christlike agent of redemption for one's victimizers through innocent suffering," and noted their potential implications for Christians – especially women.

Traditionally the Christian response to suffering has been a complex synthesis of human self-blaming and a view of God who is both omnipotent and yet a compassionate savior who intervenes in history, sending his "own son" to suffer and die to rescue humans from their sinful condition. Both God's power and goodness are vindicated in the face of suffering by teaching that God voluntarily takes on human suffering and pays for the primal sin that is its cause. This combination of belief makes for a powerful construction both to answer the question of suffering and silence the question, but when the threads of its fabric are examined, it threatens to unravel.

The Christian answer combines the following set of claims. First, it is said that God created a wholly good creation and intended the human condition to be painless. There was neither moral nor physical evil in God's original plan. Originally humans would neither have sinned nor died. Human disobedience, initiated by women, who bear the primary guilt for it, ruined this original plan and corrupted human nature and the natural world itself. As a result humans sank into a condition where they are both prone to physical evils, culminating in death, and are locked in a tendency to moral evil from which they are unable to rescue themselves, having lost their original free will. God is saved from any responsibility for evil, moral or "natural," which is placed totally on human, especially female, shoulders.

Secondly, humans are said to have incurred an infinite guilt for this situation of evil that they are incapable of paying. They have offended God infinitely and are thereby irreparably alienated from God, without any means at their disposal to make amends. But God in his graciousness has intervened to overcome this alienation and pay for this guilt. This gulf between humans and God can only be bridged through a blood sacrifice of one who is both "man," but one innocent of sin, and God. Through voluntarily suffering and dying on the cross as one himself lacking in sin and hence guilt for it, Jesus pays for human sin as a human and also acts as God to bridge the gulf created by human guilt that only God, not humans, can overcome.

The good news of redemption through the cross is that we are reconciled with God, and God now loves and accepts us in spite of our sin. We now have the possibility of growing in moral goodness through divine grace, gifted by a new capacity to obey God that we are incapable of in our present human condition, but receive through a power that comes to us from God. By accepting this good news that we are accepted, even while still sinners (and continuing to be sinners), we are assured of ultimately overcoming the mortality into which we were plunged through sin and living happily with God after death.

But what of continuing suffering here and now on earth? What of injustices that bring terrible suffering to the innocent; what about natural disasters that destroy human efforts to build secure lives? Although some Christians have held out the hope that either apocalyptic intervention from God or human progress would bring about a new paradise on earth, mainline Christianity has offered no promise that anything will get better on earth, either morally or physically, as a result of the redemption won by the cross of Christ. The action of the god-man is vertical, changing alienation from God to acceptance by God, not horizontal, changing evils that plague human history.

Sufferings, both those caused by unjust evils and by inexplicable "natural" disasters and mortality, continue unchanged by the cross of Christ. The Christian response to this continued reign of suffering on earth is a peculiar double bind. On the one hand, one should regard oneself as guilty for such continued suffering, and redouble one's repentance for guilt, and gratitude to Christ for having overcome a guilt we cannot overcome by ourselves. Indeed all other sufferings are said to pale before the sufferings endured by Christ on the cross for our sins, and it is we who caused Christ to suffer. If we had not caused sin in the first place, Christ would not have had to suffer to rescue us. Our contemplation of Christ's cross therefore should mingle gratitude for overcoming our offense with renewed guilt at having caused the terrible offense that made this infinite suffering necessary.

Secondly, even if we are innocent of having caused some particular evil that befalls us, we should endure it, accepting its blows, because thereby we imitate the cross of Christ. We become Christlike by enduring suffering like Christ, who, though innocent, suffered for our sins. Significantly, this double-bind message of the cross is first developed in the New Testament as a way of counselling slaves to passively accept not only the condition of slavery itself, but also the arbitrary beatings often inflicted on them by their masters. [...] This double bind of deserved suffering for guilt and the promise of becoming a Christlike agent of redemption for one's victimizers through innocent suffering, has been such a powerful message that Christian women have found it difficult to challenge.

Begin by considering Ruether's first paragraph. How does she portray Christianity to understand God's power and goodness as being vindicated through Christ? You might like to read John 3:16, which underlies at least part of her discussion.

Ruether regards this traditional position as being unstable, being vulnerable in a number of respects. From her account in the remaining paragraphs, what does she consider to be its weaknesses? In the middle of her analysis, Ruether interacts briefly with Anselm of Canterbury's approach, considered earlier in this chapter, though she does not specifically name Anselm. Can you find this section? What is her fundamental concern here?

Ruether notes that human suffering continues, despite the redemptive suffering of Christ. What conclusions does she draw from this? Note in particular her assertion that the traditional Christian response to this situation takes the form of a "peculiar double bind." What are the two components of this double bind? Do they have particular relevance for women?

CHAPTER 6

Spirit

There has been growing interest in the theology of the Holy Spirit in recent decades, partly due to the global rise of Pentecostalism, and partly because of the emergence of charismatic movements within mainline Christian denominations. This resurgence of interest has sometimes led to a retrieval of earlier Christian views on the Holy Spirit, as well as a more attentive reading of the biblical narratives. Both Old and New Testaments portray God as active in the world, and often speak of this activity in terms of the "Holy Spirit." The rich associations of the Hebrew term *ruach* ("spirit," "breath," or "wind") mirrored aspects of God's presence and action within the world, bringing life to individuals and empowering them to act for God. The New Testament links the person and work of the Holy Spirit to that of the Son and the Father, pointing to patterns of divine activity which are given more formal statement in the doctrine of the Trinity.

The Holy Spirit has been the subject of much theological discussion. The debates of the early patristic age focused on whether the Spirit was to be considered a divine person, or an agency through which God worked. By the end of the fourth century, there was widespread recognition that the Holy Spirit was to be regarded as divine, raising the question of how the relation of Father, Son, and Holy Spirit was to be understood.

Two quite distinct ways of understanding this relationship emerged during the fourth and fifth centuries. The Greek-speaking eastern church regarded the Son and Holy Spirit as essentially independent persons, with quite different spheres of activity. The Latin-speaking western church considered the Holy Spirit as proceeding from the Father and the Son. This disagreement is often referred to using the Latin term *filioque* (Latin: "and from the Son"), referring to an addition to the Nicene Creed made at the Third Council of Toledo (589). Toledo's version of this creed included the following statement: "I believe in the Holy Spirit who proceeds from the Father and Son (*qui ex patre filioque procedit*)." The original Greek version of the creed, however, spoke simply of believing in "the Holy Spirit who proceeds from the Father."

In this chapter, we shall consider material relating to these debates, as well as to other aspects of the theology of the Holy Spirit (often referred to as "pneumatology," from the Greek term *pneuma*, "spirit"). We begin by considering a patristic contribution to the debate about the divinity of the Spirit from the pen of Ambrose, bishop of Milan.

6.1   Ambrose of Milan on the divinity of the spirit

The fourth century was an important time of transition in Christian thinking about the identity and agency of the Holy Spirit. Gregory of Nazianzus, for example, commented that many orthodox Christian theologians were uncertain as to whether to treat the Holy Spirit "as an activity, as a creator, or as God." Although this debate initially took place in the eastern church, it was taken up in the Latin-speaking west. One important contributor to this debate was Ambrose, bishop of Milan (ca. 337–97), who was familiar with the ideas of leading Greek writers on the topic.

In his treatise *On the Holy Spirit*, written in 381, Ambrose developed a series of arguments to the effect that the Holy Spirit had to be recognized as fully divine. Ambrose's argument is best seen as an exploration of the inner trinitarian logic of the Old and New Testaments. For Ambrose, the only way of making sense of the biblical statements concerning God and divine agency was that there was a fundamental continuity of identity and action between Father, Son, and Holy Spirit.

Does anyone really deny that the Godhead of the eternal Trinity is to be worshipped? The Scriptures also express the inexplicable majesty of the Divine Trinity, as the Apostle says somewhere else: "Since God, who said that light should shine out of darkness, has shone in our hearts to give the light of the knowledge of the glory of God in the face of Jesus Christ" (2 Corinthians 4:6).

Now the apostles saw this with clarity, when the Lord Jesus shone on the mountain by the light of his Godhead. "The apostles," it says, "saw this, and fell on their faces" (Matthew 17:6). Do you not realize that they adored as they fell, since they could not endure the brightness of the divine splendor with their physical eyes, and the glory of that eternal light diminished the sharpness of their mortal sight? What else did those who saw his glory say then, other than "Come, let us adore, and fall down before him" (Psalm 94:6). For God "shone in our hearts to give the light of the knowledge of the glory of God in the face of Jesus Christ" (2 Corinthians 4:6).

Who is he, then, who "shone" so that we might know God in the face of Jesus Christ? For he said, "God shone," so that the glory of God might be known in the grace of Jesus Christ. Who else is revealed other than the Spirit? Who else is there besides the Holy Spirit, to whom this power of the Godhead is to be referred? Those who exclude this being the Holy Spirit by necessity must bring in something else, who is able to receive the glory of the Godhead along with the Father and the Son.

So let us repeat those words: God "shone in our hearts to give the light of the knowledge of the glory of God in the face of Jesus Christ." You have here Christ clearly set forth. For whose glory is said to give light but that of the Spirit? He therefore set forth God, since he spoke clearly of God. If this is said of the Father, it is still the case that the one who said that "light should shine out of darkness" and "shine in our hearts" must be understood to be the Holy Spirit, since there is none other that we can worship along with the Father and the Son. If it is understood as the Spirit, then the Apostle has called him "God," so that it is necessary that you (who now deny this) confess the divinity of the Spirit.

But how foolishly you deny this, since you have read that the Holy Spirit has a temple! For it is written: "You are the temple of God, and the Holy Spirit dwells within you" (1 Corinthians 3:16). Now God has a temple; but a creature has no true temple. Yet the Spirit, who dwells within us, has a temple. For it is written: "Your members are temples of the Holy Spirit" (1 Corinthians 6:19).

But he does not dwell in this temple as a priest, nor as a servant, but as God, since the Lord himself said: "I will dwell in them, and will walk among them, and will be their God, and they shall be my temple" (Leviticus 26:11–12). And David says: "The Lord is in his holy temple" (Psalm 10:5). Therefore the Spirit dwells in his holy temple, just as the Father dwells and as the Son dwells, who said: "I and the Father will come, and make our dwelling with him" (John 14:23).

We see, therefore, that the Father, the Son, and the Holy Spirit dwell in one and the same person through the unity of their nature. Therefore, the power of the one who dwells in this temple is divine. And just as we are temples of the Father and Son, so are we also a temple of the Holy Spirit – not many temples, but one temple, since it is the temple of one power.

Yet the Father dwells in us through the Spirit, which he has given to us. Now in what way can different natures dwell together? It is not possible. Yet the Spirit dwells with the Father and the Son. Hence the Apostle linked together the fellowship of the Holy Spirit with the grace of Jesus Christ and the love of God, saying: "The grace of our Lord Jesus Christ, and the love of God, and the fellowship of the Holy Spirit be with you all" (2 Corinthians 13:14).

Read through the passage carefully, and note the lines of argument that Ambrose develops. How would you summarize Ambrose's approach? What are his main reasons for asserting the divinity of the Spirit? What role does 1 Corinthians 6:19 play in that argument? How does the theme of individual believers as a "temple" within which God dwells feature in the later sections of Ambrose's discussion?

Note how Ambrose appeals to 2 Corinthians 4:6 in the early part of his analysis. What point does he make in doing so? How persuasive do you find this?

6.2 John of Damascus on the Holy Spirit

The patristic period saw intense debate over the status of the Holy Spirit. Some earlier writers of this era, noting that the Bible did not explicitly ascribe divinity to the Spirit, preferred to avoid speaking about the Spirit in terms that implied its divinity. During the fourth century, however, the arguments in favor of the Spirit's divinity began to gain the upper hand in both the western and the eastern church. In the previous reading, we looked at Ambrose of Milan's case for affirming the divinity of the Spirit (6.1).

Athanasius of Alexandria and Basil of Caesarea both defended the divinity of the Holy Spirit through a cumulative argument. One important element in this argument was an appeal to the formula which had by then become universally accepted for baptism within the Christian church. Since the time of the New Testament (see Matthew 28:18–20), Christians were baptized in the name of "the Father, Son, and Holy Spirit." Athanasius argued that this baptismal formula clearly pointed to the Spirit sharing the same divinity as the Father and the Son. This argument eventually prevailed.

By the time John of Damascus (ca. 675–ca. 749) wrote his classic work *On the Orthodox Faith*, the divinity of the Spirit was fully conceded, as is clear from this extract. It is interesting to note how John affirms (but does not feel the need to defend) the divinity of the Spirit. John also feels relaxed about admitting that he does not really understand the distinction between "begetting" and "proceeding." For John, the important thing is that this distinction affirms a common origination of both Son and Spirit with the Father, without implying that the Son and Spirit are identical. Each has a distinct manner of origination, and a distinct role to play within the economy of salvation.

> In the same way, we believe in the Holy Spirit, the Lord and Giver of life, who proceeds from the Father and dwells in the Son; who is adored and glorified together with the Father and the Son as consubstantial and co-eternal with them; who is the true and authoritative Spirit of God and the source of wisdom and life and sanctification; who is God together with the Father and the Son and is proclaimed as such; who is uncreated, complete, creative, almighty, all-working, infinite in power; who dominates all creation but is not dominated; who deifies but is not deified; who fills but is not filled; who is shared in but does not share; who sanctifies but is not sanctified; who, as receiving the intercessions of all, is the Intercessor; who is like the Father and the Son in all things;

who proceeds from the Father and is communicated through the Son and is participated in by all creation; who through Himself creates and gives substance to all things and sanctifies and preserves them; who is distinctly subsistent and exists in His own Person indivisible and inseparable from the Father and the Son; who has all things whatsoever the Father and the Son have except being unbegotten and being begotten.

For the Father is uncaused and unbegotten, because he is not from anything, but has his being from himself and does not have from any other anything whatsoever that he has. Rather, he himself is the principle and cause by which all things naturally exist as they do. And the Son is begotten of the Father, while the Holy Spirit is himself also of the Father – although not by begetting, but by procession. Now, we have learned that there is a difference between begetting and procession, but what the manner of this difference is we have not learned at all. However, the begetting of the Son and the procession of the Holy Spirit from the Father are simultaneous.

John of Damascus – often referred to as "the Damascene" – here sets out a comprehensive assertion of the divinity of the Spirit, emphasizing both the Spirit's divine identity and the Spirit's divine function. While insisting on the unity of Father, Son, and Spirit, he simultaneously affirms their distinctive roles within the economy of salvation. It should be remembered that, by the time John wrote this treatise, Damascus was under Islamic control, raising difficulties for the doctrine of the Trinity (which Islam regarded as compromising the absolute unity of God).

Read the passage carefully, and try to group the Damascene's statements about the Spirit under three categories: (1) what is done to the Spirit; (2) what the Spirit is; (3) what the Spirit does. What overall understanding of the Spirit emerges from this?

John declares that the Spirit "deifies but is not deified." Locate this passage within the text. The point John is making here is that the Spirit is the one who sanctifies and deifies, rather than the one who requires to be sanctified and deified. John picks up on arguments made by Didymus the Blind and others, which held that the role played by the Spirit within the economy of salvation had major implications for the identity of the Spirit. The Spirit was responsible for the creating, renewing, and sanctification of God's creatures. Yet how could one creature renew or sanctify another creature? The role of the Spirit within the economy of salvation only makes sense if the Spirit itself is divine. If the Holy Spirit performs functions which are specific to God, it must follow that the Holy Spirit shares in the divine nature.

6.3 The Formula of Concord on the Spirit and human renewal

The *Book of Concord* (1580) is one of the most important confessional resources for Lutheran churches. It takes the form of a collection of core Lutheran documents, including Martin Luther's two catechisms of 1529 and the famous Augsburg Confession (1530). One of the main reasons for assembling this collection was to encourage a consensus on a series of debated questions, including the nature of human freedom.

One of the later documents included in this collection is the "Formula of Concord" (1577). This consists of twelve articles or statements, dealing with debates and questions within Lutheranism. The work consists of two parts: a brief statement of the articles (the *Epitome*, or "summary") and a fuller reflection on their themes (the *Solida Declaratio*, or "full declaration").

Our extract is taken from the second article of the *Solida Declaratio*, dealing with human freedom. The section opens by considering the limits of natural human freedom, especially in relation to spiritual matters. True human freedom is declared to be impossible without divine renewal and transformation. As the discussion proceeds, it becomes clear that the Holy Spirit is seen as playing a significant role in establishing and preserving the spiritual freedom of believers.

> We believe that the intellect, heart, and will of people who have not been born again are unable, in spiritual and divine matters, by their own natural abilities, to understand, believe, accept, think, will, initiate, effect, do, achieve, or cooperate in achieving anything. Rather, they are dead to good and are corrupt, so that in human nature since the Fall and before regeneration, not even a spark of spiritual power remains present, by which they can, by themselves, prepare for God's grace, or accept this grace if it is offered. Nor can they be capable of this for and of themselves, nor apply or accommodate themselves to it, or by their own powers be able by themselves to assist, achieve, work, or cooperate in working anything toward their own conversion, whether in whole or in part or even in the smallest way, in that they are the servants of sin and the slaves of the devil, by whom they are moved (John 8:34; Ephesians 2:2; 2 Timothy 2:26). Hence the natural free will, by reason of its corrupted powers and depraved nature, is active and effective only in doing that which is displeasing to and which opposes God.

This pious declaration and general reply to the chief question and statement of the debate set out in this article is confirmed and substantiated by the following arguments. Although they are not acceptable to proud human reason or philosophy, yet we know that the wisdom of this perverted world is foolishness in the sight of God, and that the principles of our faith are to be judged by the Word of God.

First, although the human reason or natural intellect does indeed still have a spark remaining of the knowledge that there is a God, as also of the doctrine of the Law (Romans 1:19ff), yet it is so ignorant, blind, and perverted that when even the most ingenious and learned people in this world read or hear the Gospel of the Son of God and the promise of eternal salvation, they cannot from their own abilities perceive, apprehend, understand, or believe or regard it as true. Rather, the greater the diligence and earnestness they use, wishing to understand these spiritual things with their reason, the less they understand or believe. Before they are enlightened and are taught by the Holy Spirit, they regard all this only as foolishness, mere trifles or stories. [...]

Now just as someone who is physically dead cannot prepare or adapt themselves to obtain physical life again by their own abilities, so someone who is spiritually dead in sin cannot by their own abilities adapt or apply themselves to the acquisition of spiritual and heavenly righteousness and life, unless they are delivered and revived by the Son of God from the death of sin.

Therefore Scripture rejects that the intellect, heart, and will of natural human beings possess in themselves any suitability, skill, capacity, and ability to think, to understand, to be able to do, to initiate, to will, to undertake, to act, to work, or to cooperate in working anything that is good and right in spiritual matters. We are not sufficient in ourselves to think anything by ourselves, but our sufficiency is of God (2 Corinthians 3:5). All these things have become unprofitable (Romans 3:12). "My Word," says John 8:37, "has no place in you." The darkness does not comprehend (or receive) the light (John 1:5). Natural human beings do not receive (or, as the Greek word really means, does not grasp, comprehend, or accept) the things of the Spirit, that is, they are not capable of spiritual things; for they are foolishness to them; neither can they know them (1 Corinthians 2:14).

Still less can they truly believe the Gospel, or assent to it and recognize it as truth. The carnal mind, or the mind of the natural human being, is hostile toward God; for it is not subject to, and cannot be subject to, the law of God (Romans 8:7).

In a word, it remains eternally true what the Son of God says, "Without me you can do nothing" (John 15:5). And Paul: "It is God who works within you, both to will and to achieve his good pleasure" (Philippians 2:13). To all godly Christians who feel and experience in their hearts a small spark or longing for divine grace and eternal salvation, this most wonderful passage is very comforting. They know that God has kindled in their hearts this beginning of true godliness, and that God will further strengthen and help them in their weakness to persevere in the true faith to the end. [...]

Once God has begun and effected a beginning of the true knowledge of God and faith, kindled and brought about through the Holy Spirit in baptism, we should pray to God without ceasing that through the same Spirit and grace, by means of the daily discipline of reading and putting into practice the Word of God, God would preserve in us faith and heavenly blessings, strengthen us from day to day, and preserve us to the end.

This text can be seen as a classic statement of many aspects of classical Protestant views of the nature of sin, and the need for redemption. The most obvious point to note is the text's emphatic declaration that unregenerate human nature is incapable of desiring or securing anything that is good – above all, God. Try to summarize the key points that the document makes.

So what is to be done? It is clear that the work of Christ is seen as being essential to the transformation of the human situation. Note especially the use made of John 15:5. Yet, more importantly for the theme of this chapter, note the role played by the Holy Spirit. Work through the text, and note the specific references to the Spirit. How would you summarize these?

Note how the imagery of light and darkness (characteristic of John's gospel) features prominently in this discussion. How does the work of the Spirit fit into this context?

6.4   Charles Gore on the Holy Spirit and redemption

Charles Gore (1853–1932) was one of the most significant English theologians of the late nineteenth and early twentieth centuries, noted particularly for his exploration of "kenotic" approaches to Christology. For Gore, the incarnate Christ was subject to all human limitations, and thus did not possess omnipotence or omniscience. Yet Gore was also involved in debates concerning other areas of theology. In 1890, he published a controversial essay entitled "The Holy Spirit and Inspiration," which considered the role of the Spirit within the Christian faith, especially in relation to the inspiration of Scripture.

Our extract is taken from this essay, and deals particularly with the way in which Gore understands the relationship of the Holy Spirit to the person and work of Christ. Where some theologians drew a sharp distinction between person and work of the Son and Spirit, Gore saw them as intimately interconnected. The extract opens by considering the nature of redemption, before moving on to reflect on the role of the Spirit in enabling Christ to act as redeemer.

The work of redemption is only the reconstitution of the nature which God designed. It is the recovery within the limits of a chosen race and by a deliberate process of limitation, of a state of things which had been intended to be universal. The elect represent not the special purpose of God for a few, but the universal purpose which under the circumstances can only be realized through a few. The hedging in of the few, the drawing of the lines so close, the method of exclusion again and again renewed all down the history of redemption, represents the love of the Divine Spirit ever baffled in the mass, preserving the truth of God in a remnant, an elect body; who themselves escaping the corruption which is in the world, become in their turn a fresh centre from which the restorative influence can flow out upon mankind. Rejected in the world, He secures for Himself a sphere of operations in the Jews, isolating Abraham, giving the law for a hedge, keeping alive in the nation the sense of its vocation by the inspiration of prophets. Again and again baffled in the body of the Jewish nation, He falls back upon the faithful remnant, and keeps alive in them that prospective sonship which was meant to be the vocation of the whole nation: sometimes in narrower, sometimes in broader channels, the purpose of love moves on till the Spirit finds in the Son of Man, the Anointed One, the perfect realization of the destiny of man, the manhood in which He can freely and fully work. He came down upon the Son of God, made son of man, accustoming Himself in His case to dwell in the human race, and to repose in man, and to dwell in God's creatures, working out in them the will of the Father, and recovering them from their old nature into the newness of Christ.

In Christ humanity is perfect, because in Him it retains no part of that false independence which, in all its manifold forms, is the secret of sin. In Christ humanity is perfect and complete, in ungrudging and unimpaired obedience to the movement of the Divine Spirit, Whose creation it was, Whose organ it gave itself to be. The Spirit anoints Him; the Spirit drives Him into the wilderness; the Spirit gives Him the law of His mission; in the power of the Spirit He works His miracles; in the Holy Spirit He lifts up the voice of human thankfulness to the Divine Father; in the Spirit He offers Himself without spot to God; in the power of the Spirit He is raised from the dead. All that perfect human life had been a life of obedience, of progressive obedience, a gradual learning in each stage of experience what obedience meant; it had been a life of obedience which became propitiatory as it bore loyally, submissively, lovingly, all the heritage of pain and misery in which sin in its long history had involved our manhood, all the agony of that insult and rejection in which sin revealed itself by antagonism to Him — bore it, and by bearing it turned it into the material of His accepted sacrifice. He was obedient unto death. And because He thus made our human nature the organ of a life of perfect obedience, therefore He can go on to make that same humanity, freed from all the limitations of this lower world and glorified in the Spirit at the right hand of God, at once the organ of Divine supremacy over the universe of created things, and (itself become quickening Spirit) the fount to all the sons of obedience and faith of its own life.

Christ is the second Adam, who having "recapitulated the long development of humanity into Himself" (Irenaeus), taken it up into Himself, that is, and healed its wounds and fructified its barrenness, gives it a fresh start by a new birth from Him. The Spirit coming forth at Pentecost out of His uplifted manhood, as from a glorious fountain of new life, perpetuates all its richness, its power, its fulness in the organized society which He prepared and built for the Spirit's habitation. The Church, His Spirit-bearing body, comes forth into the world, not as the exclusive sphere of the Spirit's operations, for that breath bloweth where it listeth; but as the special and covenanted sphere of His regular and uniform operation, the place where He is pledged to dwell and to work; the centre marked out and hedged in, whence ever and again proceeds forth anew the work of human recovery; the home where, in spite of sin and imperfection, is ever kept alive the picture of what the Christian life is, that is, of what common human life is meant to be and can become.

Some points of clarification are necessary before we begin reflecting on the passage. Gore uses the term "baffle" several times in the opening sections of the extract to mean "frustrate" or "impede" (rather than in the modern sense of "puzzle" or "perplex"). The curious phrase "bloweth where it listeth" is a citation from the 1611 English translation of the Bible known as the King James Version. The text in question is John 3:8, which more modern translations render as "blows where it chooses." Gore uses the archaic word "quickening," which would now be rendered as "life-giving." Finally, note that there is no transcription error in the section dealing with Christ as "second Adam." Gore's quotation from Irenaeus disrupts the flow, but not the sense, of his sentence structure.

To begin with, note the main points of Gore's panoramic account of redemption. Gore offers a summary of the history of salvation which accentuates the role of the Spirit. Try to summarize this account in your own terms. How does Gore understand the interplay of the Holy Spirit and human nature? How does this lay the foundations for his approach to redemption in Christ?

Now consider Gore's account of Christ as redeemer. How does he understand the Spirit to equip Christ for this role? And how is the Spirit further involved in the body of Christ – the church? Gore clearly wants to affirm the ability of the Spirit to act with complete freedom, while at the same time emphasize the Spirit's covenanted reliability. Do you think he solves this problem?

6.5 Henry Barclay Swete on the Holy Spirit and the Trinity

The historical development of the doctrine of the Trinity in the early church can be seen as going through two critical stages in the fourth century – the formal recognition of the "two natures of Christ," and the subsequent acceptance that the Holy Spirit was to be regarded as divine. These two landmarks can be seen as fundamental to the church's formulation of its trinitarian faith, as set out, for example, by the Synod of Toledo. Yet it is too easy to gloss over the theological issues involved in the formal recognition of the divinity of the Holy Spirit, and assume that this was self-evidently correct. In fact, this demands closer attention, and leads to a deeper appreciation of the theological issues involved in formalizing the Christian vision of God.

Our reading, which deals with this issue, was written by Henry Barclay Swete (1835–1917), one of Victorian England's foremost theologians and biblical scholars, who ended his career as Regius Professor of Divinity at the University of Cambridge. The reading is taken from a devotional talk given by Swete at a meeting of the Exeter Church Congress in Exeter Cathedral in 1894. In this paper, Swete explored the theological options available to the church on this question, and offered a vigorous defense of its traditional teaching.

> God *is a Spirit*. Yet there is a Spirit of God, as all Scripture testifies, the Old Testament equally with the New. At first sight the two statements appear to be irreconcilable. The human spirit is a constituent of a complex nature, and stands in sharp contrast with the body and the lower life. But the Divine Nature is at once simple and purely spiritual. How shall we conceive of a Divine Spirit, differentiated in any sense from God Himself?
>
> Three answers have been given to this question.
>
> (1) Arianism attempted to solve the problem by denying the proper Godhead of the Spirit. The Spirit of God, it urged, is not called God in Scripture; He belongs to God, but not as possessing the Divine Essence. The Holy Spirit is the first of all the intelligences which were called into existence by the Word. Far above Angels and Archangels, admitted into the glorious Triad which begins with the Almighty Father, He is nevertheless infinitely removed from the majesty of the Uncreated Life.
>
> To a devout mind this answer needs no refutation. It shocks the Christian consciousness; it jars upon the ear which is attuned to the

harmony of Christian truth. The Arian hypothesis co-ordinates a creature with the Uncreated, the finite with the Infinite; in principle and in its consequences it is a return to Paganism, for it erects an order of inferior deities and thus practically disintegrates the Divine Unity. It makes the Christian life impossible; for how can a created Spirit quicken, sanctify, divinize humanity? It breaks down the analogy which S. Paul recognizes between the Spirit of God and the spirit of man. The spirit of man is human, and belongs to the being of a man. Unless the Spirit of God belongs to the Divine Essence, it does not stand in a corresponding relation to the Nature of God.

(2) The second answer, which is that of the Unitarian Theist, escapes from these difficulties. The Spirit of God, it acknowledges, is necessarily Divine. The Holy Spirit is, in fact, God Himself, but God regarded in the light of His workings upon Nature and man; the Presence of the Infinite Life pervading all that lives and is. It was this gracious operative Presence which *brooded upon the face of waters*, when the earth was yet waste and void; which reluctantly withdrew itself from the life of men as they fell under the yoke of the flesh; which is revealed as the source of wisdom in the wise, of skill in the mechanic and the artist, of prophecy in the seer, of holiness in the saint. The spirit of God, it is urged, has been identified with the Divine Presence in the parallelisms of the Psalmists: "*Cast me not away from Thy presence, and take not Thy holy Spirit from me ... whither shall I go from Thy Spirit, or whither shall I flee from Thy presence?*" All such references to the Spirit of God are sufficiently explained if we assume the working of a Divine Energy which penetrates Nature and inspires man.

(3) There is a third answer which does not exclude the second, but is complementary to it. The Catholic faith teaches all that the Old Testament teaches – that the Spirit of God is God Himself, that He is the mysterious Presence which is immanent in the world as the principle of life and which in rational creatures supplies the supernatural gift of sanctifying grace. But it goes beyond this teaching as Christ went beyond it, and to some extent corrects the conclusions to which it has led.

The Holy Ghost, it declares, is God proceeding from God. He is God in a certain eternal relation to the Father and the Son. He is not the Father or the Son, but the Spirit of Both. We identify Him with God, we distinguish Him as a Person from the other Persons in God. Thus the Catholic doctrine is not satisfied with the discrimination of God the Spirit as God present and operating in the creature; it pushes the enquiry further back, and finds a distinction within the Life of the Creator. The Spirit is God, but God is tri-personal, and the Spirit is the Third Person in the Unity of the Divine Essence. [...]

But we advance a step further when we speak of the Holy Spirit not merely as personal, but as a Person in God. We recognize that He not merely possesses the Divine Essence, but possesses It after a manner peculiar to Himself. We contrast God the Spirit with Father and God the Son, and affirm that Each of the Three possesses the Same Divine Life after a different mode. We call these modes of having the Divine Essence "Persons"; but the analogy of human personality fails us here. It can scarcely be matter for surprise that untrained minds should have gathered from this use of the terms a conception of the Holy Trinity which borders on Tritheism. The idea of One Undivided Essence, subsisting eternally after a threefold manner and in a threefold relation, finds but very partial correspondence in the nature of man or in any finite nature. When we try to express it in precise language, our terminology is necessarily at fault; the "hypostasis" of the philosophical East, the "persona" of the practical West are alike inadequate; in the things of God we speak as children, and we shall continue to do so until "*that which is perfect is come.*" Yet our imperfect terms represent eternal verities. The currency may be base, but it serves for the time to circulate amongst men the riches of God's revelation of Himself.

The passage is very clearly written. Begin by identifying the three theological options that Swete identifies in his opening discussion, and the assessment that he offers of each. Note in particular the criticisms that he offers of the first two positions. How do you respond to his concerns?

Swete clearly regards the third position as the best. Why? What reasons does he offer? And how does he relate this third position to the emergence and the specific ideas of the doctrine of the Trinity?

Finally, note Swete's reflections on the limitations of theological language. Do you think he is comfortable with the term "person" in this context? What broader conclusions might be drawn from his reflections at this point?

6.6   John Webster on the distinctiveness of the Spirit

During the 1970s, some serious criticisms were directed against the traditional notion of the Holy Spirit as a person of the Trinity. Some writers – such as the British theologian Maurice F. Wiles (1929–2005) – argued that the "Spirit" was nothing more than a sort of theological shorthand for "God's actions directed towards humanity." The term "Spirit" designated an aspect of God's work, not a distinct divine person. Others who wished to retain the traditional approach were concerned about a potential weakness within western approaches to the Trinity, which generally regard the Holy Spirit as proceeding from the Father and the Son. These were criticized as eroding any distinct identity or mission of the Holy Spirit. The Spirit thus becomes "essentially subservient and instrumental to the work of the incarnate Christ" (G. S. Hendry).

So how could such criticisms be met? One important response was made in 1983 by John Webster (1955–2016), formerly professor of divinity at the University of St Andrews, Scotland. In an essay on the distinctiveness of the Holy Spirit, Webster argued that it was possible to conceive the role of the Spirit within the western framework of a "double procession," from Father and Son, which avoided these difficulties. After surveying the criticisms directed against the traditional approach, Webster argues that it is perfectly capable of theological rehabilitation.

There is a need to ensure a properly *pluralist* doctrine of the Trinity, one, that is, in which threeness is understood as fundamental to God's unity. Unity is a *relational* term when applied to God: the divine unity is not monadic, relationless and undifferentiated. Rather, it is organic and dynamic, expressed in the personal histories of the sending of the Son and the outpouring of the Spirit. "The Divine unity is a dynamic unity actively unifying in the one Divine life the lives of the three Divine persons." Divine unity does not lie behind the threeness of God; rather, it is the event of the peace of the divine life between Father, Son and Spirit.

This will also involve careful specification of the notion of "person" as applied to God. "Person" is again to be conceived relationally: the person is not an autonomous subject but rather is constituted as person in relationship and dialogue. Understood in this way, the divine "personality" or "subjectivity" does not preclude relationship and differentiation; indeed, it is relationship. God's personality is God's relatedness to himself.

If God's triunity is thus understood as a personal, related society, then the danger of absorption of the Spirit into the person of Christ will be considerably lessened, precisely because God's being will be seen as fully plural. A pluralist understanding of God's being, moreover, will furnish the basis for understanding the distinct role of the Spirit in the divine economy, related to but properly distinguished from those of Father and Son. This will, in turn, serve to reinforce a sense of the distinct identity of the Spirit. Three areas of God's action which are properly to be attributed to the Spirit can be marked out.

First, the Spirit is the one who is sent out into the world through the church and who thus demonstrates that God's life is a life open to the creation. Because the Spirit is sent, "the triune God is the God who is open to man, open to the world, and open to time." The Spirit is a protest against monadic conceptions of God in which the divine life is seen as "a closed triangle," complete in the enjoyment of its own inner relationship and unconcerned to reach beyond itself into the history of the world.

Second, the Spirit is especially active in the mission of the church. In this, the Spirit's work is not merely that of ensuring the subjective appropriation of what was accomplished by the Son once for all in the past. Rather, we have here to do with "a great new event in the series of God's saving acts. He creates a world of his own." In this he does not supplant Christ, but rather his work continues the work which God began in Christ, and derives its validity and effectiveness from Christ's once-for-all accomplishment. Thus in the Lucan writings, Spirit and mission are inseparable: the giving of the Spirit by the exalted Christ enables the mission of the church as the agent through which Christ's kingdom is extended. This link between Spirit and mission is significant for two reasons. First, it prevents an excessive weighting of the Spirit's work towards the past work of Christ, emphasizing that that Spirit does not merely "remind" the church of Christ but also continues this work through its agency. In this way, second, it ensures a sphere of salvation history which is proper to the Spirit.

Third, in the worship of the church the Spirit is operative with an activity which differentiates him from Father and Son. The theology of prayer indicated in such passages as Romans 8:15f., 26f. and Ephesians 2:18 suggests that in the prayer which the Spirit enables God "hears his own voice." In prayer, "the Spirit's voice turns out to be … the voice of God addressing himself from within man." Such a conception of the Spirit's work in prayer and worship immediately introduces a note of differentiation in our understanding of God's being, and so safeguards both the divine plurality-in-unity and the identity of the Spirit. The way in which our prayers are caught up into God's own self-address reveals the reality of a further internal relation in the deity.

The Spirit is the one in whom God moves beyond himself in provoking mission and worship. If this is true, then we are able to see that the Spirit has an identity of his own, though one essentially bound to that of Father and Son; and we are, moreover, enabled to see a little more clearly that our understanding of the work and person of the Spirit can provide the crucible of an entire understanding of the triune life of God.

Webster's analysis is reasonably clear and easy to follow. You will find it helpful to read this through twice, perhaps comparing it with John Meyendorff's analysis of the eastern approach to the same question, which follows immediately in this collection of readings (6.7).

Find the following quotation within the extract: "The Divine unity is a dynamic unity actively unifying in the one Divine life the lives of the three Divine persons." The quote is from Leonard Hodgson's 1943 treatise *The Doctrine of the Trinity*. How does Webster develop this point? In particular, how does he affirm the distinctive natures yet fundamental unity of the persons of the Trinity?

Now identify the three "areas of God's action which are properly to be attributed to the Spirit," according to Webster. In each case, set out in your own words how the Spirit is involved in each of them. Why does Webster believe that this will help get round the difficulties noted earlier?

6.7 John Meyendorff on the Spirit and the Trinity

One of the most serious disagreements between the eastern and western churches concerns the role of the Spirit, particularly how the Spirit's relation to the Son is to be understood. As we noted in the introduction to this chapter, the *filioque* clause in western versions of the Nicene Creed continues to generate discussion and debate. Theologians within the Greek and Russian Orthodox traditions argue that the western idea that the Spirit proceeds from the Father *and* the Son limits God's work of revelation and salvation to Christ. Western theologians respond by arguing that this approach allows the Spirit to be understood as a personal being rather than an impersonal force, power, or activity.

Our extract is taken from a leading representative of the Orthodox tradition. John Meyendorff (1926–92) was for many years professor of church history and patristics at Saint Vladimir's Orthodox Theological Seminary in the United States. His writings show a deep familiarity with the historical roots and contemporary vitality of the Orthodox tradition. In this passage, Meyendorff reflects on this longstanding debate between the eastern and western churches, and offers an Orthodox perspective

It has often been noted that East and West differ in their approach to the mystery of the divine Trinity. The West takes for granted God's unity and approaches his "trinity" as a matter of speculation, while the East starts with a living experience of the *three* and then moves to affirm their equal divinity, and therefore, their unity. Thus the Greek Cappadocian fathers of the fourth century were accused of tritheism because "the groundwork of (their) thought lay in the triplicity of equal hypostases (persons), and the identity of the divine *ousia* (substance) came second in order of prominence to their minds."

The difference of approach of the trinitarian mystery is not a philosophical one. It is based on a fundamental interpretation of the New Testament by the Greek fathers who understood the Christian faith as primarily a revelation of divine *persons*. The Christian faith to them is first of all an answer to Jesus' question, "Whom say ye that I am? […] The Son of the Living God" (Matthew 16:15–16). The authority and effectiveness of Jesus' actions, as well as of His teachings, depend upon His personal identity. Only God Himself can be the *savior*, only God overcomes death and forgives sins, only God can communicate divine life to humankind. And the same approach is valid for the interpretation of Jesus' sending of "another" from the Father – the

Spirit. The primarily personal revelation of God is discovered by the early Greek fathers not only in the classic trinitarian formula – the baptismal formula of Matthew 28:19, or the three gifts personally qualified in 2 Corinthians 13:14 ("the grace of our Lord Jesus Christ, and the love of God the Father, and the communion of the Holy Spirit") but also in the Spirit speaking personally to Philip (Acts 8:19), to Peter (Acts 10:19; 11:12), to the church of Antioch (Acts 13:12), to the apostolic council of Jerusalem ("it seemed good to the Holy Spirit and us" – Acts 15:25). The Spirit is understood here as a presence distinct from that of Jesus but possessing the same divine sovereignty.

It is therefore understandable that the insistence by the Cappadocian fathers on this personal (hypostatic) distinctiveness could lead them to a trinitarian system in which their enemies saw tritheism. They were willing to run that risk in order to preserve the biblical understanding of a living and acting God, fully independent from the impersonal idealism of Greek philosophy. Even the Nicaean formulation of "consubstantiality" was long suspect in the East – and not only among the Arians – of being both unbiblical and too philosophical. It was finally accepted, but only in combination with the traditional (Origenistic) reaffirmation of the three *hypostases* in God.

The struggle against Arius, who accepted the distinction but not the substantial co-quality and co-sovereignty of the divine persons, was about the nature of salvation. This is particularly evident in the writings of Athanasius. It immediately and necessarily involved not only the person of Jesus Christ, but also that of the Spirit through whom the Son of God became man in the bosom of Mary, and through whom also, until the parousia, He is present in His body, the Church. It is in writings by Athanasius – his *Letters to Serapion* – that one finds the first elaborate patristic argument defending the divinity of the Spirit. It is the same soteriological approach that one finds in the other major fourth-century treatise on the same subject: the *De Spiritu Sancto* of St. Basil of Caesarea. Both Athanasius and Basil consider the saving activity of the Spirit accessible to the Christian experience, as being necessarily effected by God Himself. Since the *personal* character of the Spirit is taken for granted, the evidence of the Spirit's divinity is there to see.

The divine identity of the "comforter" is, therefore, a basic coordinate of the Christian idea of salvation. It is reflected not only in the theological tradition of the Christian East but also, very prominently in its liturgy. A prayer addressed personally to the Spirit, "O heavenly King," is the initial act of every liturgical action in the Orthodox

Church. The sacraments and, more particularly, the sacrament of the Christian *koinonia* itself, i.e., the eucharist, culminate in an invocation of the Spirit. Hymnology, especially that of the feast of Pentecost, proclaims the same relationship between the Spirit's act and His divine identity:

> The Spirit bestows all things: it appoints prophets; it consecrates priests; it gives wisdom to the simple; it turns fishermen into theologians; it gathers together the whole assembly of the Church. O Comforter, consubstantial in co-reigning with the Father and the Son, glory to Thee. We have seen the true light; we have received the heavenly Spirit; we have found the true faith, worshiping the undivided Trinity, who has saved us.

In the text of the Nicaean Creed, in fact the creed adopted at the Council of Constantinople in 381, the divine identity of the Spirit was defined in terms of His "procession of the Father." This definition is in accordance with the theology of the Cappadocian fathers who saw in the *person* of God the Father the very "origin of the Godhead." It is precisely as God that the Spirit "proceeds from the Father" directly, while creatures are not direct products from the Father but come into being through the operation and mediation of the Logos. Thus, the proclamation of the Spirit's "procession from the Father" is equivalent to the proclamation of His pre-eternal divinity.

Meyendorff's analysis draws attention to a series of issues that he believes to have led to misunderstanding and confusion about the eastern approach to the Trinity, and especially the role of the Spirit. What do you consider his main point to be?

For Meyendorff, the risk of "tritheism" arises on account of a greater truth which must be affirmed and preserved. What is that greater truth? And why does Meyendorff see it as being so important?

Locate the following quotation in the text: "The Spirit is understood here as a presence distinct from that of Jesus but possessing the same divine sovereignty." How does Meyendorff justify this statement? And if it is correct what are its implications for an understanding of the relation of the Spirit and Son?

CHAPTER 7

Trinity

The Christian vision of God defies simple ways of representation. The Aristotelian idea of an "unmoved mover," remote from and uninvolved with the affairs of the world, stands in obvious tension with the Christian belief in God as one who entered into human history, transforming it from within, and remaining as a living presence within the life of the church and of believers. The Christian doctrine of the Trinity is the church's intellectual response to this rich and fulsome vision of God, representing an attempt both to be faithful to the biblical witness to God on the one hand, and to do justice to the church's experience and knowledge of God on the other.

The Trinity has always been a difficult notion, and is often ridiculed as nonsensical. If the doctrine is "irrational," however, it is in the sense not of contradicting reason, but of transcending the limits of reason. The doctrine weaves together the leading elements of the Christian knowledge of God as creator, redeemer, and sanctifier into a coherent whole. The traditional trinitarian language – Father, Son, and Holy Spirit – is drawn from the New Testament, and expresses the fundamentally personal understanding of God that lies behind the doctrine. The formula "one substance, three persons," often used in theological textbooks, attempts to express the basic idea that Christians only worship one God – but that this one God is revealed as Father, Son, and Spirit.

Theology: The Basic Readings, Third Edition. Edited by Alister E. McGrath.
Editorial material and organization © Alister E. McGrath.
Published 2018 by John Wiley & Sons Ltd.

This chapter brings together a number of readings which explore and illuminate this doctrine. The first of these, dating from the second century, sets out the basic building blocks of the doctrine of the Trinity. Irenaeus of Lyons, in offering a basic account of the apostolic preaching of the church, argued that it was impossible to know the Christian God without the basic intellectual framework of the Trinity. Subsequent readings explore different aspects of this doctrine, both clarifying the reasons for believing in such a seemingly counterintuitive idea, and exploring its intellectual implications.

7.1 Irenaeus of Lyons on the trinitarian faith

In his *Demonstration of the Apostolic Preaching*, originally written in Greek but now known only in an Armenian translation, the second-century theologian Irenaeus of Lyons (ca. 130–ca. 200) sets out the basic elements of the Christian belief in the Trinity. This important early statement of a trinitarian faith is set out in a credal form, presumably to allow its readers to relate the passage to the creeds then passing into circulation. The importance of the passage lies in the way in which it clearly assigns distinct functions to each person of the Trinity, and links the three persons together as a "rule of faith," which expresses the distinctively Christian understanding of the nature of God.

> We must hold to the rule of the faith without deviation, and do the commandments of God, believing in God, fearing him as Lord, and loving him as Father. Now this doing is produced by faith: for Isaiah says: "If you do not believe, you shall not understand." And faith is produced by the truth; for faith rests on things that really exist. We believe in things that really exist, as they really are; and believing in things that really exist, as they really are, we keep firm our confidence in them. Since then faith is the means of holding fast to our salvation, we must pay especial attention to nourishing it, in order that we may have a true understanding of the things that exist.
>
> Now our faith takes the following form, as the Elders, the disciples of the Apostles, have handed it down to us. First of all, it asks us to bear in mind that we have received baptism for the remission of sins in the name of God the Father; and in the name of Jesus Christ, the Son of God, who was incarnate and died and rose again; and in the Holy Spirit of God. This baptism is the seal of eternal life, the new birth in relation to God, so that we should no longer be the children of mortals, but of the eternal and perpetual God. [...]
>
> For it is necessary that, things that are made should have the beginning of their creation from some great cause; and the beginning of all things is God. For he himself was not made by anyone, and by him all things were made. And therefore it is right for us to believe, first of all, that there is One God, the Father, who made and fashioned all things, and made what was not what it should be, and who, containing all things, alone is uncontained. Now among all these things is this world of ours, including humanity, who exists in this world. This world, then, was also created by God.

Thus then there is shown to be one God, the Father, who is not made, invisible, creator of all things; above whom there is no other God, and after whom there is no other God. And, since God is rational, he therefore created all things that were made by the Word; and God is Spirit, and by the Spirit He adorned all things. As the prophet says: "By the Word of the Lord were the heavens established, and by his spirit all their power." Since then the Word establishes (that is to say, gives substance and bestows reality of being), and the Spirit gives order and form to the diversity of the powers, it is right and appropriate that the Word is called the "Son of God," and the Spirit is called the "Wisdom of God." As Paul his apostle rightly says: "One God, the Father, who is over all and through all and in us all." For *over all* is the Father; and *through all* is the Son, for through Him all things were made by the Father; and *in us all* is the Spirit, who cries "Abba, Father," and fashions humanity into the likeness of God. Now the Spirit shows forth the Word, and therefore the prophets proclaimed the Son of God; and the Word utters the Spirit, and therefore is himself the proclaimer of the prophets, and leads and draws humanity to the Father.

This then is the sequence of the rule of our faith, the foundation of our building, and the root of our way of speaking. The first point of our faith is God, the Father, not made, not material, invisible; one God, the creator of all things. The second point is the Word of God, Son of God, Christ Jesus our Lord, who was manifested to the prophets according to the form of their prophesying and according to the method of the dispensation of the Father, through whom all things were made; who also at the end of the times, to complete and gather up all things, was made a human being among human beings, visible and tangible, in order to abolish death and show forth life and produce a community of union between God and humanity. And the third point is the Holy Spirit, through whom the prophets prophesied, and the ancients learned the things of God, and the righteous were led forth into the way of righteousness; and who in the end of the times was poured out in a new way upon humanity throughout all the earth, renewing humanity toward God.

And for this reason the baptism of our regeneration proceeds through these three points, in that God the Father bestows on us regeneration through his Son by the Holy Spirit. For all those who bear within them the Spirit of God are led to the Word, that is to the Son; and the Son brings them to the Father; and the Father causes them to possess incorruption. Without the Spirit it is not possible to behold the Word of God, nor without the Son can any draw near to the Father, in that knowledge of the Father is the Son, and the knowledge of the Son of God is through the Holy Spirit; and, according to the good pleasure of the Father, the Son ministers and dispenses the Spirit to whomsoever the Father wills, as he wills.

The passage is very clearly written, and is not difficult to understand. Notice how Irenaeus begins by emphasizing the importance of appreciating the intellectual content of the Christian faith. It is not enough simply to believe in God, or to love God. Faith involves believing certain things about God.

Irenaeus then begins to reflect on the content of faith. Locate this quotation within the reading: "For *over all* is the Father; and *through all* is the Son, for through Him all things were made by the Father; and *in us all* is the Spirit." What does Irenaeus mean by this? And how does he map this statement onto his trinitarian framework?

Irenaeus' closing argument is that knowledge of God is mediated through a trinitarian framework. This is made especially clear in this statement: "For all those who bear within them the Spirit of God are led to the Word, that is to the Son; and the Son brings them to the Father; and the Father causes them to possess incorruption." Summarize, in your own words, the point he makes in this concluding paragraph. Notice how Irenaeus clearly believes that the way in which God is known illuminates the nature of God. Since the mode of revelation is trinitarian, God must be trinitarian as well. Do you agree with this point?

7.2 The Eleventh Council of Toledo on the Trinity

Perhaps the clearest statement of the doctrine of the Trinity to be found in the later patristic period is that set out by the Eleventh Council of Toledo (675). This Council, which met in the Spanish city of Toledo and was attended by a mere eleven bishops, is widely credited with setting out the western view of the Trinity with an enviable clarity, and is regularly cited in later medieval discussions of this doctrine. In what follows, the Council explains the relation of the words "Trinity" and "God," and stresses the importance of the relationalities within the Godhead, focusing especially on the relation of the Holy Spirit to the Son and Father.

We confess and believe that the holy and ineffable Trinity, Father, Son, and Holy Spirit, is one God by nature, of one substance, of one nature as also of one majesty and power.

And we profess that the Father is neither begotten, nor created, but is unbegotten. For he himself, from whom the Son has received His birth and the Holy Spirit His procession, has his origin from no one. He is therefore the source and origin of the whole Godhead. He himself is the Father of His own essence, who in an ineffable way has begotten the Son from His ineffable substance. Yet He did not beget something different from what he himself is: God has begotten God, light has begotten light. From Him, therefore, is "all fatherhood in heaven and on earth."

We also confess that the Son was born, but not made, from the substance of the Father, without beginning, before all ages. At no time did the Father exist without the Son, nor the Son without the Father. Yet the Father is not from the Son, as the Son is from the Father, because the Father was not generated by the Son, but the Son by the Father. The Son, therefore, is God from the Father; and the Father is God, but not from the Son. He is indeed the Father of the Son, not God from the Son; but the latter is the Son of the Father and God from the Father. Yet the Son is equal to God the Father in all things, for he has never begun nor ceased to be born. We also believe that he is of one substance with the Father; wherefore He is called *homoousios* with the Father, that is, of the same being as the Father, for *homos* in Greek means "one" and *ousia* means "being," and joined together they mean "one in being." We must believe that the Son is begotten or born, not from nothing or from any other substance, but from the womb of the Father, that is from his substance. Therefore the Father is eternal, and the Son is also eternal. If he was always Father, He always had a Son, whose Father he was, and therefore we confess that the Son was born from the Father without beginning. We do not call the same Son of God a part of a divided nature, because he was generated from the Father; rather, we assert that the perfect Father has begotten the perfect Son, without diminution or division, for it belongs to the Godhead alone not to have an unequal Son. This Son of God is also Son by nature, not by adoption. We must believe that God the Father begot him neither by an act of will nor out of necessity, for in God there is no necessity, nor does will precede wisdom.

We believe that the Holy Spirit, the third person in the Trinity, is God, one and equal with God the Father and God the Son, of one substance and of one nature; not, however, begotten or created, but proceeding from both, and that He is the Spirit of both. We also believe that the Holy Spirit is neither unbegotten nor begotten, for if we called him "unbegotten" we would assert two Fathers, or if we called him "begotten," we would appear to preach two Sons. Yet he is called the Spirit not of the Father alone, nor of the Son alone, but of both Father and Son. For he does not proceed from the Father to the Son, nor from the Son to sanctify creatures, but He is shown to have proceeded from both at once, because he is known as the love or the holiness of both. Hence we believe that the Holy Spirit is sent by both, as the Son is sent by the Father. But he is not less than the Father and the Son.

This is the way of speaking about the Holy Trinity as it has been handed down: it must not be spoken of or believed to be "threefold" (*triplex*), but to be "Trinity." Nor can it properly be said that in the one God there is the Trinity; rather, the one God is the Trinity. In the relative names of the persons, the Father is related to the Son, the Son to the Father, and the Holy Spirit to both. While they are called three persons in view of their relations, we believe in one nature or substance. Although we profess three persons, we do not profess three substances, but one substance and three persons. For the Father is Father not with respect to himself but to the Son, and the Son is Son not to himself but in relation to the Father; and likewise the Holy Spirit is not referred to himself but is related to the Father and the Son, inasmuch as He is called the Spirit of the Father and the Son. So when we use the word "God," this does not express a relationship to another, as of the Father to the Son or of the Son to the Father or of the Holy Spirit to the Father and the Son, but "God" refers to Himself only [*sed ad se specialiter dicitur*].

This important text sets out some of the basic features of the emerging western understanding of the Trinity. It is of particular importance in several respects. The text stresses the importance of relationalities within the Godhead, and also clarifies the relation of the terms "God" and "Trinity." The text also explicitly avoids a serious misunderstanding which could arise from the western view that the Holy Spirit proceeds from the Father and the Son – namely, that there are *two* divine sources of the Spirit. The text makes it clear that there is only one source of the Spirit.

This is a dense text, which needs careful unpacking. It is, however, both rewarding and helpful to do this. The best way of starting to interact with this text is to read it closely, and then to set out in your own words how it understands the relation of Father, Son, and Holy Spirit. Notice how Christology plays a major role in shaping the doctrine of the Trinity – for example, consider how the term *homoousios*, explained in the text, is used to clarify the relation between Father and Son, and lay the foundations for a trinitarian approach to faith.

Toledo's approach can be seen as a definitive statement of the concepts and vocabulary of the trinitarian faith. According to this text, when – and in what kind of contexts – should the words "God" and "Trinity" be used? "Yet He is called the Spirit not of the Father alone, nor of the Son alone, but of both Father and Son." Locate this passage within the text. What does it mean? How is it to be justified? And what is its importance in clarifying the origins of the Spirit?

7.3   Richard of St Victor on the Trinity as a community of love

Some important developments in the doctrine of the Trinity took place at the University of Paris during the theological renaissance of the twelfth century. One of the major centers of theological reflection during this period was the Abbey of St Victor. The original buildings, located near the present sites of the Muséum and Jardin des plantes in Paris, were destroyed during the French Revolution. Several major theologians were based at this abbey, including the highly influential theologians Hugh of St Victor (ca. 1096–1141) and Richard of St Victor, who served as prior of the abbey from 1162 until his death in 1173. During his period as prior, Richard wrote his substantial work *On the Trinity*, from which the extract below is taken.

Richard's reflections on the relationship between the three persons of the Trinity have had a major impact on western theology, particularly on the movement known as "social trinitarianism." In this analysis of the nature of love within the Godhead, Richard argues that the idea of the "sharing of love" can only be sustained if there are three persons within the Godhead (*divinitas*).

If we concede that there exists in the true Godhead some one person of such great benevolence that he wishes to have no riches or delights that he does not wish to share with others, and if he is of such great power that nothing is impossible for him, and of such great happiness that nothing is difficult for him, then it is necessary to acknowledge that a Trinity of divine persons must exist. In order that the reasons for this may be clear, let us draw together all our arguments at this point.

If there were only one person in the Godhead, that one person would certainly not have anyone with whom he could share the riches of his greatness. But on the other hand, the abundance of delights and sweetness, which would have been able to increase for him on account of intimate love, would lack any eternal dimension. But the fullness of goodness does not permit the supremely good One to keep those riches for himself, nor does his fullness of blessedness allow him to be without a full abundance of delights and sweetness. And on account of the greatness of his honor, he rejoices at sharing his riches as much as he glories over enjoying the abundance of delights and sweetness.

On the basis of these considerations, it is clearly impossible that any one person in the Godhead could lack the fellowship of association. If he were to have only one partner, he would not be without anyone with whom he could share the riches of his greatness. However, he would not have anyone with whom he could share the delights of love. There is nothing which gives more pleasure or which delights the soul more than the sweetness of loving. Only someone who has a partner and a loved one in that love that has been shown to him possesses the sweetness of such delights.

So it follows that such a sharing of love cannot exist among fewer than three persons. As we said earlier, there is nothing more glorious and nothing more magnificent than sharing in common whatever is useful and pleasant. This fact can hardly be unknown to the supreme wisdom, nor can it fail to please the supreme benevolence. And as the happiness of the supremely powerful One cannot be lacking in what pleases him, so in the Godhead it is impossible for two persons not to be united to a third.

Richard of St Victor is one of the most important trinitarian thinkers of the Middle Ages. His understanding of the Trinity, set out in the passage above, makes much of the idea of social relationships within the Trinity – notice in particular the emphasis upon "sharing" and the use of the language of "partnership." This contrasts sharply with the more individualist approach to the Trinity adopted by Augustine of Hippo. This is an important example of the "social Trinity" model, which sees a model for the Trinity in human relationships – where Augustine chose to use the inner workings of the individual human mind as a resource for trinitarian analysis. Yet both base their analyses, at least in part, on an examination of the concept of "love," which they explore in different manners.

To begin with, set out, in your own words, the arguments and considerations which lead Richard to "acknowledge that a Trinity of divine persons must exist." Then find this passage within the text: "There is nothing which gives more pleasure or which delights the soul more than the sweetness of loving." What does Richard mean by this? And what function does this conclusion play in his argument? Finally, you might like to reflect on whether Richard's approach actually comes close to tritheism, understanding each of the persons of the Trinity as independently existing entities. Richard clearly does not believe that he has done this, nor does he intend to do so. Yet some feel his argument at this point might be vulnerable.

7.4   Karl Rahner on the economic Trinity

One of the most sophisticated modern discussions of the Trinity is due to the German Jesuit theologian Karl Rahner (1904–84). Rahner's substantial theological output often took the form of succinct essays, gathered together in the collection *Theological Investigations*. For Rahner, one of the major theological issues relating to this difficult doctrine concerned the relation of the "economic" and "essential" (or "immanent") Trinities. The "essential" Trinity, according to Rahner, refers to the way God actually is; the "economic" Trinity refers to the way in which God has made himself known.

For Rahner, these do not constitute two different Godheads; rather, they are two different manners of approaching the same Godhead. The "essential" or "immanent" Trinity can be regarded as an attempt to formulate the Godhead outside the limiting conditions of time and space; the "economic Trinity" is the manner in which the Trinity is made known within the "economy of salvation," that is to say, in the historical process itself. Rahner lays down the following axiom, which is often cited in works of theology: "The economic Trinity is the immanent Trinity, and vice versa." This means that the doctrine of the Trinity cannot be discussed in isolation (as in much scholastic theology), in that it is intimately connected with other theological topics. In the reading which follows, which is taken from his essay "Remarks on the Dogmatic Treatise 'De trinitate'," Rahner considers this point in greater detail.

> The very isolation of the treatise on the Trinity proves at once that something is wrong: the thing is impossible! For the Trinity is a mystery of salvation. Otherwise it would never have been revealed. But then it must be possible to see why it is a mystery of salvation. And then it must be possible to show in all dogmatic treatises that the realities of salvation with which they deal cannot be made comprehensible without recurring to this primordial mystery of Christianity. If the intrinsic connexion between the various treatises does not constantly appear, this can only be a sign that in the treatise on the Trinity or in the other treatises attention has not been paid to the points which show that the Trinity is a mystery of salvation in our regard and hence confronts us wherever our salvation is spoken of – that is, in the other dogmatic treatises.
>
> The basic thesis which constitutes the link between the treatises and shows the reality and not just the doctrine of the Trinity as a mystery

of salvation for us may be formulated as follows: the Trinity of the economy of salvation is the immanent Trinity and vice versa. [...] This assertion is a defined truth of faith at one point, in one case, for Jesus is not simply God in general, but the Son; the second divine Person, the Logos of God is man, and he alone. So there is at least one "sending," one presence in the world, one reality in the economy of salvation which is not merely appropriated to a certain divine person, but is proper to him. Thus it is not a matter of saying something "about" this particular divine person in the world. Here something takes place in the world itself, outside the immanent divine life, which is not simply the result of the efficient causality of the triune God working as one nature in the world. It is an event proper to the Logos alone, the history of one divine person in contrast to the others. (This is not changed by saying that the causation of this hypostatic union is the work of the whole Trinity.) There is an assertion with regard to the history of salvation which can only be made of one divine person. But if this is true once, then it is always false to say that there is nothing in the history or "economy" of salvation which cannot be predicated in the same way of the triune God as a whole and of each person in particular. And the converse is also false: that in the doctrine of the Trinity, meaning what is said of the divine persons in general and particular, there can only be assertions which describe the immanent divine life. And it is certainly correct to say that the doctrine of the Trinity cannot be adequately distinguished from the doctrine of the economy of salvation.

Is it correct to affirm that each divine person can become man? Our answer is that this pre-supposition is both not proved and false. It is not proved: the most ancient tradition, before St Augustine, never thought of the possibility and really presupposed the contrary in its theological reflexions. The Father is by definition the unoriginated who is essentially invisible and who shows and reveals himself only by uttering his Word to the world. And the Word, by definition, is both immanently and in the economy of salvation the revelation of the Father, so that a revelation of the Father without the Logos and his incarnation would be the same as a wordless utterance. [...] The thesis which we here oppose is false. For if it were true, and if it occurred anywhere except on the fringes of theological thought and were really taken seriously, it would throw the whole of theology into confusion. There would be no longer any real and intrinsic connexion between the mission of a divine person and the immanent life of the Trinity. Our sonship in grace would have absolutely nothing to do with the sonship of the Son, since it would have been absolutely the same if it could have been based on any other incarnate person of the Godhead. There would be no way of finding out, from what God is to us, what he is in himself as the Trinity. These and many other similar conclusions which would follow from the thesis in question are quite contrary to the inner movement of Sacred Scripture. This can only be denied if one does not submit one's theology to the norm of Scripture but only allows it to say what is already known from one's scholastic theology and dissolves the rest away in clever and cold-blooded distinctions. [...]

The thesis, which we presuppose as justified here, is, when understood rightly and taken seriously, not a piece of scholastic subtlety but a simple and straightforward statement. It is that each of the three divine persons communicates himself as such to man, each in his own special and different way of personal being, in the free gift of grace. This trinitarian communication (the "indwelling" of God, the "uncreated grace," to be understood not merely as the communication of the divine "nature" but also and indeed primarily as communication of the "persons," since it takes place in a free spiritual personal act and so from person to person) is the real ontological foundation of the life of grace in man and (under the requisite conditions) of the immediate vision of the divine persons at the moment of fulfilment.

This is a difficult passage. It needs to be read slowly and carefully, but will amply repay the effort this demands. Note in particular Rahner's emphasis that the God who is known in the economy of salvation corresponds to the way in which God actually is. They are the same God. God's self-communication takes on a threefold form because God is threefold. God's self-revelation corresponds to God's essential nature.

Why do you think Rahner considers this point to be so important? Write down some quotations within the text that seem to identify Rahner's points of concern.

Finally, note how Rahner often links his discussion of the Trinity to the concept of the incarnation. How does the idea of God becoming incarnate relate to Rahner's concerns here?

7.5 John Macquarrie on the function of the Trinity

One of the most interesting theological dialogues of the twentieth century concerns the place of existentialism. For writers such as Rudolf Bultmann and Paul Tillich, the analysis of human existence offered by existentialism had obvious theological implications. John Macquarrie (1919–2007), an Anglo-American writer with roots in a Scottish Presbyterian tradition, approaches the doctrine of the Trinity from an existentialist perspective. In his *Principles of Christian Theology* (1966), Macquarrie argues that the doctrine of the Trinity "safeguards a dynamic as opposed to a static understanding of God." He explores the dynamic trinitarian conception of God within the Christian tradition in the following way.

1. The Father is to be understood as *primordial Being*. By this, we are meant to understand "the ultimate act or energy of letting-be, the condition that there should be anything whatsoever, the source not only of whatever is but of all possibilities of being."
2. The Son is to be conceived as *expressive Being*. "Primordial Being" needs to express itself in the world of beings, which it does by "flowing out through expressive Being."
3. The Holy Spirit is to be understood as *unitive Being*, in that it "is the function of the Spirit to maintain, strengthen and, where need be, restore the unity of Being with the beings."

In the following passage, Macquarrie reflects on the doctrine of the Trinity as a tool to safeguard the Christian experience of God, drawing on some ideas of the Oxford philosopher of religion Ian Ramsey (1915–72).

"The catholic faith is this: that we worship one God in trinity, and trinity in unity; neither confounding the persons nor dividing the substance. For there is one person of the Father, another of the Son, and another of the Holy Ghost; but the Godhead of the Father, of the Son and of the Holy Ghost is all one." So runs part of the *Quicunque vult* or so-called Athanasian Creed. The language will probably strike us nowadays as quaint, and we may be completely puzzled to know what is meant by the idea of a God who is one in three and three in one, one substance and three persons. It must be expected, however, that any language that tries to talk to us of the mystery of God will have some obscurities. We have already seen that it will have an oblique, symbolic character. Actually, the trinitarian language has a much more coherent logic than many of its critics have allowed.

This has been well brought out by Ian Ramsey. Applying the methods of logical analysis to the Athanasian Creed, he concludes that it "may be seen for the most part as a set of logical rules for constructing the trinitarian formula." Ramsey maintains that "the early christological and trinitarian controversies are wrongly seen if they are thought to be concerned with superscientific discoveries about God, as though the early Fathers had some special high-powered telescope with which to inspect the Godhead. What the early controversies settled were rather rules for our talking, and what came out of them at the end were new symbols for our use, and in particular the trinitarian formula. The Christian does not have the single word 'God' as his key word. He substitutes for that symbol another; and this other symbol is built out from that focus of our total commitment which is made up of elements of the Christian dispensation."

I wish to draw particular attention to the last sentence quoted from Ramsey, for this emphasizes, and rightly so, the existential dimension of the trinitarian language. It is not an objective language, describing a fact laid out for our dispassionate inspection, whether with or without a high-powered telescope. It is a language rooted in existence, in the community's experience of the approach of God. At the same time, it is a language that tries to express an insight into the mystery of God. It has the mixed character that we have seen to belong to all theological language and which we express by the term "existential-ontological." Ramsey's terminology makes the same point in his talk of "commitment and discernment."

The first thing that we have to do is just to listen to this language of the one substance and three persons, to expose ourselves to it with its antiquated categories and its paradoxes, as far as possible without prejudice, to attempt that repetitive thinking in which we might hope to hear something of what the language was saying in the existential situation out of which it arose.

The Christian community believed that God, who had created heaven and earth, had become incarnate in a particular man and that furthermore he still dwelt with the community and guided it. This, we may say, was the narrative or mythological expression of their faith, and like us, they looked for an alternative interpretative language that would express the same faith in a different way. They came up with the trinitarian formula.

However puzzling its language may be to us, it was originally meant as an interpretation or elucidation. As Ian Ramsey acutely observes, the Christian could not get along with the single word "God" as his key word. A richer and fuller experience of deity demanded a more complex symbol for its expression. The Christian could not go along with a stark monotheism in which God is utterly transcendent and sovereign, and still less with a pantheism in which God is entirely and universally immanent; he could not embrace a monism in which all differences are swallowed up in the eternal unity of God, but still less a pluralism like that of the world of polytheism with its "many gods and many lords." The Christians confessed: "For us there is one God, the Father, from whom are all things and for whom we exist; and one Lord, Jesus Christ, through whom are all things and through whom we exist" (1 Corinthians 8:5–6). And in the course of further development this basic Christian conviction found expression in the doctrine of the Holy Trinity.

Thus we may say that the doctrine of the Trinity tries to elucidate the picture of God as he appears in the biblical narrative and in the history of the Christian community. He is a God who embraces diversity in unity; who is both transcendent and immanent; who is dynamic and yet has stability. These insights the trinitarian formula is meant to safeguard, though let us again remember that the success of a formula of this kind is to be judged not only in terms of what it affirms – for this will always fall short of the mystery to which it points – but also in terms of the errors and distortions which it excludes.

Macquarrie is a very clear and engaging writer. He opens his discussion of the doctrine of the Trinity by noting how it seems strange and puzzling to many today. What do you think are his main points of concern? In beginning to engage this problem, Macquarrie states that "any language that tries to talk to us of the mystery of God will have some obscurities." What does he mean by this? Notice how Macquarrie appeals to the Oxford philosophical theologian Ian Ramsey to lay the foundations for his own approach. What themes from Ramsey does Macquarrie find especially helpful?

Macquarrie believes that one of the best ways of recovering the meaning of the doctrine of the Trinity is by immersing ourselves in the situation within which it originally arose. How does he summarize the experience of the early Christian community? And how did it lead, in his view, to the formulation of the doctrine of the Trinity? What errors or distortions does it prevent?

7.6   Robert Jenson on the Trinity as God's name

A distinctive and particularly fruitful way of engaging with the doctrine of
the Trinity was developed by the American Lutheran theologian Robert
Jenson (born 1930), presently senior scholar for research at the Center
for Theological Inquiry in Princeton, New Jersey. Jenson argues that the
phrase "Father, Son, and Holy Spirit" is the proper name for Yahweh – the
God of Israel, whom Christians know in and through Jesus Christ. God
should have a proper name; so trinitarian language is Christianity's way of
naming and thus identifying its distinctive God. The doctrine of the Trinity thus comprises both a proper name – "Father, Son, and Holy Spirit" –
and an elaborate development and analysis of corresponding identifying
descriptions.

Jenson points out that ancient Israel existed and thought within a poly-
theistic context, in which the term "god" conveyed relatively little information. Which "god" do you mean? It was necessary to *name and identify*
the god in question. A similar situation was confronted by the writers of
the New Testament, who were obliged to identify the god at the heart of
their faith, and distinguish this god from the many other gods worshipped
and acknowledged in the region, especially in Asia Minor. The doctrine
of the Trinity thus *identifies* and *names* the Christian God – but identifies
and names this God in a manner consistent with the biblical witness.

Meditating on the foundation of biblical faith, the exodus, Israel's first
theologians made Moses' decisive question be: "If I come to the people of Israel and say to them, 'The God of your fathers has sent me to
you': and they ask me, 'What is his name?' what shall I say to them?" If
Israel was to risk the future of this God, to leave secure nonexistence in
Egypt and venture on God's promises, Israel had first and fundamentally to know which future this was. Then God answered, "Say this to
the people of Israel, [Yahweh], the God of your fathers, the God of
Abraham, the God of Isaac, and the God of Jacob, has sent me to you,
this is my name for ever, and thus I am to be remembered throughout
all generations" (Exodus 3:13–15).

The answer provides a proper name, "Yahweh." It also provides what
logicians now call an identifying description, a descriptive phrase or
clause, or set of them, that fits just the one individual thing to be identified. Here the description is "the God whom Abraham and Isaac and
Jacob worshipped." The more usual description is that found in a parallel account a few chapters later: God said to Moses, "Say [...] to the

people of Israel, 'I am [Yahweh], and I will bring you out from under the burdens of the Egyptians [...]; and you shall know that I am [Yahweh] your God, *who* has brought you out. [...] I am [Yahweh]' " (Exodus 6:2–7; emphasis added).

In general, proper names work only if such identifying descriptions are at hand. We may say, "Mary is coming to dinner" and be answered with, "Who is Mary?" Then we must be able to say, "Mary is the one who lives in apartment 2C, and is always so cheerful, and ...," continuing until the questioner says, "Oh, *that* one!" We may say, "Yahweh always forgives:" and be answered with, "Do you mean the Inner Self?" Then we must be able to say, "No. We mean the one who rescued Israel from Egypt, and ..."

[...] Trinitarian discourse is Christianity's effort to identify the God who has claimed us. The doctrine of the Trinity comprises both a proper name, "Father, Son, and Holy Spirit," in several grammatical variants, and an elaborate development and analysis of corresponding identifying descriptions [...]

The gospel of the New Testament is the provision of a new identifying description for this same God [as that of Israel]. The coming-to-apply of this new description is the event, the witness to which is the whole point of the New Testament. God, in the gospel, is "whoever raised Jesus from the dead." Identification of God by the resurrection did not replace identification by the exodus; it is essential to the God who raised Jesus that he is the same one who freed Israel. But the new thing that is the content of the gospel is that God has now identified himself also as "him that raised from the dead Jesus our Lord" (Romans 4:24). In the New Testament such phrases become the standard way of referring to God.

To go with this new identifying description there are not so much new names as new kinds of naming. "Yahweh" does not reappear as a name in use. The habit of saying "Lord" instead has buried it too deeply under the appellative. But in the church's missionary situation, actual use of a proper name in speaking of God is again necessary in a variety of contexts. It is the naming of Jesus that occurs for all such functions. Exorcism, healing, and indeed good works generally are accomplished "in Jesus' name" (e.g., Mark 9:37ff). Church discipline and quasi-discipline are carried out by sentences pronounced in Jesus' name (e.g., 1 Corinthians 1:10), and forgiveness is pronounced in the same way (e.g., 1 John 2:12). Baptism is described as into Jesus' name (e.g., Acts 2:38), whether or not it was ever actually performed with this formula. Undergoing such baptism is equated with that calling on the name "Yahweh" by which, according to Joel 3:5, Israel is to be saved (Acts 2:21, 38). Above all, perhaps, prayer is "in Jesus' name" (e.g., John 14:13–14), in consequence of which the name can be posited as the very object of faith (e.g., John 1:12). Believers are those "who call on the name of our Lord Jesus Christ" (e.g., Acts 9:14).

So dominant was the use of the name "Jesus" in the religious life of the apostolic church that the whole mission can be described as proclamation "in his name" (Luke 24:47), "preaching good news about the kingdom of God and the name of Jesus Christ" (Acts 8:12), indeed, as "carrying" Jesus' name to the people (e.g., Acts 9:15). [...] However various groups in the primal church may have conceived Jesus' relation to God, "Jesus" was the way they all invoked God.

One other new naming appears in the New Testament, the triune name: "Father, Son, and Holy Spirit." Its appearance is undoubtedly dependent on naming God by naming Jesus, as just discussed, but the causal connections are no longer recoverable. It is of course toward this name that we have been steering. That the biblical God must have a proper name, we have seen in the Hebrew Scriptures. In the life of the primal church, God is named by uses that involve the name of Jesus. "Father, Son, and Spirit" is the naming of this sort that historically triumphed.

Read the passage carefully, noting how Jenson focuses on the identification of God by actions – and the importance of names in recalling and celebrating those actions. The exodus from Egypt is a good example of such a divine action; so is the raising of Christ from the dead. We learn who God is from what God does.

"Trinitarian discourse is Christianity's effort to identify the God who has claimed us." Locate this statement within the text. Why, according to Jenson, do we need to "name" God? Isn't the word "God" good enough to convey our meaning?

7.7   Catherine Mowry LaCugna on the Trinity and the Christian life

The doctrine of the Trinity is often considered to be abstract, difficult to understand or visualize, and remote from the life of the church. All of these concerns have been engaged in recent theological writing. One of the most interesting defenses of the natural connections between the Trinity and the Christian life, both corporate and individual, is due to the Catholic theologian Catherine Mowry LaCugna (1952–97), who held the Nancy Reeves Dreux Chair of Theology at the University of Notre Dame before her early death from cancer.

LaCugna argued that a number of historical pressures led to the doctrine of the Trinity becoming an abstract metaphysical doctrine, detached from the realities of Christian living. One such pressure was theological controversy in the patristic age, as the church sought to develop and defend its doctrine of God against its critics; another was the desire to systematize Christian thought, which LaCugna believed to be characteristic of the scholastic age, including the writings of Thomas Aquinas. In this passage, taken from a 1992 article entitled "The Practical Trinity," LaCugna argues for the recovery of the Trinity as a relational notion, grounded in what God has done for humanity in Christ.

It used to be that a new doctrine of the Trinity meant a new way to explain "God's inner life," that is, the relationship of Father, Son and Holy Spirit to one another (what tradition refers to as the immanent Trinity). But now both Catholic and Protestant theologians who are working to revitalize the doctrine of the Trinity have shifted away from constructing theories about God's "inner life." Instead, by returning to the more concrete images and concepts of the Bible, liturgy and creeds, it has become clear that the original purpose of the doctrine was to explain the place of Christ in our salvation, the place of the Spirit in our sanctification or deification, and in so doing to say something about the mystery of God's eternal being. By concentrating more on the mystery of *God with us, God for us,* and less on the nature of God by Godself, it is becoming possible once again for the doctrine of the Trinity to stand at the center of faith – as our rhetoric has always claimed. The doctrine of the Trinity is being rehabilitated, first as the summary of what we believe about God who saves through Jesus Christ by the power of the Holy Spirit, and second as the proper context for the entire theological enterprise, whether in the areas of ecclesiology, sacraments or Christology.

The heart of Christian faith is the encounter with the God of Jesus Christ who makes possible both our union with God and communion with each other. In this encounter God invites people to share in divine life and grace through Jesus Christ by the power of the Holy Spirit; at the same time, we are called to live in new relationship with one other, as we are gathered together by the Spirit into the body of Christ. The personal and communal dimensions of Christian faith are inseparable.

The Letter to the Ephesians (1:3–14) contains a beautiful liturgical hymn that neatly summarizes this basic subject matter of trinitarian theology: God has blessed us from before all eternity; God elected us in Christ so that we would be holy and blameless before God in love; God desires to live with us in the intimacy of a familial relationship. In Jesus Christ we have been redeemed and our sins forgiven by the blood of the cross; God plans to reunite all things with God, which is why we are sealed with the Spirit of God. We also are told what our vocation is: to live for the praise of God's glory. This is the record of redemptive history, beginning with God turned toward the creature in love, and ending with all things being reunited with God.

Trinitarian theology is about this entire economy (*oikonomia* – dispensation) of providence, election, redemption and consummation. Indeed, the shape of trinitarian doctrine is dictated by the pattern of redemption; everything comes from God, is made known and redeemed through Jesus Christ, and is consummated by the power of the Holy Spirit. Theology as doctrine of God thus is dependent on theology as doctrine of salvation.

In short, the doctrine's subject matter is the mystery of God who acts and is present in the events of history – salvation history. The God of redemptive history comes to be known, loved and worshiped in the course of a yet-to-be-completed relationship between God and God's people. God is discovered first of all in creation – creation as interpreted through the religious history of Israel; the central feature of Israel's history is covenant love, initiated on Sinai and continued through the testimony of the prophets. For Christians the history of God reaches decisive expression in the life, teaching, death and resurrection of Christ. The work of God accomplished in Christ is continued in the ongoing transforming and deifying work of the Spirit, and in the eschatological consummation of creation and the fulfillment of all in God.

Once the close connection between the question of salvation and the question of God becomes apparent, it also becomes clear that the Christian doctrine of God has very little to do with an abstract state of affairs, whether heavenly or earthly. To be sure, "Trinity" is the normative Christian model for understanding who God is; but who God is can never be separated from who we are now and who we are to become. The central theme of all trinitarian theology is relationship: God's relationship with us, and our relationships with one another. The doctrine of the Trinity is not an abstract conceptual paradox about God's inner life, or a mathematical puzzle of the "one and three." The doctrine of the Trinity is in fact the most practical of all doctrines. Among other things, it helps us articulate our understanding of the gospel's demands; how personal conversion is related to social transformation; what constitutes "right relationship" within the Christian community and in society at large; how best to praise and worship God; and what it means to confess faith in and be baptized into the life of the God of Jesus Christ.

Begin by reading Ephesians 1:3–14, to which LaCugna alludes in this extract. What are its leading themes? How are they reflected in LaCugna's analysis? How do they help orientate her "practical" approach to the Trinity? You may find it helpful to set out what LaCugna identifies as some of the practical implications of the doctrine, right at the end of this extract.

LaCugna argues that the doctrine of the Trinity needs "rehabilitation," and that it is indeed being rehabilitated. What does she understand a "rehabilitated" approach to the Trinity to be? In what way could this be seen as a move away from an ontological to a relational approach to the Trinity? Or from an essential to an economic approach to the Trinity?

CHAPTER 8

Church

The doctrine of the church has long been recognized as one of the most important and contentious areas of Christian theology. What is it that gives a Christian church its distinct identity? For Irenaeus of Lyons and many other early Christian writers, it was essential that a church should be able to show continuity with the apostles. Indeed, Irenaeus emphasizes that proper Christian churches – unlike their heretical counterparts – could trace a line of connection backward to the circle of the apostles. This theme of the "apostolic succession" was a major element in the early church's struggle to maintain its identity. It became of importance all over again at the time of the Protestant Reformation in the sixteenth century.

The Donatist controversy of the late fourth century raised a new set of questions. Was holiness a defining characteristic of the church? Donatist writers held that moral excellence was not to be expected merely of individual Christians; it was a hallmark of a true Christian community. An aspiration of excellence was thus converted into a membership criterion, which applied above all to Christian leaders. Holiness was no longer seen in aspirational terms, as the true goal of the Christian life; it was the precondition for belonging to a church in the first place. For Augustine of Hippo and others, the church was to be likened to a hospital – a place in which broken, wounded, and frail people came for help, in order to find healing and renewal. This debate continues within Christian theology, and

Theology: The Basic Readings, Third Edition. Edited by Alister E. McGrath.
Editorial material and organization © Alister E. McGrath.
Published 2018 by John Wiley & Sons Ltd.

remains highly significant. In what way does the church differ from the world, if it does not possess a distinctive ethic?

In the twentieth century, a growing appreciation emerged of the importance of mission to the identity of the church. As the Swiss theologian Emil Brunner observed, "The church exists by mission as a fire exists by burning." This has led to a new interest in asking how the identity of the church is shaped by its outreach to the world. As Christianity continues to expand into hitherto unevangelized areas of the world, this question continues to be debated within the churches.

8.1　Martin Luther on the nature of the church

One of the most important debates within the area of ecclesiology (the section of Christian theology dealing with the doctrine of the church) concerns the identity of the Christian church. What criteria need to be met for a group of people to be entitled to call themselves a "Christian church"? Following a line of thought that can be traced back to writers such as Cyprian of Carthage in the third century, many argue that the church is defined *institutionally* – in other words, by historical continuity with the early church, or the apostles. During the Protestant Reformation of the sixteenth century, however, an alternative approach emerged: the church is defined by the *preaching of the gospel*.

In a major treatise on the church, first published in early modern German in 1539, the Protestant theologian Martin Luther (1483–1546) lays down seven distinguishing marks of a true Christian church, including the preaching and hearing of the word of God; the true Christian sacraments of baptism and the sacrament of the altar; the office of the keys and ministry; proper public worship; and the bearing of the cross. An episcopally ordained ministry is therefore not necessary to safeguard the existence of the church, whereas the preaching of the gospel is essential to the identity of that church. "Where the word is, there is faith; and where faith is, there is the true church." The visible church is constituted by the preaching of the word of God: no human assembly may claim to be the "church of God" unless it is founded on this gospel.

For Luther, to "believe in the church" is not to trust in the institution of the church, but to affirm that the church is ultimately called into being by God, with a mission and authorization which derives from God. Luther's idea proved very influential, and has become central to much Protestant thinking on the nature of the church. A central theme of Protestant understanding of the nature and mission of the church focuses on the presence of Christ resulting from the proclamation of the "word of God," in preaching and the sacraments. For Martin Luther, the church is therefore the community called into being by the preaching of God's word.

> First, this holy Christian people is to be recognized as having possession of the holy word of God, even if all do not possess it in equal measure, as St Paul says (1 Corinthians 3:12–14). Some possess it completely purely, others not so purely. Those who possess it purely are called those who "build on the foundation with gold, silver, and precious stones"; those who do not possess it purely are those who "build on the foundation

with wood, hay, and straw," and yet will be saved through fire. More than enough was said about this above. This is the main thing, and the most holy thing of all, by reason of which the Christian people are called holy; for God's word is holy and sanctifies everything it connects with; it is indeed the very holiness of God (Romans 1:16): "It is the power of God for salvation to every one who has faith," and 1 Timothy 4:5: "Everything is consecrated by the word of God and prayer." For the Holy Spirit himself administers it and anoints or sanctifies the Christian church with it, and not with the pope's chrism, with which he anoints or consecrates fingers, clothes, cloaks, chalices, and stones. These objects will never teach one to love God, to believe, to praise, or to be pious. They may adorn this bag of maggots [*madensack*], but afterward they fall apart and decay, along with the chrism and whatever holiness it contains, and the bag of maggots itself.

Yet this holy thing is the true holy thing, the true anointing that anoints with eternal life, even though you may not have a papal crown or a bishop's hat, but will die bare and naked, just like children (as we all are), who are baptized naked and without any such adornment. But we are speaking of the external word, preached orally by people like you and me, for this is what Christ left behind as an external sign by which his church, or his Christian people in the world, should be recognized. We also speak of this external word as it is sincerely believed and openly confessed before the world, as Christ says, "Everyone who acknowledges me before people, I also will acknowledge before my Father and his angels" (Matthew 10:32). There are many who know it in their hearts, but will not profess it openly. Many possess it, but do not believe in it or act on it, for the number of those who believe in and act on it is small. The parable of the seed (Matthew 13:4–8) says that three sections of the field receive and contain the seed, but only the fourth section, the fine and good soil, bears fruit with patience.

Now, anywhere you hear or see such a word preached, believed, confessed, and acted upon, do not doubt that the true *ecclesia sancta catholica*, a "holy Christian people" must be there, even though there are very few of them. For God's word "shall not return empty" (Isaiah 55:11), but must possess at least a fourth or a part of the field. And even if there were no other sign than this alone, it would be enough to prove that a holy Christian people must exist there, for God's word cannot be without God's people and conversely, God's people cannot be without God's word. For who would preach the word, or hear it preached, if there were no people of God? And what could or would God's people believe, if there were no word of God?

To begin with, we must contextualize Luther's views. It is important to appreciate that Luther had been formally excommunicated from the Catholic church at this stage in his career. This therefore raised a significant question concerning the status of the group of people who gathered around Luther, and sought to promote his teaching. Did they constitute a Christian church? Or were they a heretical or schismatic gathering?

To answer this question in the affirmative, it is essential to have a definition of the church which is not dependent upon institutional continuity with the medieval church. Luther's key theme in this passage is that, wherever the word of God is truly preached, a Christian church exists. Historical and institutional continuity with the medieval church is not a necessary component of the definition of the church. Note that a "chrism" is a form of anointing with oil.

"Now, anywhere you hear or see such a word preached, believed, confessed, and acted upon, do not doubt that the true *ecclesia sancta catholica*, a 'holy Christian people' must be there, even though there are very few of them." Locate this passage within the text. What are its implications for Luther's program of reform? The essential point to appreciate is that there is no requirement for a body wishing to regard itself – or be regarded by others – as a "Christian church" to demonstrate historical or institutional continuity with the medieval church. The preaching of the gospel itself establishes continuity with the apostles.

What use does Luther make of the image of a "bag of maggots"? Why do you think he downplays the importance of moral uprightness as a defining characteristic of the church? Where does Luther hold the true identity of the church to lie?

8.2   Lesslie Newbigin on a missionary ecclesiology

The growing interest in recovering the missionary calling of the church is evident from many theological works of the twentieth century, especially in the aftermath of the great World Missionary Conference, held in Edinburgh in 1910. One of the most interesting of these is a short work on the nature of the church, written in 1954 by the Protestant theologian and church leader Lesslie Newbigin (1909–98). After his theological education in Cambridge, Newbigin became a Church of Scotland missionary at the Madras Mission in India in 1937, becoming a bishop of the Church of South India in 1947. After a period working for the World Council of Churches in Geneva, Newbigin returned to India, serving once more as a bishop.

Newbigin's experience in India convinced him of the importance of incorporating the idea of mission into the self-understanding of the church. This is especially clear in his *Household of God*, which was based on the 1952 Kerr lectures at the University of Glasgow, in which New-bigin set out an ecclesiology which recovered what he regarded as a lost or neglected element of the church's identity. For Newbigin, the church is at its core defined by its identity as God's pilgrim people journeying on its way to the end of the age, and, in the meantime, taking the gospel to the ends of the earth.

We must now try to see this whole picture of the apostolate of the Church as the meaning of this present time, and show how it is related to the doctrine of the Church as a whole.

The salvation of which the Gospel speaks and which is determinative of the nature and function of the Church is – as the very word itself should teach us – a making whole, a healing. It is the summing-up of all things in Christ. It embraces within its scope the restoration of the harmony between man and God, between man and man, and between man and nature for which all things were at the first created. It is the restoration to the whole creation of the perfect unity whose creative source and pattern is the unity of perfect love within the being of the triune God. It is in its very essence, universal and cosmic.

In using the word "universal" I do not intend to exclude the possi-bility that men may finally be – as the apostle puts it – cast-aways. To exclude this possibility would obviously be to depart completely from the gravely realistic teaching of the New Testament, with its insistent reminders that there is a broad and easy way leading to destruction and that many go therein. What is intended in the use of the word universal is to emphasize first, that the nature of the salvation is governed by its source which is a love that reaches out after all men, goes to all lengths to recover one lost sheep, and cares and must ever care for the rebel and the traitor with all the passion of Calvary; secondly, that there can therefore be no private "salvation," no perfection of joy and rest until the passion of that love is quenched, until He has seen of the travail of His soul and is satisfied. It belongs to the very heart of salvation that we cannot have it in fullness until all for whom it is intended have it together.

It is because this is the nature of salvation, that our experience of it now must have the character of a foretaste, an earnest; that we who have the first fruits must yet groan waiting for adoption; that we cannot simply be quit of the old Adam and live wholly in the new Adam who is Christ, that we must live still in the flesh by faith, still involved in the old sinful order along with all humanity, while yet at the same time truly involved in the new order of righteousness along with all our brethren, the new humanity in Christ; that we know in our own selves the warfare of flesh and spirit, of bondage and freedom. We cannot enjoy the fullness of salvation until we have it together in the fullness of His body the Church. The new man into which we would fain grow up is a corporate humanity, wherein all the redeemed from every tribe and tongue are made one harmonious whole. Thus the tension which every Christian knows in his own experience between the new man and the old, between the Christ and the old Adam, is – in part at least – the tension of the uncompleted missionary task. We cannot "grow up in all things into him, which is the head" (Ephesians 4:15), except by going out into the world to make all men one with us in the fullness of His body. The eschatological tension cannot be understood apart from the tension of missionary obligation.

We see the same truth by coming at it from another side. It is because the salvation is corporate and cosmic that the manner of its revelation is through a concrete historic event at a particular point of space and time. A message whose essential meaning could be grasped by each individual apart from his relationship with his fellow men and with the rest of the created world could – one may suppose – be revealed at a great number of different places and times. Indeed the only just manner of communication would be – so to speak – a separate communication sent to each individual's address. But a salvation whose very essence is that it is corporate and cosmic, the restoration of the broken harmony between all men and between man and God and man and nature, must be communicated in a different way. It must be communicated in and by the actual development of a community which embodies – if only in foretaste – the restored harmony of which it speaks. A gospel of reconciliation can only be communicated by a reconciled fellowship. And at the heart of such a community must be the actual historical and geographical centre from which it starts and grows. In other words it will be communicated by the way of election, beginning from one visible centre and spreading always according to the law that each one is chosen in order to be the means of bringing the message of salvation to the next.

This is an important discussion, and you should read it through carefully, trying to follow Newbigin's argument. You might like to note how Newbigin believes that the church is defined by the eschatological tension of the kingdom being present now in some respects, while not yet being fully present. In what way does Newbigin think that the kingdom is present now? In what way does it remain to be fulfilled? And how does Newbigin understand this eschatological tension as emphasizing the importance of mission for the very identity of the church?

Newbigin argues that salvation "must be communicated in and by the actual development of a community which embodies – if only as a foretaste – the restored harmony of which it speaks." Locate this statement. Can you see what he means by this? If Newbigin is right here, how does this impact on his understanding of the role of the church in mission?

Earlier in this work, Newbigin commented on how someone becomes a Christian, offering a three-part response. "The first answer is, briefly, that we are incorporated in Christ by hearing and believing the Gospel." How does this fit in with the ideas he outlines in this later passage?

8.3   The Second Vatican Council on the church

The Second Vatican Council (1962–5) introduced a new vitality into the discussion of the doctrine of the church, partly through its reappropriation of biblical imagery relating to the church. The "Dogmatic Constitution of the Church" (usually referred to by its opening Latin words, *Lumen Gentium*, "A light to the nations") is notable for its rich biblical imagery on the one hand, and theological astuteness on the other. The extensive use of biblical imagery marks a significant departure from earlier Catholic documents setting forth a doctrine of the church, especially those produced by the First Vatican Council (1869–70), which tended to focus on the church as an institution.

In part, this reflects a growing realization at the Second Vatican Council of the need to reconnect Catholicism with the Bible. Yet there is a more profound influence here – the need to move away from the strongly hierarchical and institutionalized approaches to the church set out at the First Vatican Council, which increasingly seemed out of place in the modern world. While the church needs structures to survive, those structures are not in themselves adequate to define its nature or mission.

6. In the Old Testament the revelation of the Kingdom is often conveyed by means of metaphors. In the same way the inner nature of the Church is now made known to us in different images taken either from tending sheep or cultivating the land, from building or even from family life and betrothals, the images receive preparatory shaping in the books of the Prophets.

The Church is a sheepfold whose one and indispensable door is Christ. It is a flock of which God Himself foretold He would be the shepherd, and whose sheep, although ruled by human shepherds, are nevertheless continuously led and nourished by Christ Himself, the Good Shepherd and the Prince of the shepherds, who gave His life for the sheep.

The Church is a piece of land to be cultivated, the tillage of God. On that land the ancient olive tree grows whose holy roots were the Prophets and in which the reconciliation of Jews and Gentiles has been brought about and will be brought about. That land, like a choice vineyard, has been planted by the heavenly Husbandman. The true vine is Christ who gives life and the power to bear abundant fruit to the branches, that is, to us, who through the Church remain in Christ without whom we can do nothing.

Often the Church has also been called the building of God. The Lord Himself compared Himself to the stone which the builders rejected, but which was made into the cornerstone. On this foundation the Church is built by the apostles, and from it the Church receives durability and consolidation. This edifice has many names to describe it: the house of God in which dwells His family; the household of God in the Spirit; the dwelling place of God among men; and, especially, the holy temple. This Temple, symbolized in places of worship built out of stone, is praised by the Holy Fathers and, not without reason, is compared in the liturgy to the Holy City, the New Jerusalem. As living stones we here on earth are built into it. John contemplates this holy city coming down from heaven at the renewal of the world as a bride made ready and adorned for her husband.

The Church, further, "that Jerusalem which is above" is also called "our mother." It is described as the spotless spouse of the spotless Lamb whom Christ "loved and for whom He delivered Himself up that He might sanctify her," whom He unites to Himself by an unbreakable covenant, and whom He unceasingly "nourishes and cherishes," and whom, once purified, He willed to be cleansed and joined to Himself, subject to Him in love and fidelity, and whom, finally, He filled with heavenly gifts for all eternity, in order that we may know the love of God and of Christ for us, a love which surpasses all knowledge. The Church, while on earth it journeys in a foreign land away from the Lord, is like in exile. It seeks and experiences those things which are above, where Christ is seated at the right-hand of God, where the life of the Church is hidden with Christ in God until it appears in glory with its Spouse. […]

8. Christ, the one Mediator, established and continually sustains here on earth His holy Church, the community of faith, hope and charity, as an entity with visible delineation through which He communicated truth and grace to all. But, the society structured with hierarchical organs and the Mystical Body of Christ, are not to be considered as two realities, nor are the visible assembly and the spiritual community, nor the earthly Church and the Church enriched with heavenly things; rather they form one complex reality which coalesces from a divine and a human element. For this reason, by no weak analogy, it is compared to the mystery of the incarnate Word. As the assumed nature inseparably united to Him, serves the divine Word as a living organ of salvation, so, in a similar way, does the visible social structure of the Church serve the Spirit of Christ, who vivifies it, in the building up of the body.

This is the one Church of Christ which in the Creed is professed as one, holy, catholic and apostolic, which our Saviour, after His Resurrection, commissioned Peter to shepherd, and him and the other apostles to extend and direct with authority, which He erected for all ages as "the pillar and mainstay of the truth." This Church constituted and organized in the world as a society, subsists in the Catholic Church, which is governed by the successor of Peter and by the Bishops in communion with him, although many elements of sanctification and of truth are found outside of its visible structure. These elements, as gifts belonging to the Church of Christ, are forces impelling towards catholic unity.

Perhaps the best way of engaging with this important text is to begin by identifying the various biblical images that are to be woven together into an ecclesiological tapestry.

Then move on to consider the importance of the parallel that is suggested between the church and the incarnation. How does the Council understand the relationship between the sociological characteristics of the church and the work of the Holy Spirit within it? A criticism that is often directed against some earlier Catholic understandings of the church is that they were preoccupied with questions of structure, hierarchy, and order. In what way does the Second Vatican Council address this concern?

Finally, note how institutional issues are addressed in the final part of the text. How do these institutional questions relate to the biblical images cited earlier?

8.4 George Dragas on Orthodox ecclesiology

Our discussion of the Christian understanding of the church has thus far explored some documents from Catholic and Protestant sources. But what of the Orthodox tradition, now enjoying a new lease of life and theological vitality in many parts of the world? In what way do Orthodox understandings of the nature of the church differ from those of Protestantism and Catholicism? To begin to answer this question, we shall consider an important essay by George Dragas (born 1944), who is professor of church history and dogmatics at Holy Cross Greek Orthodox School of Theology in Brookline, Massachusetts.

Perhaps the most striking feature of Dragas' exposition of the doctrine of the church is its rich trinitarian foundation, expressed in his emphatic assertion that "the Church is an *eikon* of the Holy Trinity." (The Greek term *eikon*, from which the English word *icon* derives, means "an image.") The passage selected for discussion places particular emphasis on the relation between the church and Christ, seeing the eucharist as fundamental to this relationship.

The nature of the Church is to be understood as the Church of the Triune God. The Holy Trinity is the ultimate basis and source of the Church's existence and, as such, the Church is in the image and likeness of God. This being in the image of the blessed Trinity constitutes the mode of the Church's existence, which, in fact, reveals her nature. Being in God, the Church reflects on earth God's unity in Trinity. What is natural to God is given to the Church by grace.

The grace of the Trinity is the *starting point* for understanding the nature of the Church, and especially for her unity in multiplicity, as the Holy Spirit shares one life and one being. The three distinct and unique Persons are one in life and in nature. Similarly, the Church exhibits a parallel multiplicity of persons in unity of life and being. The difference between God and the Church is that, in the former, multiplicity in unity is the truth, whereas in the latter, this is only a participation in the truth. In patristic language the former is *ousia*, while the latter is *metousia*. The unity of the three divine Persons in life and being is, therefore, the prototype of the unity of the Church's persons in life and in being. As Christ Himself says in His prayer for the Church: "even as Thou O Father are in me and me in Thee, so they may be one, that the world may believe that Thou has sent me." The mark of unity is collegiality and love, and not subordination. Orthodox Triadology, based on the grace of the Trinity, supplies the basic ontological categories for Orthodox ecclesiology. The Church is an *eikon* of the Holy Trinity, a participation in the grace of God.

How does the Church participate in God's mystery and grace? How is *metousia Theou* (participation in the essence of God) achieved? How does the Church become an *eikon* of the Holy Trinity? The answer, in its simplest form, is contained in the phrase in and through Christ. Christ has established the bond between the image of the Triune God, and that which is made after the image, namely, the Church, mankind. In Christ we have both the *eikon* and the *kat' eikon* (that which is according to the image). Hence, we must say that the Church is the Church of the Triune God *as the Church of Christ.* The link between the Holy Trinity and Christology, that is, between theology and economy, demands a similar link in ecclesiology. The Church is in the image of the Triune God, and participates in the grace of the Trinity inasmuch as She is in Christ and partakes of His grace. The unity of persons in life and being cannot be achieved apart from this economy of Christ, and we here encounter what the New Testament calls the Body of Christ.

Christ is the Head of the Church and She is His Body. It is from this Christological angle that we better understand the multiplicity in unity which exists in the Church. This angle of the Body of Christ is normally connected with the divine Eucharist, because it is in the Eucharist that the Body is revealed and realized. In the divine Eucharist we have the whole Christ, the Head, and the Body, the Church. But the Eucharist is celebrated in many places and among many different groups of people. Does this then mean that there are many bodies of Christ? This is not the case because there is one Head, and one eucharistic Body (His very body which He took up in the Incarnation) into which all the groups of people in the different places are incorporated. It is the Lord Himself who is manifested in many places, as He gives His one Body to all, so that in partaking of it they may all become one with Him and with one another. In that there is one bread, the many are one Body, for we all partake of the one bread. The many places and the many groups of people where the eucharistic Body of Christ is revealed do not constitute an obstacle to its unity. Indeed, to partake of this Body in one place is to be united with Him who is not bound by place and, therefore, to be mystically (or mysterially, or sacramentally) united with all. [...] What is given in one specific place is something which also transcends it, because of its particular perfection, that is, its being Christ's risen body. The different eucharistic localities, with the eucharistic president (the bishop), the clergy, and the participants (the people) constitute or reveal the whole Church. It is a local church, and yet she reveals the catholic mystery of one Church. The one Church of Christ is equally and fully in all these localities because of the one, perfect Eucharist, the one Lord, and the one Body. This equality of the presence of the one Christ in the local churches is the ground for what is often called Orthodox eucharistic ecclesiology and its logical implication, the autocephaly of the local bishops and churches, which is rooted in, and springs from, the equal share in the fullness of the great eucharistic sacrament. Autocephaly is not autonomy. It must be understood in terms of the equality of bishops, and the participation of all in the one Body of Christ. It is their equality in grace which binds them to one another.

Dragas' exposition of the doctrine of the church begins by grounding the identity and life of the church in God. Notice how Dragas uses specifically trinitarian language from the outset, seeing this as being of importance to an understanding of the church's "unity in multiplicity." What point is Dragas making here?

Dragas endorses the traditional image of the church as the "body of Christ." However, he develops this idea in a number of interesting ways, especially in the way in which he explains the relation of the universal and local churches. Read this section carefully. How does Dragas affirm the reality and distinctiveness of individual church congregations, while at the same time holding that they each belong to, and represent, something greater and more comprehensive? What role does the eucharist play in Dragas' account of this relationship? Note the use of the term "auto-cephaly" – a distinctive Orthodox notion, which holds that each church is self-governing. Why does Dragas insist that this is not equivalent to autonomy?

8.5   Stanley Hauerwas on the church and the Christian story

Stanley Hauerwas (born 1940), who served as Gilbert T. Rowe Professor of Theological Ethics at Duke University, North Carolina, is best known as a Christian ethicist; yet his approach to ethics rests on a distinctive and influential understanding of the nature of the church. Hauerwas argues that before the Enlightenment Christian theologians did not distinguish between the ethical and theological dimensions of Christian living. The radical separation of ethics and theology was due to the agenda of the Enlightenment. According to Hauerwas, this is a false – even unsustainable – distinction. Thought and action cannot be forcibly and unnaturally separated in this way. Any Christian approach to ethics is nourished and guided by a theological vision.

This reassertion of the distinctiveness of the Christian vision can be seen partly as a response to the failure of the Enlightenment assertion of the universality of ethics and ways of reasoning. For Hauerwas, each tradition or community has its own distinctive ethics and way of reasoning, which it grounds and defends in its own distinctive way. This is a leading feature of the "post-liberal" school of theology, of which Hauerwas is presently the most distinguished representative. Post-liberalism, a movement that arose at Yale Divinity School in the late 1970s, rejected individualist approaches to "religious experience" or "rationality," and followed writers such as Alastair MacIntyre in stressing the importance of tradition and community in shaping values and ways of thinking.

Yet Hauerwas' approach to theology can also be understood as a response to the surge of interest in "narrative theology," which recognizes that the Christian faith tells a story – a grand story (or "metanarrative") of creation, fall, redemption, and consummation, which provides a framework for making sense of the world, and provides the Christian community with an identity-giving vision of its purpose and place.

For Hauerwas, the church is the community which bears witness to that vision. The church witnessed to a particular God, and to a particular way of life that results from following Jesus. Our extract is taken from Hauerwas' early book *A Community of Character* (1981), which established his name as a thinker, and introduced the theological community to his distinctive way of thinking.

To insist on the significance of narrative for theological reflection is not, however, just to make a point about the form of biblical sources, but involves claims about the nature of God, the self, and the nature of the world. We are "storied people" because the God that sustains us is a "storied God," whom we come to know only by having our character formed appropriate to God's character. [...]

The existence of the church, therefore, is not an accidental or contingent fact that can be ignored in considerations of the truth of Christian convictions. The church, and the social ethic implied by its separate existence, is an essential aspect of why Christians think their convictions are true. For it is a central Christian conviction that even though the world is God's creation and subject to God's redemption it continues eschatologically to be a realm that defies his rule. The church, which too often is unfaithful to its task, at the very least must lay claim to being the earnest of God's Kingdom and thus able to provide the institutional space for us to rightly understand the disobedient, sinful, but still God-created character of the world. The ethical significance of Christian convictions depends on the power of those convictions to shape a community sufficient to face truthfully the nature of our world.

Christian social ethics should not begin with attempts to develop strategies designed to make the world more "just," but with the formation of a society shaped and informed by the truthful character of the God we find revealed in the stories of Israel and Jesus. The remarkable richness of these stories of God requires that a church be a community of discourse and interpretation that endeavors to tell these stories and form its life in accordance with them. The church, the whole body of believers, therefore cannot be limited to any one historical paradigm or contained by any one institutional form. Rather the very character of the stories of God requires a people who are willing to have their understanding of the story constantly challenged by what others have discovered in their attempt to live faithful to that tradition. For the church is able to exist and grow only through tradition, which – as the memory sustained over time by ritual and habit – sets the context and boundaries for the discussion required by the Christian stories. As Frank Kermode has recently reminded us, the way to interpret a narrative is through another narrative; indeed, a narrative is already a form of interpretation, as the power of a narrative lies precisely in its potential for producing a community of interpretation sufficient for the growth of further narratives.

Inevitably, calling attention to the narrative shape of Christian convictions means that Christian ethics must be taken seriously as Christian. To do that seems to risk the cooperation Christians have achieved

with those who do not share their convictions; or worse, it might provide justification for the church to withdraw into a religious ghetto no
longer concerned to serve the world. Such a result would indeed be
a new and not even very sophisticated form of tribalism. The church,
however, is not and cannot be "tribal"; rather the church is the community that enables us to recognize that, in fact, it is the world we live
in which has a splintered and tribal existence.

The ability of the church to interpret and provide alternatives to the
narrow loyalties of the world results from the story – a particular story,
to be sure – that teaches us the significance of lives different from our
own, within and without our community.

Hauerwas begins by insisting upon the importance of "story." Note that
this word does not imply that this is fictional. Some stories are true;
some are false. Their defining characteristic is a narrative representation
of the faith, as opposed to an abstract metaphysical system. The particular
"story" that grounds Hauerwas' thought at this point is the story of Jesus
of Nazareth, which witnesses to the moral values of the Kingdom of God,
and thus shapes the moral vision of the church. Notice how he suggests
that the constant retelling of this story can lead to fresh insights, and the
challenging of its older interpretations and applications.

Hauerwas insists that the church is a community which is meant to
"tell these stories and form its life in accordance with them." Find this
quotation within the reading. What does he mean by this? Why does he
criticize those who begin their ethics with ideas about how to make the
world more "just"?

At several points in this passage, Hauerwas alludes to the importance
of telling the truth – of confronting the world as it really is. Why does he
consider this to be so important? And what specific contribution does he
believe that the church can make to telling the truth about things? Once
more, you need to note the importance of "storytelling" to Hauerwas'
approach.

8.6   Leonardo Boff on the reinvention of the church

Liberation theology is one of the most important theological movements to emerge from Latin America. Its origins are often traced back
to the 1960s, when calls for radical social change emerged throughout
that region. "Liberation theology" emphasized the responsibility of the
church to bring justice to the poor and oppressed, particularly through
political activism. Although some Protestant theologians became involved
in the movement, liberation theology is best seen as a movement within
the Catholic church, calling for a new commitment on the part of the
church to the poor and marginalized.

The Brazilian writer Leonardo Boff (born 1938) is widely recognized as
one of the most significant liberation theologians. Boff regarded the Second Vatican Council's "Dogmatic Constitution on the Church," *Lumen
Gentium*, as opening up new ways of thinking about the church, and actu-
alizing its vision of the kingdom of God. One of the outcomes of his
reflection was a demand for institutional reform of the church, leading to
the formation of *comunidades eclesiais de base* – "ecclesial base communities." In this section of his influential book, *Ecclesiogenesis*, Boff describes
the basic elements of these communities (here translated as "basic church
communities"). For Boff, these "grassroots communities" are to be con-
trasted with traditional hierarchical ecclesiastical structures.

The rise of the basic church communities and the praxis of these communities are of matchless value when it comes to questioning the prevailing manner of being church. They are sprung from basic, minimum
elements like faith, the reading of the word and meditation on it, and
mutual assistance in all human dimensions. As we have seen, they are
genuine church. Many functions, genuinely new ministries, appear in
them – ministries of community coordination, of catechesis, of orga-
nizing the liturgy, of caring for the sick, of teaching people to read
and write, of looking after the poor, and the like. All this is done in
a deep spirit of communion, with a sense of joint responsibility and
with an awareness of building and living actual church. The best con-
ceptualization of this experience is in the frequently heard expression,
"reinvention of the church." The church is beginning to be born at the
grassroots, beginning to be born at the heart of God's People. This experience calls into question the common fashion of considering oneself
to be church. It enables one to discover the true source of the ongoing
birth and creation of the church: the Holy Spirit.

The church can be considered from many points of view. Indeed there are as many ecclesiologies as there are basic ecclesial structures. There are those who work out their understanding of church from its priestly-episcopal-papal structure, although this yields not so much an ecclesiology as a "parochiology." There are those whose thinking begins with the word/sacrament structure, so that we have preeminently a prophetico-cultic picture of church. There are those who articulate the church from the figure of the church on a journey, and then we get a preeminently historico-salvific vision. And there are more. All these ecclesiologies have their sense, their meaning. But each is limited in itself, and must be opened out upon other forms of theoretical totalization of the mystery of church. Otherwise we have an oppressive ideologization of categories against categories, and the faith community suffers harm.

The basic church communities are aiding the whole church to overcome an internal obstacle under which it has labored for centuries, and which has prevented it from seeing the more abundant riches of the mystery of church. The church, in the Latin West, has been thought of in terms of a Christ/church polarity, within a juridical vision. The relationships between Christ and the church are formulated on the model of the relationships of a society with its founder. Christ transmits all power to the Twelve, who transmit it to their successors, the bishops and the pope. The latter have been considered as the sole depositaries of all responsibility, and have been seen as amassing for themselves all power in the church, in such wise that they are pictured as in confrontation with the community. Thus the actual community is divided between rulers and governed, between celebrants and onlookers, between producers and consumers of sacraments. In a like systematization, the hierarchy constitutes the sole representative of the universal church and the particular church.

This image suppresses the other one – that of the church as faith community (*communitas fidelium*), globally coresponsible for all the affairs of the church. Further, one begins with the shepherds who are responsible for the flock. But this is to invert the natural order: first comes the flock, and then, for the sake of the flock, the shepherd. The hierarchical function is essential in the church – but it does not subsist in and for itself. The hierarchical function must be understood – this is the simple and natural understanding of things – as subsisting within the faith community and in its service, whether by representing all the other churches vis-à-vis this particular church (the authentic face-to-face dimension of any community-and-head), or as principle of unity at the heart of the local church, of which the head is actually a member. The other understanding of church, furthermore, is predicated on a particular Christology which permits it to take Christ only in his sarkical, or fleshly, existence; it does not consider the risen Christ, with the transformations that his resurrection has conferred upon him: his cosmic ubiquity, the spiritual nature of his body (*soma pneumatikon*, 1 Corinthians 15:44), and so on. This consideration would render the institution of the church more flexible, and would reintroduce the "pneumatic" element as part and parcel of the Christological element. The church was born not only from the opened side of Christ, but from the Holy Spirit, as well, on the day of Pentecost. The unity between these two elements is found in Jesus Christ who died and was raised again as the maximum presence of the Holy Spirit in the world, in such wise that we can say: Jesus-according-to-the-flesh constituted the greatest presence of the Holy Spirit in the world; and the Holy Spirit in the church is now the presence-in-history of the risen Christ.

Boff begins this discussion by outlining the main features of the ecclesial base communities. Summarize these in your own words. These communities are often described as being popular, grassroots, and anti-authoritarian. On the basis of Boff's account of these communities, does this seem a reasonable assessment? Does the phrase "reinvention of the church" seem to be an appropriate description of the significance of these communities?

Boff sets out some significant criticisms of traditional Catholic understandings of the nature of the church. The first is what he terms a "Christ/church polarity." What does he mean by this? You might also like to read the extract from *Lumen Gentium* above (8.3). How might this important document have shaped Boff's thinking at this point? The second is his concern that an emphasis on the hierarchy of the church leads to the repression of the idea of the church as a "community of believers" (*communitas fidelium*). Why does he consider this to be so important? And what point is he making by his discussion of the relationship of flock and shepherd?

Finally, note how Boff incorporates the Holy Spirit into his ecclesiology, possibly partly in response to the rise of Pentecostalism in Latin America. What does he mean when he says that "the Holy Spirit in the church is now the presence-in-history of the risen Christ"?

CHAPTER 9

Sacraments

The term "sacrament" is generally used within Christian theology to designate certain actions or rites which are held to confer certain spiritual benefits. They are often referred to as "outward signs of inward grace." Among the many debates within Christian sacramental theology, two stand out as being of particular importance. First, what is a sacrament? How may it be defined? Significantly different answers are given by Protestantism, on the one hand, and Catholicism and Orthodoxy on the other. Protestants tend to limit the sacraments to actions that Christ explicitly commanded his followers to undertake, which are associated with physical elements. For this reason, they argue that there are only two sacraments: baptism and the eucharist (also referred to as "the Lord's Supper" and "holy communion"). Catholicism and Orthodoxy, by contrast, recognize a wider range of sacraments. In addition to baptism and the eucharist (which Catholics generally refer to as "the Mass"), they recognize penance, confirmation (or "chrismation"), marriage, ordination, and unction as sacramental.

A second major debate concerns what the sacraments achieve. What benefits do they bring to believers? All Christians believe that sacraments are an important means of sustaining the belief of individual Christians – for example, by reminding them of the foundational events of the

Theology: The Basic Readings, Third Edition. Edited by Alister E. McGrath.
Editorial material and organization © Alister E. McGrath.
Published 2018 by John Wiley & Sons Ltd.

Christian faith. There is also wide agreement that they enhance a sense of shared identity within the Christian community.

Yet Christians diverge at a number of points. For example, do the sacraments convey grace – or merely signify or represent this grace? Is infant baptism justified? In what sense is Christ present at the eucharist? Does the consecration of the bread and wine bring about the "real presence" of Christ? Or is Christ merely being remembered or symbolized, in his absence?

We shall encounter some of these issues in the readings that we shall consider in this chapter. We begin by considering an important witness to the understanding of baptism in the early church.

9.1   Cyril of Jerusalem on the meaning of baptism

The early church took baptism with enormous seriousness. The period of Lent was often used for theological instruction of new converts, culminating in their baptism early on Easter Day, in celebration of the resurrection of Christ. Our reading is an extract from a series of "catechetical lectures" given by Cyril of Jerusalem (315–86), in which he explains the significance of baptism. Cyril delivered these 23 lectures around the years 347–8. These lectures are of value in many respects, including their documentation of early Christian baptismal practices, and their theological interpretation. The lectures are notable for their rich use of Scripture, their warm and affirming pastoral tone, and the lucidity of their theological teaching.

The reading offers important insights into Cyril's theology of baptism, while also pointing to the importance of symbolic actions as a way of reinforcing theological truths. Notice how Cyril often highlights the importance of certain actions that the baptismal candidates will perform, explaining what they mean. Notice that these lectures were actually given quite late in the series, by which stage the audience had already been baptized. Cyril is thus reminding his audience of what they have done, and ensuring they appreciate its significance.

The later lectures in the series deal with "mysteries" – a theological term that is used in this reading. This term was often used by Greek-speaking theologians of the early church to refer to what we would now generally call "sacraments." The term comes from the Greek word *mysterion*, which means considerably more than a "riddle" or "puzzle" that needs to be solved. The word indicates something that is too profound to be grasped fully by the human mind.

For a long time I have wished, true-born and long-desired children of the church, to speak to you about these spiritual and heavenly mysteries. However, knowing very well that seeing is believing, I waited until the present occasion, knowing that after what you have experienced you would be a more receptive audience, now that I am to lead you to the brighter and more fragrant meadows of this paradise. In particular, you are now able to understand the more divine mysteries of divine and life-giving baptism. So now that the time has come to prepare for you the table of more perfect instruction, let me explain what happened to you on the evening of your baptism.

First you entered the antechamber of the baptistery, and turned westward. When you were told to stretch out your hands, you renounced

Satan as though he were there in person. Now you should know that
ancient history provides a type of this. When Pharaoh, the harshest
and most cruel of all tyrants, oppressed the free and noble people of
the Hebrews, God sent Moses to deliver them from this harsh slavery
which had been imposed on them by the Egyptians. They anointed
their doorposts with the blood of a lamb, so that the destroyer might
pass over the houses which bore the sign of this blood, and miracu-
lously set the Hebrew people free from their bondage. After their liberation the enemy pursued them, and on seeing the sea open in front
of them, they still continued to pursue them, only to be engulfed in the
Red Sea.

Let us now pass from the old to the new, from the type to the reality.
There Moses is sent by God to Egypt; here Christ is sent by the Father
into the world. There, Moses was to lead an oppressed people from
Egypt; here Christ was to deliver those who are under the tyranny of
sin. There the blood of the lamb turned away the destroyer; here the
blood of the unblemished lamb, Jesus Christ, puts the demons to flight.
In the past, the tyrant pursued the Hebrew people right to the sea; in
your case, the devil, the arch-evil one, followed each one of you up to
the edge of the streams of salvation. This first [tyrant] was engulfed in
the sea; this one disappears in the waters of salvation. [...]

After these things, you were led to the holy pool of Divine Baptism,
just as Christ was carried from the Cross to the sepulchre which is
before our eyes. And each of you was asked whether you believed, in
the name of the Father, and of the Son, and of the Holy Spirit. And
having made that saving confession, you descended three times into
the water, and ascended again. This is a symbol of the three days of the
burial of Christ, as our Saviour passed three days and three nights in
the heart of the earth. [...]

What a strange and inconceivable thing! We did not really die, we
were not really buried, nor were we really crucified and raised again. Yet
while our imitation of these things is purely figurative, our salvation is a
reality. Christ really was crucified, and really was buried, and really rose
again. And he really has bestowed all these things upon us, so that we,
sharing his sufferings by imitation, might gain salvation in reality. What
overwhelming loving-kindness! Christ received nails in his undefiled
hands and feet, and suffered anguish. Yet he freely bestows salvation on
me without pain or effort on account of the fellowship of His suffering.

Let no one suppose that baptism is merely the grace of remission of
sins or adoption, in the same way that John the Baptist's was a baptism

which conferred only the remission of sins. We know perfectly well, that baptism purges our sins, and provides the gift of the Holy Spirit to us, just as it is also the counterpart of the sufferings of Christ.

This passage offers us some insights into the way in which the early church at Jerusalem baptized its converts. Read the passage through, paying particular attention to the actions that are identified. Notice how each of them is interpreted in a certain way.

Notice how the exodus from Egypt is seen as an anticipation or forerunner of baptism. Early Christian theologians used the Greek word *typos* to mean an anticipation of some great New Testament theme or person in the Old Testament. A "type" is a figure or event in Old Testament history whose full embodiment (or "antitype") is found in the New Testament revelation. For Cyril, the exodus is to be seen as a "type" of baptism. This is a leading theme of early Christian baptismal theology. The imagery of "salvation by passing through water" described the baptismal ceremony itself, while recalling the deliverance of the people of Israel from their bondage in Egypt. Cyril also understands the Passover events as a "type" of the salvation achieved by Christ.

Notice how Cyril emphasizes that the benefits that Christ won for his people by his agony and death are offered without the need for them to go through the same process themselves. After listing the sufferings of Christ, Cyril comments that, "while our imitation of these things is purely figurative, our salvation is a reality." What does he mean by this? Why do you think he regarded this as being so important?

In the final paragraph, Cyril rejects any suggestion that the baptism offered by the church, and that offered by John the Baptist, achieve the same goals. For Cyril, John's baptism was purely symbolical, representing a recognition of the need for repentance and forgiveness – but not providing such forgiveness. Cyril is emphatic that such forgiveness comes only through Christ's death and resurrection, and is effected through baptism.

9.2   Huldrych Zwingli on the real presence

During the 1520s, a significant debate broke out within the emerging
Protestant movement over how to interpret Jesus' words "this is my body"
(Matthew 26:26), spoken over the bread at the Last Supper. Martin Luther
held that the words had to be taken at their face value. The bread somehow became the body of Christ. The leading Swiss Protestant theologian
Huldrych Zwingli (1484–1531), based in the city of Zurich, took a very
different view, holding that the words meant that the bread merely signified Christ's body. The debate raised important issues of biblical interpretation, as well as causing serious tensions within Protestantism at the
time.

In his 1526 treatise "A Clear Instruction concerning the Supper of
Christ," Zwingli sets out his "memorialist" view of the Lord's Supper,
which holds that Christ is remembered in his absence.

But there are two clear flaws in the argument [that the words "this is my
body" refer to the bread being the physical body of Christ]. The first
is that we are not given any reason to believe that when the Pope or
some other human person says: "This is my body," the body of Christ
is necessarily present. It is useless to say that Christ himself said: "Do
this in remembrance of me": and that the body of Christ is therefore
present. [...] The second flaw is a failure to see that before we use the
Word of God to justify anything, we must first understand it correctly.
For example, when Christ says: "I am the vine" (John 15:5), we have to
realize that he is using figurative speech in the first place. In other words,
Christ is *like* a vine. Just as the branches are nourished by the vine and
cannot bear fruit without it, so believers are in Christ, and without him
they can do nothing. Now if you object against this interpretation of
Christ's saying "I am the vine," and argue that therefore he must be a
physical vine, you end up by making Christ into a piece of vine wood.
In the same way, when you come to the words: "This is my body," you
must first make sure that he intended to give his flesh and blood in
physical form. Otherwise it is quite pointless to argue that he said it,
and therefore it is so. For it is so only as he himself understood it to be
so, and not as you misunderstand it. [...] Let us consider the basis of
the doctrine. If in Christ's saying: "This is my body," we take the little
word "is" in a substantive manner, that is literally, then it necessarily
follows that the substance of the body or the flesh of Christ is literally
and essentially present. But this gives rise to two obvious mistakes.

The first is this: if Christ is literally and essentially present in the flesh, then he is actually torn apart by the teeth and tangibly masticated in human mouths. We cannot get round the issue by saying: "With God all things are possible." [...] Therefore, if the "is" is to be taken literally, the body of Christ must be visibly, essentially, physically and tangibly present. For that reason even in this erroneous teaching itself there is a proof that the words cannot possibly mean that we partake physically of flesh and blood: for if God says literally: "This is my body," then the body ought to be there literally and physically [...]

The second error resulting from a literal interpretation corresponds to that second opinion which we mentioned alongside the first, namely, that we eat the body of Christ in or under the bread, the bread itself remaining bread. If we take the word "is" in a substantive way, that is literally, then it is clearly wrong to say that the bread remains bread and to deny transubstantiation, the changing of the substance of bread into that of flesh. And for this reason: I apply the argument used in the first error. The Word of God is living. He said: "This is my body." Therefore it is his body. But if we take the word "is" literally, as the second error obstinately maintains, then necessarily the substance of bread has to be changed completely into that of flesh. But that means that the bread is no longer there. Therefore it is impossible to maintain that the bread remains, but that the flesh is eaten in or under the bread. Notice how utterly unreasonable this position is. On no account will it allow that Christ's words: "This is my body," are figurative or symbolical. It insists that the word "is" must be taken literally. But it then proceeds to ignore that word and to say: "The body of Christ is eaten *in* the bread." Yet Christ did not say: "Take, eat, my body is eaten in the bread." He said: "This is my body." How dreadful a thing it is to get out of one's depth! If it were I who perverted the words of Christ in that way, surely the axe of judgment would strike me down. The second error is easily perceived, then, and we have only to compare the two and they cancel each other out. For the first maintains that the flesh and blood are present on account of the word "is." But if we take that word literally, it destroys the second, which tries to take it literally but still asserts that the bread remains bread. For if the word is taken literally, the bread is not bread but flesh. [...]

Yet when we expose this defect, pointing out with compelling force that there is no foundation for such ideas, they simply cry: "We remain faithful to the simple words of Christ, trusting that those Christians who follow the simple words of Christ will not go astray." But what you call the simple meaning of those words is actually the most doubtful, the most obscure, the least intelligible of all. If the simple meaning of Scripture is that which we maintain through a misunderstanding of the letter, then Christ is a piece of vine wood, or a silly sheep, or a door, and Peter is the foundation-stone of the Church. The simple or natural sense of these words is that which obtains in all similar instances, that which the minds of all believers find the most natural and the most easily understood.

Zwingli here deals with the true meaning of the Latin phrase *hoc est corpus meum* ("this is my body"), the Vulgate Latin translation of Matthew 26:26. Zwingli argues that the only acceptable meaning of the word "is" in this phrase must be acknowledged to be "signifies." The unstated object of Zwingli's criticism here is Martin Luther's view of the real presence, which Zwingli regarded as being inconsistent with his reforming principles. Luther held that the body of Christ was given "with" or "under" the bread. Although Zwingli does not name Luther, he clearly has his ideas in mind. What is the fundamental point he makes against Luther?

Set out, in your own words, Zwingli's argument against the notion of the "real presence." Why does Zwingli insist that the word "is," as it occurs in Christ's words "this is my body," is not to be interpreted literally? What is his preferred alternative interpretation? Note his appeal to the figurative sense of the "I am" sayings of John's gospel – such as "I am the good shepherd" (John 10:11) or "I am the door" (John 10:9).

9.3   The Council of Trent on transubstantiation

The Council of Trent was convened by the Catholic church in order to respond to the challenges posed to the church by the rise of Protestantism. The Council met three times between 1545 and 1563 in the city of Trent, in the north of Italy. Early sessions addressed some of the leading issues raised by the Reformation – such as the place of the Bible in Christian life and thought, and the doctrine of justification by faith. The Council's response to Protestantism extended beyond an engagement with its theological positions; it also included wide-ranging reforms of the institutions and structures of the church, in response to the perception that these were open to criticism.

The Protestant Reformation also raised some particularly serious challenges for traditional Catholic teaching concerning the sacraments, especially the idea of "transubstantiation." This doctrine, formally defined by the Fourth Lateran Council (1215), rests upon Aristotelian foundations – more specifically, on Aristotle's distinction between "substance" and "accident." The *substance* of something is its essential nature, whereas its *accidents* are its outward appearances (for example, its color, shape, smell, and so forth). The theory of transubstantiation affirms that the accidents of the bread and wine (their outward appearance, taste, smell, and so forth) remain unchanged at the moment of consecration, while their substance changes from that of bread and wine to that of the body and blood of Jesus Christ. Luther rejected this theory on account of its use of an unbiblical Aristotelian philosophy; as we saw in the previous reading, Zwingli dismissed it as resting on a misunderstanding of theological language.

The Council of Trent took some time to develop its response to the views on the sacraments associated with the Reformation. The Seventh Session of the Council of Trent concluded on March 3, 1547, and issued a brief "Decree on the Sacraments." In many ways, this is best seen as an interim measure, designed to counter Protestant views without providing a detailed Catholic rejoinder. The decree takes the form of a preface, followed by thirteen general canons, each condemning some aspect of "the heresies that in our turbulent times are directed against the most holy sacraments." It was not until the Thirteenth Session of the Council, which concluded on October 11, 1551, that Trent finally set forth the positive position of the Roman Catholic church in the "Decree on the Most Holy Sacrament of the Eucharist." Up to this point, Trent had merely criticized the reformers, without putting forth a coherent alternative position. This deficiency was now remedied.

The "Decree" opens with a vigorous attack on those who deny the real presence of Christ. Although Zwingli is not specifically mentioned, the Council's allusions to Christ sitting at the right hand of God, and to the improper use of "tropes" or "figures of speech" by some recent writers, make it clear that the Swiss reformer is the primary object of their attack.

In the first place, the holy Synod teaches, and openly and simply professes, that, in the noble sacrament of the holy Eucharist, after the consecration of the bread and wine, our Lord Jesus Christ, true God and human being, is truly, really, and substantially contained under the species of those sensible things. For neither are these things mutually opposed to one another: that our Saviour himself always sits at the right hand of the Father in heaven, according to the natural mode of existing; and that, nevertheless, he is, in many other places, sacramentally present to us in his own substance, by a manner of existing, which, though we cannot express it fully in words, yet we can, by understanding illuminated by faith, conceive that this is possible for God (as we ought most firmly to believe). For thus all our forebears, as many as were in the true Church of Christ, who have treated of this most holy sacrament, have most openly professed, that our Redeemer instituted this truly admirable sacrament at the last supper; when, after the blessing of the bread and wine, he testified, in unambiguous and clear words, that he gave them his own true body and blood. These words were recorded by the holy Evangelists, and afterwards repeated by Saint Paul. For this reason, they carry with them that proper and most obvious meaning in which they were understood by the Fathers. It is totally unworthy that they should be distorted, by certain contentious and wicked people, into fictitious and imaginary figures of speech, whereby the reality of the flesh and blood of Christ is denied, contrary to the universal sense of the Church. [...]

Wherefore, our Saviour, when about to depart out of this world to the Father, instituted this sacrament, in which he poured forth the riches of his divine love towards humanity, making a remembrance of his wonderful works. He commanded us, by sharing in it, to venerate his memory, and to show forth his death until he comes to judge the world. And he also wished that this sacrament should be received as the spiritual food of souls, for the nourishment and strengthening of those who live through his life who said, "Anyone who eats me, shall live by me." It is also an antidote, by which we may be freed from daily faults, and be preserved from mortal sins. He would, furthermore, have it to be a pledge of our glory to come, and everlasting happiness, and thus to be a symbol of that one body of which he is the head, and to which he would have us, as its members, to be united by the closest bonds of faith, hope, and charity, so that we might all confess the same things, and that there might be no schisms amongst us. [...]

Because Christ our Redeemer declared that it was truly his body that he was offering under the species of bread, it has always been the belief of the Church of God, which this sacred Council reaffirms, that by the consecration of the bread and wine a change takes place in which the entire substance of the bread becomes the substance of the body of Christ our Lord, and the whole substance of the wine becomes the substance of his blood. This change the holy Catholic Church has fittingly and correctly called "transubstantiation."

This is a very significant theological statement, important both in its own right, and as a criticism of at least some of the leading themes of the Protestant Reformation. Begin by reading the text carefully. You will find it helpful to try to summarize it using your own words.

Zwingli had argued that, since Christ was now seated at the right hand of God, he could not be in two places at one. If he was in heaven, he could not be on earth. Therefore it made no sense to speak of any kind of "real presence" of Christ at the eucharist. Christ was remembered in his absence. How does the Council respond to this challenge?

Note how the Council protests strongly against those who deny the real presence of Christ in the eucharist on account of their appeal to "fictitious and imaginary figures of speech." The Council has Zwingli in mind here. You might like to read the previous extract (9.2), which sets out Zwingli's views on this matter. How effective a rebuttal do you think Trent offers to Zwingli?

Finally, note the Council's vigorous reaffirmation of transubstantiation, both as an idea and as a word. How does it define "transubstantiation"? What benefits, according to Trent, does the eucharist offer to the faithful?

9.4   The World Council of Churches on baptism

In 1982 the Faith and Order Commission of the World Council of Churches published a highly influential theological statement entitled "Baptism, Eucharist and Ministry," sometimes known as the "Lima text," after the Peruvian city which hosted this meeting of the Commission. The statement was the outcome of several years of ecumenical study and dialogue, mainly between Protestant denominations. The document proved highly influential in catalyzing ecumenical discussions on issues relating to the sacraments and Christian ministry.

I.   THE INSTITUTION OF BAPTISM

B1. Christian baptism is rooted in the ministry of Jesus of Nazareth, in his death and in his resurrection. It is incorporation into Christ, who is the crucified and risen Lord; it is entry into the New Covenant between God and God's people. Baptism is a gift of God, and is administered in the name of the Father, the Son, and the Holy Spirit. St. Matthew records that the risen Lord, when sending his disciples into the world, commanded them to baptize (Matthew 28:18–20). The universal practice of baptism by the apostolic Church from its earliest days is attested in letters of the New Testament, the Acts of the Apostles, and the writings of the Fathers. The churches today continue this practice as a rite of commitment to the Lord who bestows his grace upon his people.

II.   THE MEANING OF BAPTISM

B2. Baptism is the sign of new life through Jesus Christ. It unites the one baptized with Christ and with his people. The New Testament scriptures and the liturgy of the Church unfold the meaning of baptism in various images which express the riches of Christ and the gifts of his salvation. These images are sometimes linked with the symbolic uses of water in the Old Testament. Baptism is participation in Christ's death and resurrection (Romans 6:3–5; Colossians 2:12); a washing away of sin (1 Corinthians 6:11); a new birth (John 3:5); an enlightenment by Christ (Ephesians 5:14); a reclothing in Christ (Galatians 3:27); a renewal by the Spirit (Titus 3:5); the experience of salvation from the flood (1 Peter 3:20–21); an exodus from bondage (1 Corinthians 10:1–2) and a liberation into a new humanity in which barriers of division whether of sex or race or social status are transcended (Galatians 3:27–28; 1 Corinthians 12:13). The images are many but the reality is one.

A.   Participation in Christ's Death and Resurrection
B3. Baptism means participating in the life, death and resurrection of Jesus Christ. Jesus went down into the river Jordan and was baptized in solidarity with sinners to fulfil all righteousness (Matthew 3:15). This baptism led Jesus along the way of the Suffering Servant, made manifest in his sufferings, death and resurrection (Mark 10:38–40, 45). By baptism, Christians are immersed in the liberating death of Christ where their sins are buried, where the "old Adam" is crucified with Christ, and where the power of sin is broken. Thus those baptized are no longer slaves to sin, but free. Fully identified with the death of Christ, they are buried with him and are raised here and now to a new life in the power of the resurrection of Jesus Christ, confident that they will also ultimately be one with him in a resurrection like his (Romans 6:3–11; Colossians 2:13, 3:1; Ephesians 2:5–6).

B.   Conversion, Pardoning and Cleansing
B4. The baptism which makes Christians partakers of the mystery of Christ's death and resurrection implies confession of sin and conversion of heart. The baptism administered by John was itself a baptism of repentance for the forgiveness of sins (Mark 1:4). The New Testament underlines the ethical implications of baptism by representing it as an ablution which washes the body with pure water, a cleansing of the heart of all sin, and an act of justification (Hebrews 10:22; 1 Peter 3:21; Acts 22:16; 1 Corinthians 6:11). Thus those baptized are pardoned, cleansed and sanctified by Christ, and are given as part of their baptismal experience a new ethical orientation under the guidance of the Holy Spirit.

C.   The Gift of the Spirit
B5. The Holy Spirit is at work in the lives of people before, in and after their baptism. It is the same Spirit who revealed Jesus as the Son (Mark 1:10–11) and who empowered and united the disciples at Pentecost (Acts 2). God bestows upon all baptized persons the anointing and the promise of the Holy Spirit, marks them with a seal and implants in their hearts the first instalment of their inheritance as sons and daughters of God. The Holy Spirit nurtures the life of faith in their hearts until the final deliverance when they will enter into its full possession, to the praise of the glory of God (2 Corinthians 1:21–22; Ephesians 1:13–14).

D. Incorporation into the Body of Christ

B6. Administered in obedience to our Lord, baptism is a sign and seal of our common discipleship. Through baptism, Christians are brought into union with Christ, with each other and with the Church of every time and place. Our common baptism, which unites us to Christ in faith, is thus a basic bond of unity. We are one people and are called to confess and serve one Lord in each place and in all the world. The union with Christ which we share through baptism has important implications for Christian unity. "There is [...] one baptism, one God and Father of us all [...]" (Ephesians 4:4–6). When baptismal unity is realized in one holy, catholic, apostolic Church, a genuine Christian witness can be made to the healing and reconciling love of God. Therefore, our one baptism into Christ constitutes a call to the churches to overcome their divisions and visibly manifest their fellowship.

The World Council of Churches' paper "Baptism, Eucharist and Ministry" is widely regarded as marking a landmark in ecumenical discussions of its themes. Baptism is here presented in a way which remains close to the language and imagery of the New Testament (note how often biblical texts are cited), while responding to some of the debates that have subsequently divided Christians. Read the text through, and try to get an understanding of its approach. Does the text seem willing to go beyond the mere repetition of what the Bible states? This is an important question, as the World Council of Churches is made up of a wide range of Protestant groups, often with widely differing baptismal policies and understandings of the nature and purpose of baptism. Inevitably, this makes documents such as the Lima text into works of theological diplomacy, trying to find common ground, and avoid creating division.

One of the most important debates in this area of theology concerns the function of sacraments. According to the Lima text, what difference does it make to someone when they are baptized? Do you think that the Lima text resolves questions like this, or tries to help its readers to see them in a new and helpful way?

The Lima text makes particular reference to the role of the Holy Spirit in baptism, and the importance of the church community. How would you summarize its teaching on both these points? Once more, notice the text's diplomacy, evident in statements such as: "God bestows upon all baptized persons the anointing and the promise of the Holy Spirit." This is consistent with the views that baptism causes the anointing of the Spirit, and that it represents a declaration on the part of the church that this anointing is already present.

9.5   Rowan Williams on the sacraments as signs

One of the most fundamental characteristics of sacraments is that they are signs. They signify something. Augustine of Hippo argued that the defining characteristic of a sacrament was that it was a sign of sacred realities. "Signs, when applied to divine things, are called sacraments." Yet these signs are not arbitrary, in that there is some connection between the sign itself and what is being represented. "If sacraments did not bear some resemblance to the things of which they are the sacraments," Augustine commented, "they would not be sacraments at all."

Thus baptism involves water, which is a sign of cleansing or purification – thus pointing to the cleansing and purification of the human soul through the grace of Christ. The eucharist involves bread and wine, which act as signs to the body and blood of Christ, and hence to the salvation that he made possible through his death on the cross. But how are sacraments to be located against the broader human activity of making sense of life, and constructing signs to help in this process? How do these "signs" emerge and gain their meaning?

Rowan Williams (born 1950), formerly archbishop of Canterbury and presently master of Magdalene College, Cambridge, has written extensively on various theological themes, and is widely regarded as one of the world's most important living theologians. Although a noted academic theologian, Williams has always recognized and valued the connection between theology and the life of the church, and many of his published writings deal with such themes. The extract is taken from a lecture given at a London church dealing with the manner in which Jesus of Nazareth instituted signs for the Christian community.

It is clear that the tradition of [Jesus of Nazareth's] deeds and words is heavily influenced by the sense that he was a sign-maker of a disturbingly revolutionary kind. He worked – we are led to understand – on the assumption that a time of crisis had begun in which the people of God would be both summoned to judgement and restored under God's kingship so as to become a people bound to God in unprecedented closeness. The covenanted faithfulness of God would once and for all overcome and cast out the unfaithfulness of the people. Thus Jesus acts for a community that does not yet exist, the Kingdom of God: he chooses rabbis and judges for the twelve tribes of the future, he heals and forgives, he takes authority to bring the outcasts of Israel into this new world by sharing their tables. His strange isolation, the suspicion and incomprehension he meets, have to do with the fact that his acts are signs of a form of human life yet to be realized and standing at odds with the political and cultic status quo. The "sense" he is making is entirely rooted in the fundamental Jewish conviction that God is the God who, by his free commitment, brings a people into being; yet the "people" in whose name he acts, whose forms and signs he constructs in his healing and fellowship, both is and is not identical with the Israel that now exists.

This paradox is most evident in the last of the "signs" of the kingdom which he performs, the unexpected variation on the passover theme in which he announces a new covenant sealed in his forthcoming death. The Last Supper is not a simple, primitive fellowship meal; as far back as we can go in the tradition about Jesus, it is seen as "intending," meaning, the event that finally sets Jesus and his followers apart from the continuities of Israel and makes the beginnings of a new definition of God's people. Maundy Thursday *means* Good Friday and Easter, the sealing of the new and everlasting covenant. In the costly gift of his chosen and beloved to the risk of rejection and death, God uncovers the scope of his commitment in a way that alters the whole quality of human trust and commitment to him: he creates *faith*. And he creates a community of faith called, exactly as Israel is called, to show his nature in their life by following out the logic of Torah itself. Every act must speak of God, but not in such a way as to suggest a satisfying of divine demands, an *adequacy* of response to God's creative act. What we do is now to be a sign, above all, of a gift given for the deepening of solidarity – or, in Paul's language, ethics is about "the building up of the body of Christ." If our acts with one another speak of mutual gift and givenness, they are signs of the radical self-gift which initiates the Church.

So, it is readily intelligible that the most characteristic (i.e. self-identifying) acts of the Church from its beginnings should be the signs of the paschal event. Baptism is already, in the tradition about Jesus, something that stands not only for commission and empowerment, but for the specific commission to die at the hands of the powerful of this earth, to realize God's power through the gift of one's own life to him (Mark 10:38–39, cf. Luke 12:50), so that the washing of the convert becomes an identification with this death, this gift and this empowering. The supper draws us into the event of the covenant's sealing, placing us with the unfaithful disciples at table whose unfaithfulness is to be both judged and set aside by God – for the supper is also celebrated as the meal shared with the risen Jesus.

Williams argues that a normal part of human communal life is to create signs, and that it is therefore to be expected that such actions or signs should play an important role in the life of the Christian community. For Williams, these actions are linked with the "paschal event," both demonstrating and enhancing the believer's identification with Jesus of Nazareth and the redemption and transformation which he achieves. Note that Maundy Thursday is the day before Good Friday, marking the occasion of the Last Supper of Jesus and his disciples.

Read through the passage, and try to follow the line of argument that Williams develops. How does Williams understand the relationship between the church and Israel? And how is this related to his understanding of the role of sacraments? In trying to answer this question, you will find it helpful to pick up some themes and institutions of the Old Testament that Williams alludes to – such as the Passover – and work out how he incorporates them into his understanding of the sacraments. How does this relate to Williams' statement that "the 'people' in whose name [Christ] acts, whose forms and signs he constructs in his healing and fellowship, both is and is not identical with the Israel that now exists."

It is clear that Williams regards the "paschal event" as being of critical importance. For those not familiar with this way of expressing things, the "paschal event" is normally understood to mean the events in the life of Jesus of Nazareth that are associated with Easter, especially the betrayal, arrest, scourging, crucifixion, and resurrection of Christ. Explain, in your own words, how Williams understands baptism and the eucharist to relate to the "paschal event." In what way are they signs of the kingdom? How do they emerge from his ministry?

Williams explores the idea, characteristic of Christian reflection on the meaning of baptism, that to be baptized is to identify oneself with the death of Christ, and the benefits this brings. What difference might this make to someone?

9.6 Benedict XVI on the eucharist

What theological insights lie at the heart of the eucharist? And how do these help motivate and shape the life and mission of the church? These questions were discussed at a General Assembly of the Synod of Bishops in the Vatican in 2005, focusing on the theme The Eucharist: Source and Summit of the Life and Mission of the Church. Although this Assembly had been convened by John Paul II, it took place under the guidance of his successor, Benedict XVI (formerly Joseph Ratzinger, born 1927), who issued an "apostolic exhortation" after the Assembly affirming some of its central themes. Ratzinger was elected to succeed Pope John Paul II after the latter's death in April 2005, and chose to be known as "Benedict XVI." He resigned on grounds of ill health in 2013, and was succeeded by Pope Francis.

The exhortation *Sacramentum Caritatis* ("The Sacrament of Charity") was delivered by Benedict XVI at Saint Peter's, Rome, on February 22, 2007. The section of this exhortation which has been chosen for study focuses on the themes that lie at the heart of the eucharist, which is to be seen as "the sum and summary of our faith."

The Church's eucharistic faith
6. *"The mystery of faith!"* With these words, spoken immediately after the words of consecration, the priest proclaims the mystery being celebrated and expresses his wonder before the substantial change of bread and wine into the body and blood of the Lord Jesus, a reality which surpasses all human understanding. The Eucharist is a "mystery of faith" par excellence: "the sum and summary of our faith."[13] The Church's faith is essentially a eucharistic faith, and it is especially nourished at the table of the Eucharist. Faith and the sacraments are two complementary aspects of ecclesial life. Awakened by the preaching of God's word, faith is nourished and grows in the grace-filled encounter with the Risen Lord which takes place in the sacraments: "faith is expressed in the rite, while the rite reinforces and strengthens faith."[14] For this reason, the Sacrament of the Altar is always at the heart of the Church's life: "thanks to the Eucharist, the Church is reborn ever anew!"[15] The more lively the eucharistic faith of the People of God, the deeper is its sharing in ecclesial life in steadfast commitment to the mission entrusted by Christ to his disciples. The Church's very history bears witness to this. Every great reform has in some way been linked to

the rediscovery of belief in the Lord's eucharistic presence among his people.

THE BLESSED TRINITY AND THE EUCHARIST

The bread come down from heaven
7. The first element of eucharistic faith is the mystery of God himself, trinitarian love. In Jesus' dialogue with Nicodemus, we find an illuminating expression in this regard: "God so loved the world that he gave his only Son, that whoever believes in him should not perish but have eternal life. For God sent the Son into the world, not to condemn the world, but that the world might be saved through him" (*Jn* 3:16–17). These words show the deepest source of God's gift. In the Eucharist Jesus does not give us a "thing," but himself; he offers his own body and pours out his own blood. He thus gives us the totality of his life and reveals the ultimate origin of this love. He is the eternal Son, given to us by the Father. In the Gospel we hear how Jesus, after feeding the crowds by multiplying the loaves and fishes, says to those who had followed him to the synagogue of Capernaum: "My Father gives you the true bread from heaven; for the bread of God is he who comes down from heaven, and gives life to the world" (*Jn* 6:32–33), and even identifies himself, his own flesh and blood, with that bread: "I am the living bread which came down from heaven; if anyone eats of this bread, he will live forever; and the bread which I shall give for the life of the world is my flesh" (*Jn* 6:51). Jesus thus shows that he is the bread of life which the eternal Father gives to mankind.

A free gift of the Blessed Trinity
8. The Eucharist reveals the loving plan that guides all of salvation history (cf. *Eph* 1:10; 3:8–11). There the *Deus Trinitas*, who is essentially love (cf. *1 Jn* 4:7–8), becomes fully a part of our human condition. In the bread and wine under whose appearances Christ gives himself to us in the paschal meal (cf. *Lk* 22:14–20; *1 Cor* 11:23–26), God's whole life encounters us and is sacramentally shared with us. God is a perfect communion of love between Father, Son and Holy Spirit. At creation itself, man was called to have some share in God's breath of life (cf. *Gen* 2:7). But it is in Christ, dead and risen, and in the outpouring of the Holy Spirit, given without measure (cf. *Jn* 3:34), that we have become sharers of God's inmost life.[16] Jesus Christ, who "through the eternal Spirit offered himself without blemish to God" (*Heb* 9:14), makes us, in

the gift of the Eucharist, sharers in God's own life. This is an absolutely free gift, the superabundant fulfilment of God's promises. The Church receives, celebrates and adores this gift in faithful obedience. The "mystery of faith" is thus a mystery of trinitarian love, a mystery in which we are called by grace to participate. We too should therefore exclaim with Saint Augustine: "If you see love, you see the Trinity."[17]

Notes

13   *Catechism of the Catholic Church*, 1327.
14   *Propositio* 16.
15   Benedict XVI, Homily at the Mass of Installation in the Cathedral of Rome (7 May 2005): AAS 97 (2005), 752.
16   Cf. *Propositio* 4.
17   *De Trinitate*, VIII, 8, 12: CCL 50, 287.

Read the passage carefully, and try to summarize its paragraphs in your own words. Benedict's argument is relatively easy to follow, and is developed in close engagement with the New Testament and the Catholic tradition. The first section explores the centrality of the eucharistic mystery to the faith of the church. Benedict argues that "rediscovery of belief in the Lord's eucharistic presence among his people" lies at the heart of revival and reform within the church, in effect setting an agenda for rediscovery and renewal.

The document then turns to focus on the eucharistic bread. Notice how this section draws heavily on John's gospel. Why do you think this is so? And how is the central image of bread developed in this section? Locate the following sentence in this extract: "In the Eucharist Jesus does not give us a 'thing,' but himself." What does Benedict mean by this? How does he develop this insight in the passage as a whole?

The next section explores how the eucharist fits into the broader trinitarian logic of the Christian faith. Try to summarize this section in your own words. What is the core point that Benedict wants to make? And in what way does a trinitarian theological framework help him to make this point? You might find it helpful to focus on this statement toward the end of this section: "The 'mystery of faith' is thus a mystery of trinitarian love, a mystery in which we are called by grace to participate." Try to piece together how Benedict arrives at this conclusion, and what specific elements of trinitarian and eucharistic theology he uses in getting there.

CHAPTER 10

Heaven

Most works of Christian theology follow the pattern of the creeds, and end with a discussion of heaven and eternal life. In theological terms, Christian thinking about heaven is located within the broad area of theology generally known as "eschatology" – the "last things" (Greek: *ta eschata*). Just as "Christology" refers to the Christian understanding of the nature and identity of Jesus Christ, so "eschatology" refers to the Christian understanding of such things as heaven and eternal life, while also including topics such as the Christian expectations of resurrection and judgment.

This chapter focuses on the idea of heaven, which is associated with powerful images such as that of the "New Jerusalem" (Revelation 21:1–4) or a restored paradise, such as the Garden of Eden. Such images depict heaven as a place of security, refreshment, and rest for believers, in which they are finally able to delight in the presence of God.

The term "heaven" is used frequently in the Pauline writings of the New Testament to refer to the Christian hope. Although it is natural to think of heaven as a future entity, Paul's thinking appears to embrace both a future reality and a spiritual sphere or realm which coexists with the material world of space and time. Thus "heaven" is referred to both as the future home of the believer (2 Corinthians 5:1–2; Philippians 3:20) and as the present dwelling-place of Jesus Christ, from which he will come in final judgment (Romans 10:6; 1 Thessalonians 1:10; 4:16).

Theology: The Basic Readings, Third Edition. Edited by Alister E. McGrath.
Editorial material and organization © Alister E. McGrath.
Published 2018 by John Wiley & Sons Ltd.

One of Paul's most significant statements concerning heaven focuses on the notion of believers being "citizens of heaven" (Philippians 3:20), and in some way sharing in the life of heaven in the present. The tension between the "now" and the "not yet" is evident in Paul's statements concerning heaven, making it very difficult to sustain the simple idea of heaven as something which will not come into being until the future, or which cannot be experienced in the present.

Probably the most helpful way of conceiving the New Testament statements concerning heaven is to see it as a consummation of the Christian doctrine of salvation, in which the presence, penalty, and power of sin have all been finally eliminated, and the total presence of God in individuals and the community of faith has been achieved.

The hope of heaven has played an important role in Christian theological speculation, providing spiritual consolation in times of persecution or personal distress, as well as a stimulus to reflection on the nature and destiny of humanity. We begin our exploration of the theme by considering the place it plays in the thought of Cyprian, bishop of Carthage, who was martyred in 258.

10.1   Cyprian of Carthage on paradise as the Christian homeland

Cyprian of Carthage (died 258) wrote his treatise *De Mortalitate* ("On Mortality") in Latin during the great plague (probably smallpox) which broke out in the Roman world during the early 250s. The treatise is gener-ally thought to represent the published text of a sermon originally deliv-ered orally to the Christians of Carthage, exploring questions raised by the outbreak. Cyprian's detailed descriptions of the plague – which the Roman authorities blamed on the rise of Christianity – have led some scholars to refer to this epidemic as the "plague of Cyprian."

The outbreak raised some theological questions. Why, some Christians wanted to know, did the plague seem to affect both Christians and pagans? Others were worried that dying of the plague might rob them of the chance to become martyrs for their faith in an increasingly hostile cultural environment. One of Cyprian's main concerns, however, is to set out his vision of the Christian hope. Christians ought not to be afraid of death, in that it enables them to return to their homeland (*patria*). Cyprian invites his readers to imagine themselves returning home, and anticipating the joy of reunion with friends and family – and, above all, the risen Christ. Cyprian himself suffered a martyr's death at the hands of the Roman authorities in 258.

> For those who fight for God, my dearest brothers and sisters, ought to see themselves as those who are already placed in the heavenly camp, hoping for divine things, so that they may not be perturbed by the storms and whirlwinds of the world, nor experience any disturbance, since the Lord had foretold that these things would take place. The Lord predicted, through his foreseeing word, that wars, and famines, and earthquakes, and pestilences would arise in each place; and he thus instructed, prepared, and strengthened the people of his Church to endure all things that were to come. And in case any unexpected and dreadful calamities should shake us, he forewarned us that adversity would increase more and more in the last times. Now the very things that he spoke about are taking place; and since these things that were foretold are now happening, it also follows that whatever other things were promised will also follow. As the Lord himself promises, "when you see all these things happening, you will know that the kingdom of God is at hand." The kingdom of God, my beloved brothers and sisters, is beginning to draw near. The reward of life, rejoicing in our eternal

salvation, and the perpetual gladness at possessing a once-lost paradise, are now coming, with the passing away of the world. Already heavenly things are taking the place of earthly, great things of small ones, and eternal things of things that will fade away. What room is there here for anxiety and concern? Who, in the midst of these things, is trembling and sad, except anyone who is without hope and faith? Those who fear death are those who are not willing to be with Christ. Who would be unwilling to go to Christ, who does not believe that they are about to reign with Christ? […]

Those who wish to remain long in the world are those whom the world delights – those whom this life, flattering and deceiving, welcomes by its enticements of earthly pleasure. And, since the world hates the Christian, why should you love that which hates you? Why would you not rather follow Christ, who both redeemed you and loves you? John in his epistle exhorts that we should not follow fleshly desires and love the world. "Do not love the world," he says, "nor the things which are in the world." […] Rather, beloved brothers and sisters, let us be prepared for the whole will of God with a sound mind, a firm faith, and strong virtue. Let us lay aside the fear of death, and reflect on the immortality which follows it. By this let us show ourselves to be what we believe – that we do not grieve over the departure of those dear to us, and that when the day of our own summons shall arrive, we shall depart without delay and without resistance to the Lord when He himself calls us.

And although this is how God's servants should always behave, it is all the more important now – now that the world is collapsing and is oppressed with the storms of evil and sin. We who recognize that terrible things have begun, and know that still more terrible things are about to take place, may regard it as the greatest advantage to depart from it as quickly as possible. If the walls of your house were shaking with age, the roofs above you were trembling, and the structure of the house, now worn out and wearied, were about to collapse on account of its age, would you not get out as quickly as possible? If you were on a voyage when you encountered a fierce and raging tempest, with violent waves suggesting that you were about to be shipwrecked, would you not quickly find a harbour? See, the world is changing and passing away, and witnesses to its ruin not so much by its age, but by the end of things. And do you not give God thanks and congratulate yourself that you managed to get away earlier, and so were delivered from the imminent shipwrecks and disasters?

We should always consider, dearly beloved brothers and sisters, that we have renounced the world, and are in the meantime living here as guests and strangers. Let us greet the day which sees each of us return to our own homes, which snatches us from here and sets us free from the snares of the world, and restores us to paradise and the kingdom. Which of us, when placed in foreign lands, does not want to hurry back to our own country? Who that is eager to return to his friends would not earnestly desire a prosperous gale, so that he might the sooner embrace those dear to him? We regard paradise as our native land. We have already begun to consider the patriarchs as our parents. Why do we not hasten and run, so that we may catch sight of our native land, and greet our parents? There a great number of our dear ones is awaiting us, and a dense crowd of parents, brothers, children, is longing for us, already assured of their own safety, and still anxious for our salvation. To attain to their presence and their embrace – what a joy, both for them and for us!

This passage has been very influential in shaping Christian attitudes to death. Its most famous statement is this: "We regard paradise as our native land." What does Cyprian mean by this? The Latin word *patria* (here translated "native land") is deeply evocative, suggesting a place where we really belong – where we have roots. So if paradise is our native land, how are we to understand our life on earth? What difference does belief in heaven make to the way we evaluate the world, and our place within it? A central theme of the passage is the danger of falling in love with the world. Identify the issues that Cyprian regards as being important here.

Toward the end of the passage, Cyprian uses two illustrations to reinforce his theological points – a house teetering on the brink of collapse, and a ship at sea which has encountered a tempest which threatens to sink it. What point does he want to make using these images? How effective is he? Is there anything in the passage which suggests that the threat of martyrdom is imminent? And, if so, how might Cyprian's message enable believers to face it?

10.2 Methodius of Olympus on the resurrection body

How is the resurrection body related to the body that we possess while on earth? This highly speculative question has intrigued Christian theologians, who have offered some equally speculative answers. The image of a seed, used by Paul in 1 Corinthians 15, was taken by many writers to mean that there was some organic connection between the earthly and heavenly body. Resurrection could thus be conceived as the unfolding of a predetermined pattern within the human organism. Yet even this image had to be treated with caution.

Methodius of Olympus (martyred 311) is an excellent example of a theologian who felt the need to develop analogies for the resurrection which went beyond the modest statements of the New Testament. Although Methodius clearly believed that his ideas were completely in line with Scripture, there are points at which they seem to develop a life of their own. Methodius' fundamental analogy for the resurrection of the body is the melting and recasting of a damaged statue, so that it can be restored to its former glory. In his dialogue with Aglaophon on the resurrection, Methodius sets out his basic ideas.

Now since there is a need for many examples in matters of this kind, let us examine them particularly from this point of view, not stopping until our discussion ends in clearer explanation and proof. It is as if some skilled artificer had made a noble image, cast in gold or other material, which was beautifully proportioned in all its features. Then the artificer suddenly notices that the image had been defaced by some envious person, who could not endure its beauty, and so decided to ruin it for the sake of the pointless pleasure of satisfying his jealousy. So the craftsman decides to recast this noble image. Now notice, most wise Aglaophon, that if he wants to ensure that this image, on which he has expended so much effort, care, and work, will be totally free from any defect, he will be obliged to melt it down, and restore it to its former condition.

But if he does not cast it all over again, nor reconstruct it, but allows it to remain just as it is, while repairing and restoring it, it must follow that the image, having passed through the fire and having been forged, can no longer be preserved unchanged, but will be altered and wasted. For this reason, if he should wish it to be perfect, beautiful, and faultless, it must be broken up and recast, in order that all the disfigurements and mutilations inflicted upon it by treachery and envy may be eliminated by breaking it up and recasting it. In this way, the image will be restored again to its original state, and made as like its original as possible. For it is impossible for an image under the hands of the original artist to be lost, even if it be melted down again, for it may be restored. Yet it is possible for blemishes and injuries to be eliminated in this way, for they will melt away and cannot be restored. In every work of art the best craftsman looks not for blemish or failure, but for symmetry and correctness in his work.

Now it seems to me that God's plan was much the same as this human example. He saw that humanity, his most wonderful creation, had been corrupted by envy and treachery. Such was his love for humanity that he could not allow it to continue in this condition, remaining faulty and deficient to eternity. For this reason, God dissolved humanity once more into its original materials, so that it could be remodeled in such a way that all its defects could be eliminated and disappear. Now the melting down of a statue corresponds to the death and dissolution of the human body, and the remolding of the material to the resurrection after death. That is what the prophet Jeremiah says, for he addresses the Jews in these words, "So I went down to the potter's house, and there he was working at his wheel. The vessel he was making of clay was spoiled in the potter's hand, and he reworked it into another vessel, as seemed good to him. Then the word of the Lord came to me: 'Can I not do with you, O house of Israel, just as this potter has done?' says the Lord. Just like the clay in the potter's hand, so are you in my hand, O house of Israel" (Jeremiah 18:3–6).

Now I draw your attention to the fact, as I said, that after humanity's transgression, the Great Hand was not content to leave as a trophy of victory its own work, debased by the Evil One, who wickedly injured it from motives of envy. Rather, he moistened and reduced it to clay, as a potter breaks up a vessel, so that by remodeling it all the blemishes and bruises in it may disappear, and it may be made faultless and pleasing all over again.

Yet it is not satisfactory to say that the universe will be utterly destroyed, and that the sea, air and sky will no longer exist. For the whole world will be deluged with fire from heaven, and burned for the purpose of purification and renewal. It will not, however, come to complete ruin and corruption. For if it were better for the world not to exist than to exist, why did God, in making the world, choose to take the worse course? But God did not work in vain, or do that which was worse. God ordered the creation with a view to its existence and continuance, as the Book of Wisdom confirms, when it says: "For God created all things so that they might have their being; and the generations of the world were healthy, and there is no poison of destruction in them" (Wisdom 1:14). And Paul clearly confirms this […] saying that the creation was made subject to vanity, and that he expects that it will be set free from such servitude, as he intends to call this world by the name of creation. For it is not what is unseen but what is seen that is subject to corruption. The creation, then, after being restored to a better and more seemly state, remains, rejoicing and exulting over the children of God at the resurrection, for whose sake it now groans in labor, waiting for our redemption from the corruption of the body. When we have risen and shaken off the mortality of our flesh, according to that which is written, "Shake off the dust, and arise, and sit down, O Jerusalem" (Isaiah 52:2), and have been set free from sin, it also shall be freed from corruption and be subject no longer to vanity, but to righteousness.

This passage is very accessible, and relatively easy to understand. Begin by trying to summarize the argument in your own words, focusing on the central image used by Methodius – the metal statue. Why does it have to be recast? Why could it not just be repaired? You also might like to compare and contrast this analogy with the points that Methodius makes using a second image – the potter and his clay.

The imagery of fire is used throughout this passage. Does Methodius see fire as a symbol of destruction, or of renewal? How does this affect his thinking on the future resurrection, and the transformation of the present order of things?

10.3   Peter Abelard on the hope of heaven

Christian thinking on the nature of heaven developed extensively during the Middle Ages, especially in relation to the way in which it was visualized. Works such as Dante's *Divine Comedy* depicted the journey of the soul to heaven in highly visual ways. Dante (1265–1321) wrote the *Divine Comedy* partly to give poetic expression to the Christian hope. The poem is an important representation of the medieval worldview, in which the souls of the departed were understood to pass through a series of purifying and cleansing processes, before being enabled to catch a glimpse of the vision of God – the ultimate goal of the Christian life. For many, its most distinctive feature is its vivid depiction of the spiritual geography of the last things.

The image of the "New Jerusalem" played a particularly important role in medieval Christian spirituality and hymnody, as well as theological reflection. "I saw the holy city, the New Jerusalem" (Revelation 21:2). This vision of heaven as a city captivated the Christian imagination. This image of heaven resonates strongly with one of the leading themes of Paul's theology – that Christians are to be regarded as "citizens of heaven" (Philippians 3:19–21). The New Jerusalem is characterized by the pervasive presence of God, and the triumphant and joyful response of those who had long awaited this experience, who now had the right of permanent abode in this city. They were wayfarers and sojourners on earth; they were now settled citizens of the New Jerusalem.

One of the most important theological poems of the Middle Ages to develop the image of the New Jerusalem was written by Peter Abelard (1079–1142). Like many religious poems of this age, this focused on the hope of heaven, using striking visual imagery. The poem is generally known by its Latin title – "O quanta qualia sunt illa sabbata" (which can be translated as "O How Many and How Great are the Sabbaths") – and has been widely used in the worship of Christian churches. Four of its seven verses are set out below, in the 1854 English translation of John Mason Neale. Neale's translation is not an exact rendering of the original Latin, as the poetry makes this difficult. It does, however, provide a reliable rendering of some of Abelard's key theological concerns.

> O what their joy and their glory must be,
> Those endless Sabbaths the blessèd ones see;
> Crown for the valiant, to weary ones, rest;
> God shall be all, and in all ever blessed.

Truly, "Jerusalem" name we that shore,
City of peace that brings joy evermore;
Wish and fulfillment are not severed there,
Nor do things prayed for come short of the prayer.

Now, in the meanwhile, with hearts raised on high,
We for that country must yearn and must sigh;
Seeking Jerusalem, dear native land,
Through our long exile on Babylon's strand.

There, where no troubles distraction can bring,
We the sweet anthems of Zion shall sing;
While for thy grace, God, their voices of praise
Thy blessèd people eternally raise.

The hymn is well known, and it is likely that you have already come across it. If you can read Latin, you can easily consult the original Latin text on the Web, and make this the basis of your reflections. Begin by reading through the English translation, and noting its leading ideas, particularly the emphasis on the "New Jerusalem" (Revelation 21:1–7). Then focus on the first verse. What are its dominant themes? Why does the poem focus so much on rewarding the righteous and valiant, and giving rest to the weary?

The second verse sets out the theme of fulfillment of human aspirations and longing in heaven. The first line of Neale's translation reads a little awkwardly; the point is that the true name of this shore or city that we seek is "Jerusalem." The core theme is that heaven is a place in which our longings find their final fulfillment – something that was not possible under the limiting conditions of earthly life. How is this theme expressed in the statement: "Wish and fulfillment are not severed there"?

The third verse develops a theme we noted earlier (see 10.1) in Cyprian of Carthage's reflections on paradise as the Christian's "homeland" or "native land" (Latin: *patria*). For Abelard, the New Jerusalem is the Christian's "dear native land." In this verse, Abelard reflects on how this future hope affects life in the present. He depicts life on earth as an exile. Just as the people of Jerusalem were exiled to the city of Babylon, so believers are exiled on earth – "our long exile on Babylon's strand." Yet the hope of returning to the homeland sustains that period of exile. There are clear connections being made here between theology and spirituality. Try to set out, in your own words, how Abelard thinks that the Christian hope of entering the New Jerusalem affects life on earth.

The fourth verse builds on ideas developed earlier, emphasizing the notion of safety, security, and freedom from distractions and concerns. What points do you think Abelard is trying to make here?

10.4   John Wesley on the final restoration of nature

The rise of Methodism in eighteenth-century England was of theological importance for many reasons, not least on account of its emphasis on the "religion of experience." Yet the Methodist revival also led to the development of means by which theology could be expressed and communicated more effectively. One of the most significant methods was the use of hymns, which proved to be highly effective in communicating and applying important theological ideas. Another was the revival of the sermon as a means of educating the Christian public. The "standard sermons" of the great Methodist leader and theologian John Wesley (1703–91) became virtually the equivalent of a Methodist confession of faith, setting out its distinctive themes.

In his sermon "The General Deliverance," Wesley reflects on the nature of the final restoration envisaged by the Christian vision of heaven. The sermon addresses a range of questions concerning the animal kingdom, and contains one of the most interesting and potentially significant theological reflections on how the fall and the final restoration affect the "brute creation." The sermon argues that God makes amends for the pain and suffering of animals in this lifetime by delivering them from their bondage of corruption and giving them "large amends" in a restored nature.

If the Creator and Father of every living thing is rich in mercy towards all; if he does not overlook or despise any of the works of his own hands; if he wills even the meanest of them to be happy, according to their degree; how comes it to pass, that such a complication of evils oppresses, yea, overwhelms them? How is it that misery of all kinds overspreads the face of the earth? This is a question which has puzzled the wisest philosophers in all ages: And it cannot be answered without having recourse to the oracles of God. But, taking these for our guide we may inquire,

    I. What was the original state of the brute creation?
    II. In what state is it at present? And,
    III. In what state will it be at the manifestation of the children of God?

We may inquire, in the first place, What was the original state of the brute creation? And may we not learn this, even from the place which was assigned them; namely, the garden of God? All the beasts of the field, and all the fowls of the air, were with Adam in paradise. And there is no question but their state was suited to their place: It was paradisiacal; perfectly happy. Undoubtedly it bore a near resemblance to the state of man himself. By taking, therefore, a short view of the one, we may conceive the other. [...]

[Wesley then describes the impact of the fall and its "deplorable consequences" for every aspect of the creation.]

But will "the creature," will even the brute creation, always remain in this deplorable condition? God forbid that we should affirm this; yea, or even entertain such a thought. While "the whole creation groaneth together" (whether men attend or not), their groans are not dispersed in idle air, but enter the ears of Him that made them. While his creatures "travail together in pain," he knoweth all their pain, and is bringing them nearer and nearer to the birth, which shall be accomplished in its season. He seeth the "earnest expectation" wherewith the whole animated creation "waiteth for" that final "manifestation of the sons of God," in which "they themselves also shall be delivered" (not by annihilation; annihilation is not deliverance) "from the present bondage of corruption into" a measure of "the glorious liberty of the children of God." [...]

A general view of this is given us in the twenty-first chapter of the Revelation. When He that "sitteth on the great white throne" hath pronounced "Behold, I make all things new," when the word is fulfilled, "the tabernacle of God is with men, and they shall be his people, and God himself shall be with them, and be their God" – then the following blessing shall take place (not only on the children of men; there is no such restriction in the text; but) on every creature according to its capacity. [...]

The whole brute creation will then, undoubtedly, be restored, not only to the vigour, strength, and swiftness which they had at their creation, but to a far higher degree of each than they ever enjoyed. They will be restored, not only to that measure of understanding which they had in paradise, but to a degree of it as much higher than that, as the understanding of an elephant is beyond that of a worm. And whatever affections they had in the garden of God, will be restored with vast increase; being exalted and refined in a manner which we ourselves are not able to comprehend. The liberty they then had will be completely restored, and they will be free in all their motions. They will be delivered from all irregular appetites, from all unruly passions, from every disposition that is either evil in itself, or has any tendency to evil. No rage will be found in any creature, no fierceness, no cruelty, or thirst for blood. So far from it that "the wolf shall dwell with the lamb, the leopard shall lie down with the kid, the calf and the young lion together; and a little child shall lead them. The cow and the bear shall feed together, and the lion shall eat straw like an ox. They shall not hurt nor destroy in all my holy mountain" (Isaiah 11:6–7). [...]

But though I doubt not that the Father of All has a tender regard for even his lowest creatures, and that, in consequence of this, he will make them large amends for all they suffer while under their present bondage; yet I dare not affirm that he has an *equal* regard for them and for the children of men. [...] May I be permitted to mention here a conjecture concerning the brute creation? What, if it should then please the all-wise, the all-gracious Creator to raise them higher in the scale of beings? What, if it should please him, when he makes us "equal to angels," to make them what we are now – creatures capable of God; capable of knowing and loving and enjoying the Author of their being? If it should be so, ought our eye to be evil because he is good? However this be, he will certainly do what will be most for his own glory.

This important sermon addresses a question that is often neglected in standard theological textbooks: will there be animals in heaven? And, if so, what will their status be? Wesley offers a provocative response to this question, arguing that the restoration of creation must extend to include the animal kingdom. Read the sermon through, and try to get an understanding of the general flow of argument that it presents. Note how it begins by asserting that animals played an important role in paradise.

In formulating his vision of the restored creation, Wesley makes an appeal to Isaiah 11:6–7. Locate this section of the text. What point does Wesley make on its basis? And how does he develop this in his "bold conjecture" toward the end? What specific proposal does Wesley offer by which God might make "large amends" to animals "for all they suffer while under their present bondage"?

10.5   The *Catechism of the Catholic Church* on the resurrection

In 1985 an extraordinary Synod of Bishops gathered in Rome to celebrate the twentieth anniversary of the Second Vatican Council and find ways to develop its work further. There was considerable pressure for the production of a new vernacular catechism, reflecting the needs of the church in the late twentieth century. The *Catechism of the Catholic Church*, published in 1992, resulted from this process, and soon established itself as a major teaching resource. Its clarity of presentation of key theological issues makes it an ideal resource for study. What follows is the *Catechism's* succinct summary of the fundamental elements of belief in the resurrection of the body, a central theme in any Christian account of heaven.

I.   CHRIST'S RESURRECTION AND OURS

The progressive revelation of the Resurrection
992 God revealed the resurrection of the dead to his people progressively. Hope in the bodily resurrection of the dead established itself as a consequence intrinsic to faith in God as creator of the whole man, soul and body. The creator of heaven and earth is also the one who faithfully maintains his covenant with Abraham and his posterity. It was in this double perspective that faith in the resurrection came to be expressed. In their trials, the Maccabean martyrs confessed: "The King of the universe will raise us up to an everlasting renewal of life, because we have died for his laws.[540] One cannot but choose to die at the hands of men and to cherish the hope that God gives of being raised again by him."[541]

993 The Pharisees and many of the Lord's contemporaries hoped for the resurrection. Jesus teaches it firmly. To the Sadducees who deny it he answers, "Is not this why you are wrong, that you know neither the scriptures nor the power of God?"[542] Faith in the resurrection rests on faith in God who "is not God of the dead, but of the living."[543]

994 But there is more. Jesus links faith in the resurrection to his own person: "I am the Resurrection and the life."[544] It is Jesus himself who on the last day will raise up those who have believed in him, who have eaten his body and drunk his blood.[545] Already now in this present life he gives a sign and pledge of this by restoring some of the dead to life,[546] announcing thereby his own Resurrection, though it was to be of another order. He speaks of this unique event as the "sign of Jonah,"[547] the sign of the temple: he announces that he will be put to death but rise thereafter on the third day.[548]

995 To be a witness to Christ is to be a "witness to his Resurrection," to "[have eaten and drunk] with him after he rose from the dead."[549] Encounters with the risen Christ characterize the Christian hope of resurrection. We shall rise like Christ, with him, and through him.

996 From the beginning, Christian faith in the resurrection has met with incomprehension and opposition.[550] "On no point does the Christian faith encounter more opposition than on the resurrection of the body."[551] It is very commonly accepted that the life of the human person continues in a spiritual fashion after death. But how can we believe that this body, so clearly mortal, could rise to everlasting life?

How do the dead rise?

997 *What is "rising"?* In death, the separation of the soul from the body, the human body decays and the soul goes to meet God, while awaiting its reunion with its glorified body. God, in his almighty power, will definitively grant incorruptible life to our bodies by reuniting them with our souls, through the power of Jesus' Resurrection.

998 *Who will rise?* All the dead will rise, "those who have done good, to the resurrection of life, and those who have done evil, to the resurrection of judgment."[552]

999 *How?* Christ is raised with his own body: "See my hands and my feet, that it is I myself",[553] but he did not return to an earthly life. So, in him, "all of them will rise again with their own bodies which they now bear," but Christ "will change our lowly body to be like his glorious body," into a "spiritual body":[554] But someone will ask, "How are the dead raised? With what kind of body do they come?" You foolish man! What you sow does not come to life unless it dies. And what you sow is not the body which is to be, but a bare kernel. [...] "What is sown is perishable, what is raised is imperishable. [...] The dead will be raised imperishable. [...] For this perishable nature must put on the imperishable, and this mortal nature must put on immortality."[555]

1000 This "how" exceeds our imagination and understanding; it is accessible only to faith. Yet our participation in the Eucharist already gives us a foretaste of Christ's transfiguration of our bodies: "Just as bread that comes from the earth, after God's blessing has been invoked upon it, is no longer ordinary bread, but Eucharist, formed of two things, the one earthly and the other heavenly: so too our bodies, which partake of the Eucharist, are no longer corruptible, but possess the hope of resurrection."[556]

1001 *When?* Definitively "at the last day," "at the end of the world."[557] Indeed, the resurrection of the dead is closely associated with Christ's Parousia: "For the Lord himself will descend from heaven, with a cry of command, with the archangel's call, and with the sound of the trumpet of God. And the dead in Christ will rise first."[558]

Notes

540 *2 Maccabees* 7:9.
541 *2 Maccabees* 7:14; cf. 7:29; *Daniel* 12:1–13.
542 *Mark* 12:24; cf. *John* 11:24; *Acts* 23:6.
543 *Mark* 12:27.
544 *John* 11:25.
545 Cf. *John* 5:24–25; 6:40, 54.
546 Cf. *Mark* 5:21–42; *Luke* 7:11–17; *John* 11.
547 *Matthew* 12:39.
548 Cf. *Mark* 10:34; *John* 2:19–22.
549 *Acts* 1:22; 10:41; cf. 4:33.
550 Cf. *Acts* 17:32; *1 Corinthians* 15:12–13.
551 St. Augustine, *En. in Ps.* 88, 5: PL 37, 1134.
552 *John* 5:29; cf. *Daniel* 12:2.
553 *Luke* 24:39.
554 Lateran Council IV (1215): DS 801; *Philippians* 3:21; *1 Corinthians* 15:44.
555 *1 Corinthians* 15:35–37, 42, 52, 53.
556 St. Irenaeus, *Adv. haeres.* 4, 18, 4–5: PG 7/1, 1028–1029.
557 *John* 6:39–40, 44, 54; 11:24; LG 48 § 3.
558 *1 Thessalonians* 4:16.

The *Catechism* here sets out a brief account of the relationship between the resurrection of Christ and the general Christian hope of the resurrection of believers on the last day. It is rich in biblical citations and allusions, as the annotations indicate. Work through its argument, noting its key elements. Why was the hope of resurrection revealed gradually, according to this text? Note especially its cautious statements about how the dead rise (999–1000). In what way does the *Catechism* establish a link between the hope of resurrection and the eucharist?

10.6 Wolfhart Pannenberg on eschatology and evil

The area of Christian theology dealing with the "last things" – such as heaven – is often referred to as "eschatology" (from the Greek phrase *ta eschata*, "the last things"). One of the themes of a Christian eschatology, as we have seen from earlier readings, is that of the restoration of all things to their original intended pattern.

This theme is found in the biblical image of the "New Jerusalem" (Revelation 21:1–5), which depicts a restored creation in which suffering, evil, and pain have passed away: "Death will be no more; mourning and crying and pain will be no more, for the first things have passed away." The theme of the New Jerusalem incorporates motifs drawn from the Genesis creation account – such as the presence of the "tree of life" (Revelation 22:2) – suggesting that heaven can be seen as the restoration of the bliss of Eden, when God dwelled with humanity in harmony. The pain, sorrow, and evil of a fallen world have finally passed away, and the creation has been restored to its original intention.

This raises an important question: what does the Christian hope of heaven have to say in the face of evil and suffering in the world? How are we to think of the final overcoming of evil? And how does this affect the way in which we experience and understand evil and suffering in the present world? This question is addressed by the German Lutheran theologian Wolfhart Pannenberg (1928–2014), who established his scholarly reputation during the 1960s by engaging with the question of the relevance of the resurrection of Christ for the Christian understanding of history. In his three-volume *Systematic Theology*, Pannenberg considers the implications of the Christian hope in relation to the existence of evil.

In all its forms and individual themes biblical eschatology has to do with the overcoming of wickedness and evil. This is obvious in the views of world judgment and also in the dramatic depictions of the battles of Michael against the dragon and of the rider on the white horse against the ungodly empires of the end time and the kings of the earth (Revelation 12:7ff.; 19:11ff.). But the resurrection of the dead is also an overcoming of sin and evil because there is achieved in it a victory over the death and corruptibility under whose dominion the present world is sighing. The society of the kingdom of God rests on the defeat of the injustice that is the root of the lack of peace in human relations and in those between states and peoples. Finally the praise of God offered by the perfected community will represent the overcoming of all false worship, of all idolatry, which for its part culminates in the worship of antichrist.

The specific Christian accent in this expectation falls on its relation to the saving event of the reconciliation of the world in the death of Christ. This event is in itself already an overcoming of evil, and it effects deliverance from the power of sin and death. Nevertheless, there is still need of a consummation, which is possible for its part only after this earthly life and to which the expectation of Christians is directed. The saving event relates to this as a real anticipation that calls for a final enforcement on which its own power and truth retrospectively depend because it always derives already from this future of God's salvation and is to be understood as its inbreaking into this present world. In Jewish history eschatology arose out of the question of the righteousness of God in the lives of individuals and out of the hope of the consummation of the covenant righteousness of the electing God vis-à-vis his elect people. For Christian faith, however, the theme of reconciliation and its consummation has replaced those concerns.

In the previous section we discussed the element of change that is contained in the last judgment but more comprehensively in the whole work of the Spirit as the dynamic of glorification. This is the change that according to what the apostle says in 1 Cor. 15:50ff. awaits the earthly life of believers but that by the power of the Spirit has broken in already in the case of those who believe and have been baptized. The concept of reconciliation also contains this element of change. The life of those who accept the invitation that God has issued in Jesus Christ for reconciliation with himself is changed thereby from a state of distance and estrangement from God to one of fellowship with him. In the process there is present already in the sense of reconciliation the future fellowship with God by participation in his eternal life that is still future for believers. Included also is the overcoming of all the wickedness and evil that go along with the creature's self-separation from God and its consequences and that seem to give the creature that is thus separated occasion for complaint against God. [...]

If, however, our earthly lives are to undergo such far-reaching changes from the standpoint of eternity, can we speak of an identity of the future life with our present life? Is it still our own life that we shall find again in this form that is so changed from an eternal stand-point?

Obviously there is not an identity of content in the sense that nothing is added or subtracted. Nevertheless, we may maintain an identity of the eschatological consummation with human life as it now is on earth if we consider what it is that constitutes the identity of a person even now in this earthly life. On the one side are the concrete conditions and experiences and realities of life that we cannot suppress but that we are to integrate into the unity of our selfhood. On the other side is this selfhood, our destiny as human beings and as specific individuals, and what exactly constitutes this selfhood we can grasp only provisionally because we are still on the way to it, and in one form or another we constantly go beyond what we already are and were. All the same, we are also already in some sense what we shall be. Hence in the process of building identity we always find together both identity and change, including change in the significance of what we experienced earlier.

Pannenberg's account of the Christian hope here opens by noting how the hope of the overcoming of evil is a constant theme in the Bible. Note the examples that he offers. What does he mean when he states that "the resurrection of the dead is also an overcoming of sin and evil because there is achieved in it a victory over the death and corruptibility under whose dominion the present world is sighing"?

Pannenberg then sets out an account of how the resurrection of Christ is involved in this general idea of the overcoming of evil. Summarize his argument at this point. How does he use the notion of "reconciliation" to develop this point? And how does this relate to the resurrection of Christ?

The final paragraph offers an important reflection on the question of the maintenance of human identity before and after the resurrection. What is the point at issue? And how does Pannenberg deal with the problem of continuity of identity or "selfhood" in this passage?

10.7   Kathryn Tanner on eternal life

What is eternal life? In her 2001 book *Jesus, Humanity and the Trinity*, Kathryn Tanner (born 1957), presently professor of systematic theology at Yale Divinity School, sets out a creative synthesis of Christian beliefs, rooted in tradition, yet orientated toward the future. Tanner's discussion of the concept of "eternal life" is of particular interest, on account of its constructive engagement with the Christian theological tradition.

Because it runs across the fact of death, life in Christ is eternal life. There is a life in the triune God that we possess now and after death, in Christ through the power of the Holy Spirit. Ante and post mortem do not mark any crucial difference with respect to it. Death makes no difference to that life in God in the sense that, despite our deaths, God maintains a relationship with us that continues to be the source of all life-giving benefit. Even when we are alive, we are therefore dead in so far as we are dead to Christ. Separation from Christ (and from one's fellows in Christ) is a kind of death despite the apparent gains that might accrue to one in virtue of an isolated, simply self-concerned existence. Eternal life, moreover, is one's portion or possession despite all the sufferings of life and death in a way that should comfort sufferers of every kind of tribulation. In all the senses of death, including the biological, we therefore live even though we die if we are alive to Christ. "If we live, we live to the Lord, and if we die, we die to the Lord; so then, whether we live or whether we die, we are the Lord's" (Romans 14:8).

This understanding of eternal life follows the Old Testament suggestion, then, that all the goods of life ("life" in its extended senses) flow from relationship with God (the second biblical sense of life in relationship): "ye that did cleave unto the Lord are alive ... this day" (Deuteronomy 4:4, KJV). The effort to turn away or separate oneself from God has, in this understanding of things, the force of death, broadly construed. (It is literally the effort to unmake oneself.) Eternal life as *life in God* is a way of indicating this priority of the second biblical sense of life as relationship with God. It is also a way of specifying a character of relationship with God that might survive death. If the world, human society, and individual persons live in virtue of a relationship with God beyond the fact of their deaths, they must live *in* God and not simply in relationship *with* God. After death, the only powers of life our bodies have are God's own powers of life via the life-giving humanity of Christ in the power of the Spirit. *Eternal* life means a deepened affirmation that one's relation with God is not conditional; it is not conditioned even by biological death or the cessation of community and cosmos. The Bible maintains that God remains the God of Israel and the church, remains the God of the world that God creates and of all the individuals in it, whatever happens; the idea of eternal life is simply a way of continuing this affirmation of God's loving and steadfast faithfulness across the fact of death.

While continuing and consummating God's faithful commitment to the creature's good as that is manifest in creation, eternal life is itself a greater gift (and brings in its train greater gifts) than the relationship with God that creatures enjoy simply as creatures. The evident unconditionality of eternal life marks one such difference. With eternal life it becomes clear how relation with God as the source of all benefit cannot be broken by either sin or death (in all its senses including the biological); relations with a life-giving God are maintained unconditionally from God's side. Whatever might happen, God remains faithful to a life-giving relation to us and empowers us, through Christ, for faithfulness, too. The relationship is also unconditional, then, in that what we should be in it – the image of God's own relationship with us – is maintained or shored up from God's side (in virtue of the free favor and mercy of God in Christ) despite our own failings, sufferings, and sin. In the relationship of eternal life, God sets us in and upholds our position in relation to God, whatever we do, whatever happens to us. Despite the fact of human failing, faithlessness and death, we *are* alive in God.

Eternal life is, secondly, not the same sort of relationship as the rather external one that exists between God and creatures: our very identity as creatures is redefined so as to be essentially constituted by relationship with God. Separation from God is now impossible in a way it was not for us simply as creatures. The very meaning of this new identity is that our dependence upon God for our existence is now complete: in Christ we essentially *are* that relationship to God in a way that simply being creatures of God does not entail.

The model for this aspect of life in God is the incarnation. Jesus is the one who lives in God, the one who is all that he is as a human being without existing independently of God, the human being whose very existence is God's own existence – that is the meaning of the hypostatic union. Otherwise expressed, in Jesus God becomes the bearer of our very human acts and attributes. By grace – by virtue, that is, of a life-giving relationship with Jesus that is ours in the power of the Spirit – we enjoy something like the sort of life in God that Jesus lives. We (and the whole world) are to live in God as Jesus does, through him. In short, there is an approximation to the hypostatic union that the world enjoys through grace, most particularly after the world's death, when it transpires that, like Christ, the only life or existence we have is in and through God.

Eternal life is, in the third place, a greater gift than the relations enjoyed simply by creatures because of the gifts it brings with it. As a consequence of the incarnation, the powers and character of Godself shine through Jesus' human acts and attributes – giving Jesus' acts and attributes a salvific force (for example, so as to overcome and heal the consequences of sin) and eventuating in the manifest glorification of Jesus' own human being in the resurrection. So for us, life in Christ brings not just created goods but divine attributes such as imperishability and immortality, which are ours only through the grace of Christ in the resurrection of our bodies. When the fire of our own lives grows cold, we come to burn with God's own flame.

In this extract, Tanner sets out a strongly relational understanding of eternal life, establishing an important connection between eternal life and Jesus Christ, particularly through her interpretation of the concept of the incarnation. Set out, in your own words, the three basic points that Tanner wants to make concerning eternal life. Notice how eternal life is something that we may be said to possess *now* – a present reality with future implications. What do you think she means by stating "eternal life is itself a greater gift (and brings in its train greater gifts) than the relationship with God that creatures enjoy simply as creatures"?

Tanner emphasizes that eternal life will be qualitatively different from the form of life that we presently experience. It is not to be seen as an infinite expansion of our existence, but as its radical transformation. Locate the following statement in the text: "our very identity as creatures is redefined so as to be essentially constituted by relationship with God." What does Tanner mean by this?

A Brief Glossary of Theological Terms

What follows is a brief discussion of a series of technical terms that you may encounter while reading the texts in this collection, or material arising from them. It is not intended to be exhaustive, but simply to help clarify some otherwise puzzling terms that you may come across in your reading.

adoptionism
The heretical view that Jesus was "adopted" as the Son of God at some point during his ministry (usually his baptism), as opposed to the orthodox teaching that Jesus was Son of God by nature from the moment of his conception.

Anabaptism
A term derived from the Greek word for "re-baptizer," and used to refer to the radical wing of the sixteenth-century Reformation, based on thinkers such as Menno Simons or Balthasar Hubmaier.

analogy of being (*analogia entis*)
The theory, especially associated with Thomas Aquinas, that there exists a correspondence or analogy between the created order and God, as a result of the divine creatorship. The idea gives theoretical justification to the

Theology: The Basic Readings, Third Edition. Edited by Alister E. McGrath.
Editorial material and organization © Alister E. McGrath.
Published 2018 by John Wiley & Sons Ltd.

practice of drawing conclusions from the known objects and relationships of the natural order concerning God.

analogy of faith (*analogia fidei*)
The theory, especially associated with Karl Barth, which holds that any correspondence between the created order and God is only established on the basis of the self-revelation of God.

anthropomorphism
The tendency to ascribe human features (such as hands or arms) or other human characteristics to something nonhuman, such as God.

anti-Pelagian writings
The writings of Augustine relating to the Pelagian controversy, in which he defended his views on grace and justification. *See also* "Pelagianism."

Apocalyptic
A type of writing or religious outlook in general which focuses on the last things and the end of the world, often taking the form of visions with complex symbolism. The book of Daniel (Old Testament) and Revelation (New Testament) are examples of this type of writing.

apologetics
The area of Christian theology which focuses on the defense of the Christian faith, particularly through the rational justification of Christian belief and doctrines.

apophatic
A term used to refer to a particular style of theology, which stressed that God cannot be known in terms of human categories. "Apophatic" (which derives from the Greek *apophasis*, "negation" or "denial") approaches to theology are especially associated with the monastic tradition of the Eastern Orthodox church.

apostolic era
The period of the Christian church, regarded as definitive by many, bounded by the resurrection of Jesus Christ (ca. AD 35) and the death of the last apostle (ca. AD 90). The ideas and practices of this period were widely regarded as normative, at least in some sense or to some degree, in many church circles.

appropriation
A term relating to the doctrine of the Trinity, which affirms that, while all three persons of the Trinity are active in all the outward actions of the Trinity, it is appropriate to think of those actions as being the particular work of one of the persons. Thus it is appropriate to think of creation as the work of the Father, or redemption as the work of the Son, despite the fact that all three persons are present and active in both these works.

Arianism
A major early Christological heresy, which treated Jesus Christ as the supreme of God's creatures, and denied his divine status. The Arian controversy was of major importance in the development of Christology during the fourth century.

atonement
An English term originally coined in 1526 by William Tyndale to translate the Latin term *reconciliatio*, which has since come to have the developed meaning of "the work of Christ" or "the benefits of Christ gained for believers by his death and resurrection."

Barthian
An adjective used to describe the theological outlook of the Swiss theologian Karl Barth (1886–1968), and noted chiefly for its emphasis upon the priority of revelation and its focus upon Jesus Christ. The terms "neo-orthodoxy" and "dialectical theology" are also used in this connection.

beatific vision
A term used, especially in Roman Catholic theology, to refer to the full vision of God, which is allowed only to the elect after death. However, some writers, including Thomas Aquinas, taught that certain favored individuals – such as Moses and Paul – were allowed this vision in the present life.

Calvinism
An ambiguous term, used with two quite distinct meanings. First, it refers to the ideas of religious bodies (such as the Reformed church) and individuals (such as Theodore Beza) who were profoundly influenced by John Calvin, or by documents written by him. Second, it refers to the religious ideas of John Calvin himself. Although the first sense is by far the more common, there is a growing recognition that the term is misleading.

canonical
A word deriving from the Greek term *kanon* ("a rule"), referring to works that are included in the Christian Bible. Protestants and Catholics have slightly different understandings of which books are included in this collection.

Cappadocian Fathers
A term used to refer collectively to three major Greek-speaking writers of the patristic period: Basil of Caesarea, Gregory of Nazianzen, and Gregory of Nyssa, all of whom date from the late fourth century. "Cappadocia" designates an area in Asia Minor (modern-day Turkey) in which these writers were based.

catechism
A popular manual of Christian doctrine, usually in the form of question and answer, intended for religious instruction.

catholic
An adjective which is used both to refer to the universality of the church in space and time, and also to a particular church body (sometimes also known as the Roman Catholic church) which lays emphasis upon this point.

Chalcedonian definition
The formal declaration at the Council of Chalcedon that Jesus Christ was to be regarded as having two natures, one human and one divine.

charisma, charismatic
A set of terms especially associated with the gifts of the Holy Spirit. In medieval theology, the term "charisma" is used to designate a spiritual gift, conferred upon individuals by the grace of God. Since the early twentieth century, the term "charismatic" has come to refer to styles of theology and worship which place particular emphasis upon the immediate presence and experience of the Holy Spirit.

charismatic movement
A form of Christianity which places particular emphasis upon the personal experience of the Holy Spirit in the life of the individual and community, often associated with various "charismatic" phenomena, such as speaking in tongues.

Christology
The section of Christian theology dealing with the identity of Jesus Christ, particularly the question of the relation of his human and divine natures.

confession
Although the term refers primarily to the admission of sin, it acquired a rather different technical sense in the sixteenth century – that of a document which embodies the principles of faith of a Protestant church, such as the Lutheran Augsburg Confession (1530), which embodies the ideas of early Lutheranism, and the Reformed First Helvetic Confession (1536).

consubstantial
A Latin term, deriving from the Greek term *homoousios*, literally meaning "of the same substance." The term is used to affirm the full divinity of Jesus Christ, particularly in opposition to Arianism.

consubstantiation
A term used to refer to the theory of the real presence, especially associated with Martin Luther, which holds that the substance of the eucharistic bread and wine are given together with the substance of the body and blood of Christ.

creed
A formal definition or summary of the Christian faith, held in common by all Christians. The most important are those generally known as the "Apostles' Creed" and the "Nicene Creed."

deism
A term used to refer to the views of a group of English writers, especially during the seventeenth century, the rationalism of which anticipated many of the ideas of the Enlightenment. The term is often used to refer to a view of God which recognizes the divine creatorship, yet which rejects the notion of a continuing divine involvement with the world.

dialectical theology
A term used to refer to the early views of the Swiss theologian Karl Barth (1886–1968), which emphasized the "dialectic" between God and humanity.

Docetism
An early Christological heresy, which treated Jesus Christ as a purely divine being who only had the "appearance" of being human.

Donatism
A movement, centering upon Roman North Africa in the fourth century, which developed a rigorist view of the church and sacraments.

Ebionitism
An early Christological heresy, which treated Jesus Christ as a purely human figure, although recognizing that he was endowed with particular charismatic gifts which distinguished him from other humans.

ecclesiology
The section of Christian theology dealing with the theory of the church.

Enlightenment, the
A term used since the nineteenth century to refer to the emphasis upon human reason and autonomy, characteristic of much of western European and North American thought during the eighteenth century.

eschatology
The section of Christian theology dealing with the "end things," especially the ideas of resurrection, hell, and eternal life.

eucharist
The term used in the present volume to refer to the sacrament variously known as the "Mass," the "Lord's supper," and "holy communion."

evangelical
A term initially used to refer to reforming movements, especially in Germany and Switzerland, in the 1510s and 1520s, but now used of the movement, especially in English-language theology, which places especial emphasis upon the supreme authority of Scripture and the atoning death of Christ.

exegesis
The science of textual interpretation, usually referring specifically to the Bible. The term "biblical exegesis" basically means "the process of interpreting the Bible." The specific techniques employed in the exegesis of Scripture are usually referred to as "hermeneutics."

exemplarism
A particular approach to the atonement, which stresses the moral or religious example set to believers by Jesus Christ.

fathers
An alternative term for "patristic writers."

feminism
A general cultural movement which seeks to establish the intellectual, social, political, and economic equality of the sexes. Theologically, this movement has raised important questions about the apparent "maleness" of much traditional theological language (such as the trinitarian formula "Father, Son, and Holy Spirit"), and explored the issues arising from Christianity's central figure, Jesus of Nazareth, being male.

fideism
An understanding of Christian theology which refuses to accept the need for (or sometimes the possibility of) criticism or evaluation from sources outside the Christian faith itself.

Five Ways, the
A standard term for the five "arguments for the existence of God" associated with Thomas Aquinas.

fourth gospel
A term used to refer to the gospel according to John. The term highlights the distinctive literary and theological character of this gospel, which sets it apart from the common structures of the first three gospels, usually known as the "synoptic gospels."

fundamentalism
A form of American Protestant Christianity, which lays especial emphasis upon the authority of an inerrant Bible.

hermeneutics
The principles underlying the interpretation, or exegesis, of a text, particularly of Scripture, and particularly in relation to its present-day application.

historical Jesus
A term used, especially during the nineteenth century, to refer to the historical person of Jesus of Nazareth, as opposed to the Christian

interpretation of that person, especially as presented in the New Testament and the creeds.

historico-critical method
An approach to historical texts, including the Bible, which argues that their proper meaning must be determined only on the basis of the specific historical conditions under which a text was written.

history of religions school
The approach to religious history, and Christian origins in particular, which treats Old and New Testament developments as responses to encounters with other religions, such as Gnosticism.

homoousios
A Greek term, literally meaning "of the same substance," which came to be used extensively during the fourth century to designate the mainline Christological belief that Jesus Christ was "of the same substance as God." The term was polemical, being directed against the Arian view that Christ was "of similar substance (*homoiousios*)" to God. *See also* "consubstantial."

humanism
In the strict sense of the word, an intellectual movement linked with the European Renaissance. At the heart of the movement lay not (as the modern sense of the word might suggest) a set of secular or secularizing ideas, but a new interest in the cultural achievements of antiquity. These were seen as a major resource for the renewal of European culture and Christianity during the period of the Renaissance.

hypostatic union
The doctrine of the union of divine and human natures in Jesus Christ, without confusion of their respective substances.

incarnation
A term used to refer to the assumption of human nature by God, in the person of Jesus Christ. The term "incarnationalism" is often used to refer to theological approaches which lay especial emphasis upon God becoming human.

justification by faith, doctrine of
The section of Christian theology, particularly emphasized by Protestant writers, dealing with how the individual sinner is able to enter into

fellowship with God. The doctrine was to prove to be of major significance at the time of the Reformation.

kenoticism
A form of Christology which lays emphasis upon Christ's "laying aside" of certain divine attributes in the incarnation, or his "emptying himself" of at least some divine attributes, especially omniscience or omnipotence.

kerygma
A term used, especially by Rudolf Bultmann (1884–1976) and his followers, to refer to the essential message or proclamation of the New Testament concerning the significance of Jesus Christ.

liberal Protestantism
A movement, especially associated with nineteenth-century Germany, which stressed the continuity between religion and culture, flourishing between the time of F. D. E. Schleiermacher and Paul Tillich.

liberation theology
Although this term designates any theological movement laying emphasis upon the liberating impact of the gospel, the term has come to refer to a movement which developed in Latin America in the late 1960s, which stressed the role of political action and orientated itself toward the goal of political liberation from poverty and oppression.

liturgy
The written text and set forms of public services, especially of the eucharist. In the Greek Orthodox church, the word "liturgy" often means "the [liturgy of the] eucharist."

logos
A Greek term meaning "word," which played a crucial role in the development of patristic Christology. Jesus Christ was recognized as the "Word of God"; the question concerned the implications of this recognition, and especially the way in which the divine "logos" in Jesus Christ related to his human nature.

Lutheranism
The religious ideas associated with Martin Luther, particularly as expressed in the Lesser Catechism (1529) and the Augsburg Confession (1530).

Manicheism

A strongly fatalist position associated with the Manichees, to which Augustine of Hippo attached himself during his early period. A distinction is drawn between two different divinities, one of which is regarded as evil, and the other good. Evil is thus seen as the direct result of the influence of the evil god.

memorialism

The approach to the eucharist, associated with Huldrych Zwingli and others, which holds that Christ is remembered in his absence. Since Christ is now in heaven, it is argued, he cannot also be present in the bread and wine.

modalism

A trinitarian heresy, which treats the three persons of the Trinity as different "modes" of the Godhead. A typical modalist approach is to regard God as active as Father in creation, as Son in redemption, and as Spirit in sanctification.

monophysitism

The doctrine that there is only one nature in Christ, which is divine (from the Greek words *monos*, "only one," and *physis*, "nature"). This view differed from the orthodox view, upheld by the Council of Chalcedon (451), that Christ had two natures, one divine and one human.

neo-orthodoxy

A term used to designate the general position of Karl Barth (1886–1968), especially the manner in which he drew upon the theological concerns of the period of Reformed Orthodoxy.

ontological argument

A term used to refer to the type of argument for the existence of God especially associated with the scholastic theologian Anselm of Canterbury.

orthodoxy

A term used in a number of senses, of which the following are the most important: orthodoxy in the sense of "right belief," as opposed to heresy; orthodoxy in the sense of the forms of Christianity which are dominant in Russia and Greece; orthodoxy in the sense of a movement within

Protestantism, especially in the late sixteenth and early seventeenth century, which laid emphasis upon need for doctrinal definition.

parousia
A Greek term, which literally means "coming" or "arrival," used to refer to the second coming of Christ. The notion of the *parousia* is an important aspect of Christian understandings of the "last things."

patripassianism
A theological heresy, which arose during the third century, associated with writers such as Noetus, Praxeas, and Sabellius, focusing on the belief that the Father suffered as the Son. In other words, the suffering of Christ on the cross is to be regarded as the suffering of the Father. According to these writers, the only distinction within the Godhead was a succession of modes or operations, so that Father, Son, and Spirit were just different modes of being, or expressions, of the same basic divine entity.

patristic
An adjective used to refer to the first centuries in the history of the church, following the writing of the New Testament (the "patristic period"), or thinkers writing during this period (the "patristic writers"). For many writers, the period thus designated seems to be ca. 100–451 (in other words, the period between the completion of the last of the New Testament writings and the landmark Council of Chalcedon).

Pelagianism
An understanding of how humans are able to merit their salvation which is diametrically opposed to that of Augustine of Hippo, placing considerable emphasis upon the role of human works and playing down the idea of divine grace.

perichoresis
A term relating to the doctrine of the Trinity, often also referred to by the Latin term *circumincessio*. The basic notion is that all three persons of the Trinity mutually share in the life of the others, so that none is isolated or detached from the actions of the others.

Pietism
An approach to Christianity, especially associated with German writers in the seventeenth century, which places an emphasis upon the personal

appropriation of faith, and the need for holiness in Christian living. The movement is perhaps best known within the English-language world in the form of Methodism.

post-liberalism
A theological movement, especially associated with Duke University and Yale Divinity School in the 1980s, which criticized the liberal reliance upon human experience, and reclaimed the notion of community tradition as a controlling influence in theology.

postmodernism
A general cultural development, especially in North America, which resulted from the general collapse of confidence in the universal rational principles of the Enlightenment.

Protestantism
A term used in the aftermath of the Diet of Speyer (1529) to designate those who "protested" against the practices and beliefs of the Roman Catholic church. Prior to 1529, such individuals and groups had referred to themselves as "evangelicals."

Radical Reformation
A term used with increasing frequency to refer to the Anabaptist movement – in other words, the wing of the Reformation which went beyond what Luther and Zwingli envisaged, particularly in relation to the doctrine of the church.

Reformed
A term used to refer to a tradition of theology which draws inspiration from the writings of John Calvin (1510–64) and his successors. The term is now generally used in preference to "Calvinist."

Sabellianism
An early trinitarian heresy, which treated the three persons of the Trinity as different historical manifestations of the one God. It is generally regarded as a form of modalism.

sacrament
A church service or rite which was held to have been instituted by Jesus Christ himself. Although Roman Catholic theology and church practice

recognize seven such sacraments (baptism, confirmation, eucharist, marriage, ordination, penance, and unction), Protestant theologians generally argue that only two (baptism and eucharist) were to be found in the New Testament itself.

scholasticism

A particular approach to Christian theology, associated especially with the Middle Ages, which lays emphasis upon the rational justification and systematic presentation of Christian theology.

Scripture principle

The theory, especially associated with Reformed theologians, that the practices and beliefs of the church should be grounded in Scripture. Nothing that could not be demonstrated to be grounded in Scripture could be regarded as binding upon the believer. The phrase *sola scriptura*, "by Scripture alone," summarizes this principle.

soteriology

The section of Christian theology dealing with the doctrine of salvation (Greek: *soteria*).

synoptic gospels

A term used to refer to the first three gospels (Matthew, Mark, and Luke). The term (derived from the Greek word *synopsis*, "summary") refers to the way in which the three gospels can be seen as providing similar "summaries" of the life, death, and resurrection of Jesus Christ.

theodicy

A term coined by Leibniz to refer to a theoretical justification of the goodness of God in the face of the presence of evil in the world.

Theopaschitism

A disputed teaching, regarded by some as a heresy, which arose during the sixth century, associated with writers such as John Maxentius and the slogan "one of the Trinity was crucified." The formula can be interpreted in a perfectly orthodox sense and was defended as such by Leontius of Byzantium. However, it was regarded as potentially misleading and confusing by more cautious writers, including Pope Hormisdas (died 523), and the formula gradually fell into disuse.

transubstantiation
The doctrine according to which the bread and the wine are transformed into the body and blood of Christ in the eucharist, while retaining their outward appearance.

Trinity
The distinctively Christian doctrine of God, which reflects the complexity of the Christian experience of God. The doctrine is usually summarized in maxims such as "three persons, one God."

two natures, doctrine of
A term generally used to refer to the doctrine of the two natures, human and divine, of Jesus Christ. Related terms include "Chalcedonian definition" and "hypostatic union."

Zwinglianism
The term is used generally to refer to the thought of Huldrych Zwingli, but often used to refer specifically to his views on the sacraments, especially on the "real presence" (which for Zwingli was more of a "real absence").

Sources of Readings

Chapter 1: Faith

Chapter 2: God

Theology: The Basic Readings, Third Edition. Edited by Alister E. McGrath.
Editorial material and organization © Alister E. McGrath.
Published 2018 by John Wiley & Sons Ltd.

2.3 Jürgen Moltmann, "The 'Crucified God': God and the Trinity Today," in *New Questions on God*, ed. J. B. Metz (New York: Herder & Herder, 1972), 31–5.

2.4 Hans Urs von Balthasar, *The Glory of the Lord: A Theological Aesthetics*, 7 vols (Edinburgh: T&T Clark, 1989), vol. 7, 268–70.

2.5 Elizabeth A. Johnson, *She Who Is: The Mystery of God in Feminist Theological Discourse* (New York: Crossroad, 1992), 55–7.

2.6 Sarah Coakley, *Powers and Submissions: Spirituality, Philosophy and Gender* (Oxford: Blackwell, 2002), 32–6.

Chapter 3: Creation

3.1 Giovanni Pico della Mirandola, *Oration on the Dignity of Humanity*, 4.10–5.23.

3.2 Jonathan Edwards, *The Images of Divine Things*, ed. Perry Miller (New Haven, CT: Yale University Press, 1948), 61, 69, 109, 134.

3.3 William Paley, *Natural Theology*, in *The Works of William Paley* (London: William Orr, 1844), 25–6.

3.4 John Henry Newman, *An Essay in Aid of a Grammar of Assent* (London: Longmans, Green & Co., 1903), 396–9.

3.5 G. K. Chesterton, *Orthodoxy* (London: Bodley Head, 1909), 136–44.

3.6 Dorothy L. Sayers, *The Mind of the Maker* (London: Methuen, 1941), 81–3.

3.7 John Polkinghorne, *The Faith of a Physicist* (Princeton, NJ: Princeton University Press, 1994), 73–5. This work was published by SPCK in the United Kingdom with the title *Science & Christian Belief*.

Chapter 4: Jesus

4.1 Athanasius of Alexandria, *On the Incarnation*, III, 11–14.

4.2 Leo the Great, "Letter 28 to Flavian" (June 13, 449), in J. P. Migne, *Patrologia Latina* (Paris, 1841–55), 54.758B–760A, 764A–768B.

4.3 Martin Kähler, *Der sogenannte historische Jesus und der geschichtliche, biblische Christus* (Munich: Kaiser Verlag, 1953), 40–5.

4.4 George Tyrrell, *Christianity at the Cross-Roads* (London: Longmans Green & Co, 1909), 46–9.

4.5 Austin Farrer, *Love Almighty and Ills Unlimited: An Essay on Providence and Evil* (London: Collins, 1962), 124–30.

4.6 Morna D. Hooker, "Chalcedon and the New Testament," in *The Making and Remaking of Christian Doctrine*, ed. Sarah Coakley and David A. Pailin (Oxford: Clarendon Press, 1993), 73–93.

4.7 N. T. Wright, "Jesus and the Identity of God," *Ex Auditu* 14 (1998): 42–56.

Chapter 5: Salvation

5.1 Rufinus of Aquileia, *Exposition of the Creed*, 14–17.

5.2 Maximus of Constantinople, *Questions for Thalassius*, 22.

5.3 Anselm of Canterbury, *Why God Became Man*, II. 4, 6–7.

5.4 Friedrich Schleiermacher, *The Christian Faith* (Edinburgh: T&T Clark, 1928), 429–31.

5.5 Bernard Lonergan, *The Collected Works of Bernard Lonergan, vol. 6: Philosophical and Theological Papers, 1958–1964* (Toronto: University of Toronto Press, 1996), 8–13.

5.6 Colin E. Gunton, *The Actuality of Atonement* (Edinburgh: T&T Clark, 1988), 47–51.

5.7 Rosemary Radford Ruether, *Introducing Redemption in Christian Feminism* (Sheffield: Sheffield Academic Press, 1998), 97–100.

Chapter 6: Spirit

6.1 Ambrose of Milan, *On the Holy Spirit*, III.xii.85–92.

6.2 John of Damascus, *On the Orthodox Faith*, I, 8.

6.3 Formula of Concord, "Full Declaration," II.7–16.

6.4 Charles Gore, *Lux Mundi: A Series of Studies in the Religion of the Incarnation* (London: John Murray, 1890), 233–5.

6.5 Henry Barclay Swete, "The Person of the Holy Spirit," in *The Official Report of the Church Congress Held at Exeter*, ed. C. Dunkley (London: Bemrose & Sons, Ltd., 1894), 692–8.

6.6 John Webster, "The Identity of the Holy Spirit: A Problem in Trinitarian Theology," *Themelios* 9, no. 1 (1983): 4–7.

6.7 John Meyendorff, *The Byzantine Legacy in the Orthodox Church* (Crestwood, NY: St Vladimir's Seminary Press, 1982), 154–6.

Chapter 7: Trinity

7.1   Irenaeus of Lyons, *Demonstration of the Apostolic Preaching*, 3–6.
7.2   Council of Toledo, *Statement of Faith on the Trinity and Incarnation*, 1–14.
7.3   Richard of St Victor, *On the Trinity*, III, 14.
7.4   Karl Rahner, "Remarks on the Dogmatic Treatise 'De trinitate'," in *Theological Investigations* (London: Darton, Longman & Todd, 1966), 77–102.
7.5   John Macquarrie, *Principles of Christian Theology*, rev. ed. (London: SCM Press, 1977), 190–2.
7.6   Robert Jenson, "The Triune God," in *Christian Dogmatics*, ed. C. E. Braaten and R. W. Jenson, vol. 1 (Philadelphia, PA: Fortress Press, 1984), 87–92.
7.7   Catherine Mowry LaCugna, "The Practical Trinity," *Christian Century* 109, no. 22 (1992): 678–82.

Chapter 8: Church

8.1   Martin Luther, *On the Councils and the Church* (1539), in *D. Martin Luthers Werke: Kritische Gesamtausgabe*, vol. 50 (Weimar: Böhlau, 1914), 628–30.
8.2   Lesslie Newbigin, *The Household of God: Lectures on the Nature of the Church* (London: SCM Press, 1953), 140–1.
8.3   Second Vatican Council, *Lumen Gentium* ("Dogmatic Constitution on the Church"), 6, 8.
8.4   George Dragas, "Orthodox Ecclesiology in Outline," *Greek Orthodox Theological Review* 26 (1981): 185–92.
8.5   Stanley Hauerwas, *A Community of Character: Toward a Constructive Christian Social Ethic* (Notre Dame, IN: University of Notre Dame Press, 1981), 91–2.
8.6   Leonardo Boff, *Ecclesiogenesis: The Base Communities Reinvent the Church* (Maryknoll, NY: Orbis, 1986), 23–4.

Chapter 9: Sacraments

9.1   Cyril of Jerusalem, *Catechetical Lectures*, XIX.2–3, XX.4–6.
9.2   Huldrych Zwingli, "A Clear Instruction concerning the Supper of Christ" (1526), in *Corpus Reformatorum: Huldreich Zwinglis sämtliche Werke*, vol. 91 (Leipzig: Heinsius, 1927), 796–800.

9.3 Council of Trent, "Decree on the Most Holy Sacrament of the Eucharist," preface, chapters 1–2, 4.

9.4 World Council of Churches, "Baptism, Eucharist and Ministry," Faith and Order Paper 111 (Geneva: World Council of Churches, 1982), 2–3.

9.5 Rowan Williams, *On Christian Theology* (Oxford: Blackwell, 2000), 203–4.

9.6 Benedict XVI, "Post-Synodal Apostolic Exhortation *Sacramentum Caritatis*," given at Saint Peter's, Rome, on February 22, 2007, http://w2.vatican.va/content/benedict-xvi/en/apost_exhortations/documents/hf_ben-xvi_exh_20070222_sacramentum-caritatis.html.

Chapter 10: Heaven

10.1 Cyprian of Carthage, *On Mortality*, 2, 24–6.

10.2 Methodius of Olympus, *On the Resurrection*, I, 6–8.

10.3 Peter Abelard, "O quanta qualia sunt illa sabbata," in *Oxford Book of Medieval Latin Verse*, ed. F. I. E. Raby (Oxford: Clarendon Press, 1959), p. 243. Translation by John Mason Neale (1818–66).

10.4 John Wesley, Sermon 60: "The General Deliverance," in John Wesley, *Works*, 16 vols (Grand Rapids, MI: Baker, 1996), vol. 6, 242–3, 248–50.

10.5 *Catechism of the Catholic Church* (Collegeville, MN: Liturgical Press, and other publishers, 1994), paras 992–1001.

10.6 Wolfhart Pannenberg, *Systematic Theology*, 3 vols (Grand Rapids, MI: Eerdmans, 1988–98), vol. 3, 637–40.

10.7 Kathryn Tanner, *Jesus, Humanity and the Trinity: A Brief Systematic Theology* (Minneapolis, MN: Fortress Press, 2001), 108–10.

Index

Theology: The Basic Readings, Third Edition. Edited by Alister E. McGrath.
Editorial material and organization © Alister E. McGrath.
Published 2018 by John Wiley & Sons Ltd.